THE TWAINING OF AMERICA

by

B. J. FISKE

DORRANCE PUBLISHING CO., INC.
PITTSBURGH, PENNSYLVANIA 15222

DEDICATION

To my late beloved wife and "twaining" partner, who gave me the idea for this book, its
title, and central theme.

Contents

(Illustrations follow pages 69, 153, 221 and 291)

PREFACE

"East is east and west is west, and never the twain shall meet."
Rudyard Kipling, *The Ballad of East and West*, 1889.

Mr. Kipling apparently was unaware of the "twaining of America"—from the new United States east of the Mississippi to Spanish California on the Pacific coast, and all the people of different backgrounds and nationalities who joined together to create the phenomenal growth of America in the nineteenth century.

Fact and fiction are herein combined, with a predominance of historical facts and anecdotes. The fictional characters are "low-key" so as to blend in with and not distract attention from actual events and persons of the period. Any similarity of fictitious persons to actual persons, living or dead, is not intended to be inferred.

ACKNOWLEDGMENTS

My late wife encouraged me in this endeavor; contributed original writings which are used herein; and provided invaluable comments, suggestions, and assistance throughout the preparation of this work.

Special thanks to John S. D. Eisenhower, author of *So Far From God—The U.S. War with Mexico 1846–1848*, for words of advice and encouragement, and for providing an excellent literary example.

Thanks to the following for permission to reprint excerpts, as follows:

1. Quotation from Robert Louis Stevenson's *An Immigrant Crosses America*, reproduced in *Eyewitness to History*, by John Carey, copyright 1987, reprinted with permission of Harvard University Press, 7–11–89. (Ch. 13 herein.)

2. Quotation from Frederick Remington reproduced in *A Visual Feast from the Santa Fe Railway Collection of Southwestern Art*, by Arrell M. Gibson, copyright 1983, reprinted with permission of Santa Fe Railway Co., 8–30–89. (Ch. 16 herein.)

3. Quotation from Richard Henry Dana, reproduced in *The Thirty-first Star*, by James A.B. Scherer, copyright 1942, G.B. Putnam & Sons, courtesy of the Putnam Publishing Group, 8–9–89. (Ch. 6 and 9 herein.)

4. Quotation from a New York Sun article of 1838, reproduced in *The Epic of America*, by James Truslow Adams, copyright 1931, courtesy of Little, Brown & Co., 8–29–89. (Ch. 2 herein.)

5. Quotation from Edward H.R. Green reproduced in *The Witch of Wall Street—Hetty Green*, by Boyden Sparks and Samuel Taylor Moore, copyright 1930, Doubleday Doran & Co., reprinted with permission of Bantam, Doubleday, Dell Publishing Group, Inc., 9–14–89. (Ch. 14 herein.)

6. Quotation from Mrs. Hall reproduced in Philip Glazebrook's article titled "Rome Revisited" in the *Washington Post* Travel Section, 3–19–89, reprinted with permission of Georges Borchardt Inc., Literary Agent for Philip Glazebrook, 11–14–89. (Ch. 12 herein.)

7. Quotation from Ralph Waldo Emerson reproduced in *Americans and the California Dream*, 1850–1915, by Kevin Starr, copyright 1973, Oxford University Press; and from Tiburcio Vasquez reproduced in *Inventing the Dream—California Through the Progressive Era*, by Kevin Starr, copyright 1985, Oxford University Press; both reproduced with permission of Oxford University Press, 1–15–91. (Chapter 13 herein.)

8. Descriptions of "Hard Times Tokens" (Chapter 5) and Bryan satirical "dollars" (Chapter 16) from Stack's Catalog for Public Auction September 8 and 9, 1988, and from Stack's American Historical Medals Fixed Price List 1991, reproduced with permission of Stack's, New York, 5–20–91.

Acknowledgement for assistance in providing research materials is extended to: U.S. Department of State, Office of Historian and Reference Library, Washington DC; Department of the Army, Public Information Office, Washington DC; Library of Congress, Washington DC—Local History and Genealogy Section; U.S. Archives, Washington DC; U.S. Commission of Fine Arts, Washington DC; Martin Luther King Memorial Library, Washington DC—History and Biography Section; Georgetown Branch of DC Public Library, including Peabody Room.

And to: Utah State Historical Society, Salt Lake City, UT; Church of Jesus Christ of L.D.S., Salt Lake City, UT—Library Service; Mormon Public Communications Office, Washington DC; Mormon Family History Center, Kensington, MD; the Historical Society of Washington DC; The Claretian Missionaries, Mission San Gabriel Arcangel, San Gabriel, CA; San Clemente Chamber of Commerce, San Clemente, CA.

And further to: The Association of American Railroads, Washington DC; The National Association of Railroad Passengers, Washington DC; Santa Fe Pacific Corp., Chicago IL; CSX Corp., Richmond, VA; Chemical Bank of New York, NY; American Heritage Division of Forbes Corp., New York, NY; The Wall Street Journal and Dow Jones, Inc., New York, NY.

Also to: Commission for Historic Districts and Landmarks, New Orleans, LA; and the Office of the City of New Orleans in Washington DC; the Newberry Library, Burlington Archives, Chicago, IL; and the Wells Fargo Bank, Private Banking Div., Los Angeles, CA.

And finally to Mabel Mason and Mary Beth Mason, who helped immeasurably in final review, manuscript preparation, and generally helping me get this project moving again after my wife died in January 1992.

BJF

INTRODUCTION

When Uncle Tony died at age 100, outliving all other relatives, I volunteered to go through his things and decide on their disposition. I called him "uncle" because our families had been close, but he actually was a more distant relative on my father's side of the family.

As I looked through old papers from an attic trunk in the house in which he lived and died, I learned Uncle Tony's father had a cousin named Ramón Clemente, born 100 years before me in the same part of California. I wondered what his life in the 19th century was like and what my life would have been like a century earlier.

Uncle Tony inherited Ramón Clemente's papers and kept most of them with his own in the attic trunk. After going through all the old letters, journals, documents, pictures, and clippings, I put together the story related herein.

PART I
GROWING UP
(1819–1840)

PROLOGUE
TURNING POINT

On a crisp sunny January morning in 1836, Ramón Clemente stood by a window in his father's room. He felt the growing warmth of the Alta California air, which accentuated the beauty of the plants and flowers around the tiled fountain in the hacienda courtyard. He sensed its stark contrast to the scene within as he listened to his father's dying gasps for air.

A few moments before, Padre Carlos Borgoña had pronounced the last rites and told the family that Don Guillermo would soon be gone. Ramón felt his own life fall apart with the Padre's words. His mother, Doña Caterina, was too distraught to attend her husband's final unconscious moments, and went outside to the courtyard. Ramón witnessed his father's death alone, except for Padre Borgoña and Antonio Morales, the ranch foreman, who assured him they would take care of the burial arrangements.

He prayed for his father in the promised life beyond and for the grieving family left behind. He worried about how his mother would react. It would be hard enough for him losing his father but devastating for her to lose her husband with whom she had been so close for so long. He wished his older sister Cristina were here to share the burden of grief but she was visiting friends in Monterey and not expected back for several days—as long as it would take to get word to her and for her to return. Ramón knew she would be distressed not to have seen their father before he died.

Only yesterday he had talked with his father about future plans, as they often had done. The only visible sign that this would be their last conversation was that Don Guillermo looked unusually drawn and tired. He had asked his son to look after certain family papers stored in a Spanish oak chest at the foot of his bed, something only Don Guillermo himself had handled before. Ramón thought at the time his father was acknowledging his son's approaching maturity in beginning to turn some things over to him but now realized it may have been a premonition of death.

Ramón went downstairs to tell his mother it was "all over." She stood by the fountain, her usually erect frame twisted with grief and disbelief. Ramón put his arm around her stooped shoulders and led her to a carved wooden bench in the shade at the end of the court-yard. She turned and fell against him, sobbing, "How can I ever live without him?" then: "He used to say that if anything happened, I could always count on you, my son."

Ramón winced inwardly as he felt the yoke of responsibility tightening around him. He noticed his mother's face looked more drawn and older than he had ever seen it. Her formerly light brown hair was now nearly all gray. He held her hands, now so much more wrinkled than when she had cared for him as a child. As her wrenching sobs continued, he tried to comfort and calm her by getting her to talk about Don Guillermo. "Mother, tell me again how you and father came to this land—how you met and married."

While Doña Caterina was composing herself and collecting her thoughts, Ramón turned to Maria, the housekeeper who was standing nearby waiting for instructions about the noon meal, and asked her to bring them something light on trays.

After a long silence, Doña Caterina spoke, haltingly at first. "Your father was born in 1772 in the Spanish colony of Santa Fe, where his father's great-great grandfather, Don Juan Clemente, was among the first settlers. Don Juan was named after Don Juan de Onate, who set up colonies in New Spain after Coronado's expedition from Mexico. Guillermo's family came west to California over the Spanish Trail in 1801, eighteen years before you were born."

She broke down in tears again, then following what seemed an interminable pause, she continued in a stronger, more confident voice. "My family, the Calderons, settled near the Spanish Presidio at Tubac, far to the south and west of Santa Fe. My father helped organize de Anza's expedition to open a southern overland trail to California.[1] We came west on it just a month before it was closed by the Yuma Indian massacre of 1781. Since then fewer people have come west to spoil it. We have been living in a world of our own here and want to keep it that way."

Ramón tried to assure her that it would probably remain that way for many years. After a long sigh, she went on, now more in control of herself. "I was only a child when we came west, but I was told we arrived just after Governor de Neve and the San Gabriel Mission padres christened our town El Pueblo de Nuestra Señora La Reina de Los Angeles. My father received a large grant of land south and east of town from the governor to produce food for the presidios."

After another long pause, she continued, "I first saw your father when I was twenty-two years old and already promised to another. Guillermo and I each were walking with our families in opposite directions on the Plaza in Los Angeles after attending Sunday Mass. I couldn't keep my eyes off of him, and he seemed to notice me too. We met formally at a grand reception the governor gave for a visitor from Madrid to meet the most prominent families in town. I knew then he was the only man for me. I determined we would be married and we were, but not for several years. For a wedding present, my father gave us a portion of his lands near the Mission San Gabriel. Guillermo named it Rancho Alhambra, after the palace in Granada from near where his family lived in Spain."

Doña Caterina stopped talking as Maria brought a tray of fresh fruit and corn tortillas, which they glanced at and set aside to have later. Then she continued. "I lost our first child—a little girl who died at birth. Guillermo and I were desolate. Then Cristina came and we were ecstatic—she made us forget our sorrow and come alive again. Of course we were pleased also when you arrived."

Doña Caterina seemed to have completely regained her composure and even seemed a bit annoyed at having been cajoled into so lengthy a revelation. Ramón felt he had been helpful in relieving her grief, at least momentarily. He passed her the plate of fruit and tortillas. She selected a small bunch of grapes and ate about half of them very slowly. She looked extremely tired. Ramón thought she might rest now and escorted her to her room for a siesta.

As he walked with her upstairs, Ramón recalled how his father used to stop several times to catch his breath going up these stairs. He was suddenly overwhelmed by a cold empty feeling at the realization that he never would see Don Guillermo again. After closing his mother's door, Ramón returned to the courtyard to contemplate his own loss.

There was so much more Ramón wanted to learn from his father, such as his experiences growing up and at the time of his life that Ramón was going through. Now he would never know and would have to rely on what he had learned so far during his sixteen years. This made him feel very sad and alone yet with a certain fascination about things to come. He left the courtyard and began walking about the grounds adjacent to the hacienda, recalling his past and thinking about how it might affect his future.

CHAPTER 1
CHILDHOOD IN ALTA CALIFORNIA

Ramón Luis Clemente-Calderon was born on February 1, 1819, near the former Indian village of Yang-Na, later named El Pueblo de Nuestra Señora La Reina de Los Angeles de Porciuncula, in the south of Spain's new world province of Alta California.

So far during his lifetime, Ramón's homeland had been under two flags—first that of Spain, then Mexico, which became an independent nation when he was three years old.

In the early days, government was of little concern to the average Californio. What government there was emanated from the Presidio at Santa Barbara, which was subject to the Commandante at Monterey in the north, who was answerable to the central government in Mexico City and, until Mexico's independence, to the supreme authority in Madrid.[1]

The Spanish Californians' indifference to government changed after 1825 when California became a territory of the Republic of Mexico. They were given a governor, a territorial legislature, a superior court, prefects, district judges, alcaldes (minor judges), and ayuntamientos (town councils). The first governor, Jose Maria Echeandia, was liberal and just. He was replaced in 1830 by the dictatorial Governor Victoria, against whom a group of citizens led a rebellion. The Californians defeated Victoria's troops at Cahuenga Pass in 1831, causing his return to Mexico.

The Californians' new sense of political responsibility went so far as an open revolt in 1836 to proclaim the "Free and Sovereign State of Alta California." Concessions were made by Mexico which brought California back into the republic, at least for the time being.

Life in Alta California was a continuous round of hospitality and outdoor sport, mostly involving horses.

Horse racing was a favorite pastime, usually with only two horses run at a time, accompanied by betting with cattle put up for stakes. There were no inns or hotels, and every door was open to friend or stranger. There were few schools. Music, games and conversation constituted most of the education that young people received, except for private tutors for those who could afford it. There were many balls and festivals, particularly when foreign ships arrived at California ports. The American author Richard Henry Dana came from Boston on one such ship. He sailed up and down the coast from 1834 to 1836, enjoying the casual California social life on frequent excursions ashore.

Dances lasted until all hours, and there were instances when they wouldn't stop even for an earthquake. Many of the Spanish dances were exhibitions in which one girl or one couple took turns performing. There was also much singing with guitar accompaniment and impromptu renditions of verse or humorous couplets about some current topic. In later years, when there was a possibility of California being taken over by another country, one man began a couplet:

> "Ay si viennen los ingleses, ay!
> California esta Perdida!"
> (If the English come California will be lost)
> His lady partner completes it with:
> "Mas si viennen los Francesces, ay!
> La mujer esta rendida!"
> (But if the Frenchmen come the women will be conquered.)[1]

After the American "conquest" of California, the music of the U.S. Army bands did more to win over the people than any oratory or government proclamations.

If one symbol were chosen to represent the life of a Californian, it would have to be the horse. On a typical day most men's waking hours were spent in the saddle. The usual costume included a large hat with conical crown, broad brim, glazed surface, and a band under the chin. A handkerchief covered the head underneath the hat. A shirt with collar open at the neck was covered by a tight-fitting vest ornamented with buttons and much braid. A bright sash topped tightly fitted trousers open up to the knee, which were worn over white cotton drawers. Below the trousers were embroidered buckskin leggings and shoes or high-heeled leather boots. Finely woven, colorful serapes were generally worn, or ponchos of a finer texture when a more waterproof garment was needed.[2]

When there was a wedding on a ranch, the groom would array himself in his finest and call for the bride on horseback, he riding behind her on the same horse on their way to the church. After the ceremony the couple would leave for their honeymoon on two horses, arrayed with the finest equipment obtainable, such as saddles with decorative carving and silver mountings and silver ornamentation on bridles, bits, and the rider's spurs.[3]

During some dances the men remained on horseback while the women danced in the center of a circle formed by the horses. The men pushed and shoved trying to force their horses to the front of the circle, singing, jesting, and making a lot of noise. After a while some of the men would dismount, hang their spurs on the saddle horn, slip their sombreros back behind their heads, and pick out a partner for the dance. Afterwards the men would return to their horses.[4]

An important part of Ramón's life was the Mission San Gabriel adjacent to his family's Rancho Alhambra. The mission was founded in 1771 by Padre Junipero Serra and was the fourth of twenty-two missions the Spanish established in Alta California.

Like all the California missions, San Gabriel was established to further Spanish colonization—to convert the local Indians, mostly of the Chumash and Coahuilla tribes, to Catholicism and to put them to work for the benefit of the Spanish colonial economy. In this latter respect, the objective was to treat them as well as was necessary to maintain them in good physical working condition. Ramón later learned this was comparable to the treatment of negro slaves in the southern United States, with attendant abuses in both cases.

The Mission San Gabriel, near the Rio de Jesus de Los Temblores (River of Earthquakes), was the largest of the California missions. Its designer, Father Antonio Cruzado, was born and raised in Cordova, Spain.[6] The sprawling, open style of mission construction, an adaptation of Mediterranean Spanish architecture with its Moorish influence, was typical of all the California missions. The sun-baked adobe walls, red-tiled roofs, and flower-filled courtyards with tiled fountains were seen in many other buildings in Alta California.

Unlike most others, Mission San Gabriel was enclosed in walls, giving the appearance of a Moorish fortress. Inside was a maze of gardens and courtyards. The main church building, about 30 feet wide by 150 feet long, could accommodate 400 people. Its four-foot thick walls and seven-foot thick buttresses were made of stone, brick, and mortar, topped by a pitched tile roof supported by beams cut from local trees. Outside the walls was a stairway to the choir loft. In 1812 an earthquake destroyed the original bell tower, which was replaced by a new "campanile" or belfry constructed as part of the wall.[7]

In addition to the main church was the "convento" or common building, containing the monastery, friar's quarters, refectory, kitchen, offices, weaving rooms, blacksmith shop, tannery, wine press, and warehouses. The pueblo or town where the mission Indians known as "Gabrielenos" were housed made up the rest of the square of which the church and convento formed one side. Outside the walls were vegetable gardens, grain fields, and large herds of cattle, sheep and goats cared for by the Mission Indians. In 1825 epidemics of cholera and smallpox killed many of the Mission Indians, who were buried in the "Campo Santo" or cemetery inside the mission grounds.

Father Jose Maria Zalvidea was the guiding light of the San Gabriel Mission from 1806 to 1827 and made it the wealthiest of all the California missions.[6] The Clementes had a financial interest in this mission, so to speak, for by decree of the Pope, the California missions were authorized to exact contributions from nearby ranchos amounting to a "diezmo" or one-tenth of their yearly increase in cattle. This was collected regularly until after the missions were secularized by the Mexican government.[9]

While lands were used primarily for cattle raising, the mission padres initiated the growth of tropical fruits such as oranges, lemons, figs, dates, and grapes. Ramón frequently visited the mission and gratefully received samples of these products, which he enjoyed immensely. The mission held other treasures of great interest to Ramón such as: a four-pound cannon called "Frijollera" or beanshooter, part of the original arsenal; and a small reed organ brought from France in 1821—only four feet long and two and a half feet deep, made of rosewood with iron handles at each end. It had a transposing keyboard which could be shifted any fraction of an entire octave, making it possible to use any key desired while still playing as if in the key of C. Most fascinating to Ramón were the primitive paintings of the fourteen stations of the cross, done by mission Indians on sailcloth with paints made from crushed petals of local wildflowers and oil pressed from olives of the mission orchards.[10]

Because of the aridity of this part of California it was necessary to devise systems of irrigation and water conservation, such as "La Zanja Madre" (mother ditch) built in 1782 to bring water from the sometimes dry river into the pueblo of Los Angeles.[16]

Before coming to California, Don Guillermo had experience in channeling water from the mountains near Santa Fe to the lower arid plains of New Mexico and made his expertise available to the Mission San Gabriel. He worked with Father Zalvidea in developing irrigation systems, including aqueducts made of clay pipe to transport water from lakes in the nearby foothills, which facilitated the mission's agricultural activities.[12]

In his youth, Ramón spent much of his spare time at the Mission San Gabriel, which was the closest center of activity outside the ranch. It lay at the junction of El Camino Real or "King's Highway," which connected the California missions, and the old Spanish trail to the east. Here he first saw Americans, such as Jebediah Smith and Kit Carson. Smith, an explorer, trapper, and trader, arrived in 1826 from the great Salt Lake, after losing half of his fifty horses during the hazardous journey. He was feared and distrusted by local officials, who refused permission for him to travel north to Monterey. After conference with Governor Echeandia, Smith was told to return the way he came. He started to do so, but after crossing the San Bernardino mountains he turned west through the Tehachapi Pass and north into the San Joaquin valley.[11]

It was reported by persons who met Smith along the way that he was seeking the legendary "Rio Buenaventura," thought by early explorers to be a navigable river flowing west from the Rocky Mountains to the Pacific.[5] He kept going north and ultimately reached the Hudson Bay Post at Fort Vancouver, from whence word spread of this vast unspoiled area to the south. Soon other bands of trappers set out for California. One of these from New Mexico arrived at Mission San Gabriel in 1830. Ramón observed the group closely and listened intently to their conversations. He learned they preferred associates such as hard-working Scotsmen who were used to outdoor hardships, and that they did not want city-bred young men who were used to high-living and licentiousness. He was particularly impressed by a buckskin clad, broad-shouldered, clear-eyed mountain man named Kit Carson, who was about ten years his senior. Ramón thought briefly that he might follow in Carson's footsteps some day, but as with most boys his age, he soon had other things on his mind.

Ramón's earliest knowledge of agriculture and animals was learned not only from the mission padres but also from Antonio Morales, Don Guillermo's majordomo or ranch foreman. Antonio taught Ramón to ride horseback at an early age, in the absence of Don Guillermo whose work on irrigation projects and subsequent illness kept him from teaching the boy himself.

Most of the California horses were descended from Arabian stock brought from Spain. While there were many horses available for riding at the Clemente ranch, each family member had one horse more or less regularly assigned. For Don Guillermo it was the white stallion Ricardo. Ramón's first was originally his sister's horse with the French name Chevalier. When Cristina desired another mount, Chevalier was passed down to Ramón. Horse and boy viewed each other with diffidence, and it was never a great relationship. In his fifteenth year, Ramón asked his father for permission to be assigned a horse of his own choice, which was granted. He rode all over the ranch and viewed many horses before he saw a young horse, just past a year old, which at once struck his fancy. Its color was a rich dark brown that appeared lighter or darker depending on how the sunlight struck his hide. He had a white stripe down his forehead and four white bands above his hooves that gave the appearance of short white stockings. But the quality that most attracted Ramón's attention was the horse's independence and individuality, not following the others but darting about to find out things for himself. Ramón wanted to train this young horse from scratch and felt thereby they could learn more from and about each other.

Ramón went to Don Guillermo and said, "I've found the horse I want, Father, and I'd like to train him myself."

Don Guillermo replied, "You may have him, son, but one of Antonio's more experienced horsemen will break him first to the saddle, then you may break him to the bit."

Ramón knew not to argue with his father and so accepted this partial victory.

The boy named his horse Bolivar after the soldier-statesman who liberated much of South America from Spain. When turned over to Ramón, the horse was presumably ready for saddle riding, but he still bucked a little and sometimes "crowhopped" when running. Once he threw Ramón to the ground, then stopped and cropped grass, waiting for the boy to remount. When riding Bolivar, Ramón first used a "bosal" or noseband of woven leather thongs attached to a leather headpiece called a "cabestro" or halter, to control the horse. Then he began inserting a metal bit into Bolivar's mouth and taking it out right away, to let him feel what it was like, but also let him know that he was not being forced to retain it. A few weeks later Ramón started riding Bolivar with the bit for short periods then going back to the bosal. He gradually increased the time with the bit and by the end of three months Bolivar accepted it easily, and he and Ramón seemed to have reached a mutual understanding.

Rodeos were held in the spring and fall, originally to keep the cattle from becoming too wild. The animals were herded to the rodeo grounds once a week to accustom them to going to one place. When rodeo time came, notices were sent out and everyone came, including wives and children, from the surrounding area. Although it was looked on by all as an occasion for much feasting and merrymaking, the main function was to separate the cattle into groups that belonged to individual owners. A system of branding had been introduced to identify the animals, and each brand was registered with the alcalde under the name of the owner. For example, Don Guillermo's brand was **AC** for Alhambra/Clemente, and the San Gabriel Mission brand was **TS** for "temblores" or earthquakes.[13] There were other distinctive symbols for the brands of neighboring ranchos San Pascual, Santa Anita, La Puente, San Bernardino, etc.[6] Besides the branding of additions to the herds, old marks were inspected, wandering animals were returned to claimants, and sick or injured animals were cut from the rest to be cared for. The whole was presided over by a "Juez de Campo" or field judge, chosen from amongst the owners, who settled all disputes concerning ownership.[14]

In the evening after the work was done, guitars were tuned and there was singing and dancing, all of which Ramón enjoyed immensely. What he didn't like about ranch life were the slaughtering seasons or "matanzas," at which time young steers were killed for sale or home use, but he recognized it as an economic necessity.

In addition to the ranch hands and vaqueros who handled the livestock, the Clementes had Indian servants who worked inside the hacienda and cared for the outside gardens. These Indians had been schooled and trained at the mission and were an important part of Ramón's childhood development. Some had young children who were his and his sister's early playmates. As he grew older, Ramón often wondered how people so like him and his family in every respect except skin color, dress, and speech pattern, and seemingly equally deserving of life's benefits, were not accorded the same deferential treatment as his family expected and received from them. He knew they were treated in a kind and fair manner at Rancho Alhambra but soon learned this was not always the case at other ranchos and in other parts of the country.

As the Clemente hacienda was quite a distance from other ranchos, Ramón and his sister Cristina had few other regular playmates. Most of their education was received at home from their parents and tutors from the mission, such as Padre Borgoña. Don Guillermo's widowed sister Isabel, who shared with the children a mutual affection, was very religious in the orthodox sense and contributed to their spiritual training and guidance in a way that stayed with them throughout their lives. In addition to biblical studies, the children's aunt told them stories of local history, some with religious significance. One was about the very old painting of "Our Lady of Sorrows" which hung in the San Gabriel Mission. Isabel told Cristina and Ramón how when the founding missionaries arrived from San Diego to select a site for the mission, they were approached by a band of hostile Indians who threatened to drive them away. One of the padres unfurled the painting of "Our Lady of Sorrows" and spread it on the ground for the Indians to see. Greatly impressed and seemingly transfixed by its beauty, the Indians put down their weapons, and the chieftains removed beads from around their necks and placed them before the picture as a gesture of peace and respect.[15]

In 1824 Don Guillermo built a new home a few miles further north towards the mountains, which he named "Casa Loma" or Hill House. Ramón sensed that his father was happier here in a home of his own making than in the one which was a gift from his father-in-law Don Julio Calderon. It was in this new home, twelve years later, that Don Guillermo died of a respiratory illness contracted while working on the irrigation systems and aqueducts at a particularly cold and damp location in the north.

By this time more colonists had come to Alta California by sea and overland, mostly from Mexico City. More varied styles of living were adopted after the Spanish fashion, built around an inner court filled with plants watered by a fountain in the center. The newer homes had more decorative tiles and much iron grillwork, particularly for window gratings, than those built earlier.

It was in such a home that Ramón lived until 1836, the year his sister Cristina became engaged to marry Raimundo Carillo of Monterey, and Ramón became one of the first students from Alta California, Mexico, to attend college in the United States of America.

CHAPTER 2
EARLY EXPERIENCES IN THE UNITED STATES

Having always been fascinated by the landscape of California and curious about the formation of its mountains, deserts, and seashores, Ramón began at an early age to read all he could find on the subject of geology. Through the writings of Benjamin Silliman, a pioneer in scientific education and founder of the study of geology in America who graduated from Yale College in 1796, Ramón became interested in attending that college.

His interest was further encouraged by a distant relative, Henry Clement, who graduated from Yale in 1830. He had written Ramón about Yale's major collection of scientific instruments and described their library as one of the finest in the world.

Having set his sights on learning more about geology, Ramón wrote to the president of Yale, Jeremiah Day,[1] for information concerning admission, courses of study, tuition costs, living accommodations, etc. To generate interest and a positive attitude on the part of the institution towards his intended application, Ramón included with his request letters of recommendation from alumnus Henry Clement; Governor Jose Figueroa; and Augustin Olvera, Alta California representative to the Mexican Congress.

While awaiting a reply, Ramón began looking into travel arrangements. He had help from his aunt Isabel, who had made the journey herself eight years before. She travelled the whole way by sea around Cape Horn to New York, as opposed to crossing the Isthmus of Darien, now called Panama. The land crossing was not only dangerous because of unhealthy conditions and hostile natives, but could take many weeks or even months including the wait at

Chagres on the eastern shore for a ship to New York. All things considered, the Cape Horn route seemed best for Ramón if he were accepted by Yale.

After a long, anxious wait, Ramón received the requested information from Yale, returned the application, and resigned himself to more waiting. Finally he received the hoped-for notification of his acceptance for the academic year beginning in September 1836. The news came shortly before Don Guillermo's death, so Ramón was able to share the good news with his father. It was a poignant moment for both father and son to realize that while one was just starting out on this new adventure, the other's life experience was drawing to a close.

Because of the length of the journey around Cape Horn, Ramón planned to be away from home the entire four years required to complete his undergraduate studies. His mother, Doña Caterina, was grieving her husband's death, a grief which Ramón naturally shared. He could easily have given in to the emotional pressure not to leave at that time and be away for so long. However, everyone agreed that life must go on as they believed Don Guillermo would have wanted. Cristina Beatriz was occupied with planning for her new married life, and everything else was going on as usual.

With his earlier enthusiasm somewhat subdued, Ramón packed a few belongings and completed arrangements for the long journey ahead. He would travel by coach along El Camino Real to the Presidio at Monterey, where he would board the American bark Valiant that would take him around Cape Horn to New York and a new stage in his life.

Realizing that customs of dress might differ between Alta California and the eastern United States, Ramón took very little with him, only what was needed for the sea voyage. He intended to fill out his wardrobe upon arrival in New York, after observing what was the customary attire for that part of the world.

After bidding final farewells, Ramón rode with Antonio to the Mission San Gabriel, where he boarded the coach, and Antonio returned to his ranch duties. Ramón began to feel a twinge of homesickness which he quelled with a determination to enjoy the scenery along the way.

Leaving the mission on El Camino Real, the coach passed through the plaza of Los Angeles, where Ramón heard the angelus tolled from the belfry of the Iglesia de Nuestra Señora and thought it would be a long time before he heard that again.

The coach's first stop on El Camino Real was at Mission San Fernando, a short distance northwest. Ramón had visited the mission often and always admired its blending of moorish architecture with Roman style arches in a long, open corridor. Next the coach stopped at Mission San Buenaventura, where passengers first saw the Pacific Ocean, then continued up the coast to the Mission Santa Barbara.

From points along the coast between the Missions San Buenaventura and Santa Barbara, looking out over the blue Pacific, Ramón could see a few miles offshore the three northernmost of the chain of Santa Barbara or Channel Islands. On one of them was said to be buried Juan Rodriguez Cabrillo, who first explored the California coast in 1542. These distant islands, glimmering in the sunshine, were very appealing to Ramón who hoped one day to visit and explore them himself.

The coach travelled up a hillside road from the presidio and pueblo of Santa Barbara to the mission which had been rebuilt following the 1812 earthquake. After a brief halt, the coach continued north on El Camino Real, turned inland and up a steep slope into the mountains where the Mission Santa Iñes is located, then passed Mission La Purisima Conçepcion in its small coastal valley and went on to Mission San Luis Obispo de Tolosa once again near the Pacific Ocean. Here the coach stopped to change horses and give the passengers a brief overnight rest. They arose early for a scenic side trip of about twelve miles through "La Cañada de los Osas," named by de Portola in 1769 for the many grizzly bears in the area,[2] to see the beautiful blue bay with its white sand dunes and massive rocks that served as a landmark for early Spanish explorers.[2]

Returning to El Camino Real, the coach went inland and up another coastal valley, stopping at missions San Miguel Arcangel, San Antonio de Padua, and Nuestra Senora de la Soledad, before turning off to Monterey. One of the oldest communities in Alta California, Monterey was selected by de Portola as the site for the first presidio. The town was founded in 1770 by Franciscan fathers who also established Mission San Carlos Borromeo, which later was moved further south along the Rio Carmelo. Monterey had been the capital of Alta California since 1775, and had an active history that included being pillaged by a French pirate in 1818 (comparable to the British burning the White House in Washington a few years earlier).

Ramón was almost sorry to stop his tour of California missions without seeing the others further north. Somewhat reluctantly he stepped down from the coach to begin the next leg of his journey.

From among several two-masted trading schooners in the bay loading and unloading their cargoes at the Monterey wharf, Ramón spotted the three-masted bark *Valiant*, which would carry him to New York. After identifying himself to the captain, Ramón was welcomed aboard and shown to a small cabin which would be his home for the next three months.

Shortly after leaving port, the *Valiant* encountered one of the fierce storms that belied the ocean's name, "Pacific," and which brought on Ramón's first attack of seasickness. Also he could not deny an attack of homesickness on his first extended absence from home. Both played a part in the general feeling of depression that descended over him.

His gloom lifted somewhat with the occasional stops for provisions and deliveries of hides and tallow from California ranchos such as his. The *Valiant* first put in at La Orilla at the mouth of Rio de las Balsas on the west coast of Mexico. He recovered briefly at the sight and feel of land but on departure lapsed back into his earlier feeling of torpor, interrupted only by bouts of nausea. He did not get off at the next three stops.

He had wanted to visit the Bolivian port of Antofagasta, which was situated almost exactly on the Tropic of Capricorn. As this was as far south of the equator as the Tropic of Cancer, where the tip of Baja California was located, was north of the equator, Ramón was interested in noting similarities and differences between the two areas. However, a border dispute with Chile over the small Bolivian coastline had recently erupted into violence, so it was considered unsafe to land at that time.

Strangely, he began to feel better as the weather worsened. The midsummer of the northern hemisphere and the constant warmth at the equator had turned into mid-winter as the *Valiant* approached Cape Horn. Ramón aroused himself from near hibernation since leaving La Orilla and began to take more interest in his surroundings. They were approaching Tierra del Fuego at the southern end of South America—actually a large island separated from the mainland by the Strait of Magellan, which he learned was named for a Portuguese explorer in the service of Spain who first traversed it in 1520 on his way to the orient. Magellan was followed nearly sixty years later by Sir Francis Drake, who had the good sense to continue north up to the California coast, as Ramón knew from his history studies.

Instead of passing through this strait, the *Valiant* went further south through Beagle Channel, named after the ship in which naturalist

Charles Darwin had sailed on a surveying expedition five years previously, as explained to Ramón by a crew member. It was not just chilly now but bitter cold. Earlier sights of snow-capped peaks were replaced by glaciated mountains rising sharply from the water's edge, which was described by a fellow passenger, Robert Woodward, as resembling the spectacular fjords of Norway.

After sighting Cape Horn on the southernmost island of a group at the tip of the continent, and starting the journey north, Ramón began to feel more like joining his shipmates for regular meals and sharing in shipboard story-swapping. He learned that Buenos Aires on the Rio de la Plata in Argentina, which they were approaching, was beginning to rival New York as a port for European trade and was becoming more of a European than a South American city. He could not view this first hand, as the Valiant did not put in at Buenos Aires, but continued on to the Brazilian port of Rio Grande, at the entrance of Dos Patos Bay. He was a bit disappointed after the buildup of his expectations for Buenos Aires, but on going ashore at the smaller port was surprised to find the local citizens preparing to celebrate the centennial of the city's founding.

The next stop was at Salvador, Brazil, which was founded two years before Rio Grande and had been Brazil's capital until 1763.[18] He took the occasion to visit the church at the Portuguese Monastery of Sao Francisco and gave thanks for having survived the journey thus far and for returning to a warmer climate.

Their last stop in South America was Recife, a flourishing port for the cotton, sugar, and slave trade. Here Ramón saw first hand the slave markets he had only read about but believed represented much worse treatment of negroes than the Spanish/Mexican treatment of Indians in California. A more pleasant experience was exploring this two-century old city called the "Venice of Brazil" for being built on three rivers with many connecting bridges.[3] Coming from California, where major settlements were little more than a half century old, he was impressed by these Brazilian communities dating to the 16th century.

A final stop before reaching the United States was at the port of Santo Domingo on the island of Hispaniola in the West Indies. Ramón learned that Santo Domingo is the oldest European settlement in the Western Hemisphere and claims to house the remains of Christopher Columbus in its ancient cathedral. Alternating between French, Spanish, and native rule, it was now a part of a Haitian Republic following a rebellion led by former slave Pierre

Toussaint-L'Ouverture. Ramón was not overly impressed with the town or the country, and found the climate oppressive, but was moved by the political energy of former slaves in building their own nation, as compared with the slaves he had seen on the trading block in Recife and the comparatively docile mission Indians of Alta California.

Ramón's excitement mounted as the Valiant approached the American shores. His initial landings at the ports of Savannah and Charleston were fascinating to him, and he looked forward to returning. Their climate and leisurely living customs recalled his native Alta California and reactivated some homesickness, but that was soon replaced by new thoughts as the ship approached its destination.

He had learned from his fellow passenger Richard Woodward, who lived in nearby New Jersey, something of New York's phenomenal growth as a seaport. The Erie Canal in northern New York State was completed in 1825, which greatly reduced travel time and shipping costs from the west, opened up the Great Lakes for trade, and made New York the chief seaport on the Atlantic coast. Even before that New York had some special advantages. In the 1700s, the city extended only two or three streets from its wooden wall at the water's edge but already was a "boom town" with 3500 inhabitants. The reason was New York Governor Benjamin Fletcher's liberal attitude towards maritime affairs, including piracy. Thus the port of New York came to rival Newport to the north, and Charleston to the south, as a place to unload cargo with no questions asked. Fletcher was replaced as governor by the Earl of Bellomont, who reversed his predecessor's policies, but the die was cast and New York continued in a competitive position as an Atlantic seaport until the Erie Canal made it preeminent.[4]

Ramón was unprepared for and fascinated by the urban bustle of the city but, with the need to concentrate on selection of appropriate clothing, there was little time for sightseeing, so he made a mental note to return at the first opportunity.

Richard Woodward, who was slightly older than Ramón, gave him some advice on what to wear and directed him to a retail shop founded in 1818 by Henry Brooks as "a gentleman's store run by gentlemen." Here he received appropriate sartorial guidance and was able to fill most of his needs at a reasonable cost. He was referred to Lord and Taylor on Catherine Street for the remainder of his requirements.

One of the main problems Ramón encountered was exchanging the Spanish reales used in California for the coinage of the United States, which had undergone revision two years before, so both old and new coins were circulating at the same time, making it doubly confusing to a newcomer.

Although the Spanish "Pillar" dollar minted in Mexico and valued at eight reales was the principal coin of both Spanish and English colonists in the "new world," the newer American decimal coinage was now in fuller use in the United States. Ramón had to learn the value of the half cent and one cent copper pieces, the silver half disme and disme, and the larger quarter and half dollar pieces. There was no one dollar coin minted at that time, and those minted earlier were infrequently seen.

There were also gold coins in denominations of quarter and half eagles ($2 1/2 and $5) which had been redesigned in 1834, but no full eagles ($10) until 1838.

This was all very confusing to Ramón but perhaps this confusion and the need to learn the new system in a hurry gave rise to his interest in numismatics, and U.S. coins in particular, that remained with him the rest of his life. He noted with interest that the obverse of American coins bore the head of a fictitious female known as "Lady Liberty" rather than the likeness of a current ruler or head-of-state, such as used on Spanish, British, and most other national coinage but considered too "monarchial" for United States coins.

Another more serious problem Ramón had was lack of fluency in English. Although he had studied the language at home and practiced it aboard ship, he had difficulty with idiom and when conversation was fast, particularly as spoken in New York. To alleviate the problem, he planned to obtain tutoring in New Haven.

He left New York reluctantly but hurriedly to arrive in time to register before classes began. The trip by coach to New Haven over what was known as the Boston Post Road took a long and bumpy two days, relieved by an overnight stay at the Silvermine Tavern, a country inn on the banks of the Silvermine River near Norwalk, Connecticut.[5] Ramón enjoyed the respite and the evening meal in a dining room that overlooked a millpond and was decorated with paintings by local artists. The menu, featuring New England specialties such as broiled lobster and "white" clam chowder, as opposed to the clear or "red" style with tomatoes as served in New York, was especially interesting to this visitor who was accustomed to the Spanish style of cooking.

Ramón arrived in New Haven with two suitcases, just in time for registration and the beginning of classes and little time for anything else. He was fortunate in securing lodging in a private home that let rooms to students, in which he could also obtain English language tutoring. The house was that of a French born professor of medicine, and the tutor was his daughter—an attractive young woman only a few years older than Ramón. He might have had romantic inclinations towards her had he not been preoccupied with getting settled into his new life.

The professor's house, and Ramón's home for the time being, was a short distance from the Yale School of Medicine where, it was reported, students had engaged in grave-robbing and body-snatching from the nearby West Haven cemetery as recently as 1824. The Medical School building, constructed originally as a hotel, was acquired by Yale in 1813 as a home for its first professional school and later expanded to include the Sheffield Scientific School. The building was rumored to have a tunnel leading from the dissecting laboratory to the cemetery across the street, which enabled over-eager medical students to carry out their nocturnal activities.[16]

While enjoying other courses in history, science, and languages, Ramón was most interested in geology and was pleased that the class took field trips to outlying areas such as East Rock and up the Quinnipiac River to observe regional rock formations. They also studied what was available concerning the western United States acquired in the Louisiana Purchase, using books and drawings such as accounts of the Lewis and Clark expeditions of 1804–06 from St. Louis into the northwest regions.

Ramón was glad to be able to contribute something from his own knowledge of the topography of Alta California and of earthquakes such as that of 1812 recorded by the San Gabriel Mission.[8] There was also much interest in the formations, geologic and otherwise, of the new Republic of Texas, which had just won its independence from Mexico earlier that year. Students and teacher speculated on whether it might join the United States.

The American tradition of Thanksgiving first became known to Ramón when he learned that many students who lived nearby planned to leave for a few days in November to spend the holiday with families and friends. Expecting to be alone on his first vacation away from home, he was pleasantly surprised by an unexpected invitation from Royal and Helen Clement, distant relatives of the Clemente family who lived near Worcester, Massachusetts, a long days ride by coach from New Haven. It seemed that Ramón's aunt Isabel had kept in touch with these American cousins since visiting them in 1828 and had informed them that Ramón would be attending college at New Haven, might be feeling lonely, and would benefit from making their acquaintance.

By November there had been some early snows, and the harsh New England weather had become harsher when Ramón boarded the coach and travelled northeast to Worcester. On arrival late in the evening, he was warmly received by the Clements at their large white clapboard farmhouse. Royal Clement was a tall, robust man with white hair and ruddy complexion as might be expected of a successful farmer in this rugged New England climate. Ramón noticed a slight resemblance to his father before Don Guillermo lost much of his vigor due to illness. Helen Clement, Royal's wife, was plump and jolly with graying hair and an open, friendly face. She seemed to live for cooking good things for her large family and reminded Ramón not at all of Doña Caterina, who prided herself on having little knowledge of culinary arts. The Clements' eldest son, Lawrence, five years older than Ramón, was tall and lean with blond hair. He had attended Harvard college in Massachusetts, a traditional rival of Yale, so he and Ramón had much to talk about. There were four younger sons, three daughters, and many other relatives at the family gathering. Unfortunately Henry Clement, who was instrumental in Ramón's going to Yale, was unable to attend.

Ramón was charmed by the openness and friendliness of these American cousins as shown to their distant Spanish/Mexican relative and grateful for their patience with his newly acquired English and his unfamiliarity with Thanksgiving customs. The tastes of roast turkey, cranberries, and pumpkin pie were all new to him and well received by his palate, which usually welcomed new and tasteful experiences but was still recovering from the discomforts of the long journey around Cape Horn. Ramón entertained his relatives with tales of California, the sea voyage, visits to foreign ports, and the sometimes unnerving experiences of a foreign students' first arrival at an American college.

Although the hospitality left nothing to be desired, Ramón felt something of an outsider. Moreover, he had a longing for the familiar surroundings of sunny California and a strong desire not to be surrounded by white snowdrifts and buffeted by wintry winds. He was just as glad when it came time to meet the coach for the return trip to New Haven and left amid promises to return next year, which both sides probably knew would not be fulfilled. However, he was glad to have met the Clements of Worcester and to have learned more about this English branch of his father's side of the family.

Ramón remained fully occupied with his studies until Christmas time, when a classmate named Homer Bradford invited him to spend the holiday with his family in New York City. This fulfilled his earlier wish to return there after his first brief visit. He was also glad of the opportunity to meet more Americans, outside the collegiate community of New Haven, and particularly in such a cosmopolitan city as New York. He was accepted graciously by the Bradfords and found himself attracted to Homer's sister, Jeanette. Ironically being his classmate's sister reminded Ramón of his own sister, tending to place Jeanette outside the bounds of romantic consideration.

This New York visit was a memorable experience and one requiring Ramón to augment his relatively sparse wardrobe with appropriate attire for the rounds of balls and other festivities which were the custom in that city, especially during the holidays. Most enjoyable were festive occasions at Delmonico's Restaurant on William Street[18] and at Fraunce's Tavern on Wall Street. After the elegance of Delmonico's, he was relieved by Fraunce's Tavern's less impressive surroundings, such as its narrow stairway to the second floor dining room. He enjoyed the widely varied menu including unusual items such as bear.

Ramón remained impressed with the vitality of this busy community, in which people were constantly on the move. Even the horse-drawn carts proceeded at a brisk trot and often at full gallop. People gulped down meals and hurried from the table as if in fear of being late going somewhere else. They always seemed busy at something, and even in repose, men's jaws were busy chewing tobacco, near the ever present brass spittoons, more discreetly called cuspidors.

Ramón noted the lack of aesthetic interest amid the constant concern with making money. An earlier visitor had remarked that scenery meant nothing to Americans who considered a waterfall, for instance, "only as motive power for machinery."[6]

Though he found it exciting, compared with the more pastoral life of Alta California, Ramón was relieved when the time came to leave the fast pace of New York and return to his studies. The work became harder but increasingly interesting as he learned more and began to satisfy some of his thirst for knowledge, particularly of the earth's history and geologic formation.

In the spring, near Easter time, students were allowed time off for extended reading in their chosen fields of study. Ramón took advantage of the time to revisit one of the southern cities he so admired on a stopover during the prior year's sea voyage. He had made the acquaintance of a fellow student named Hosea Stewart from Charleston, South Carolina, and gladly accepted the Stewarts' invitation to visit. Hosea Beauregard Somerville Stewart was the grandson of early French and English immigrants. His given biblical name sounded like the Spanish "Jose," which Ramón liked to call his new friend, who in turn called him "Ray." Other classmates called Hosea by the initials of his two middle names—"B.S.," giving it a scatological connotation. Otherwise normal in every respect, Hosea was afflicted by an obsessive concern with the conquest of young women and was referred to by his colleagues as being "girl crazy." He was downcast at this particular time because his latest, and to him most serious girlfriend was seeing another man—an actor no less, a profession which was looked down upon in Charleston high society. Hosea hoped to correct the situation on this Charleston visit, and Ramón was going along for new adventures of his own.

While there were many railroad lines under construction since the Baltimore & Ohio began in 1828, none went all the way from New York to Charleston, or even Washington. The boys went by coach to Baltimore, where they boarded the B&O's new Washington branch, opened two years before.[7] The fare was $2.50 and well worth it for Ramón's first ride on a railroad. Everything about it was new and exciting to him. First the "Grasshopper" steam engine, so-called because of four vertical rods pumping up and down to move the four wheels. Power came from the vertical steam boiler, fueled by anthracite coal. Next came the baggage car which carried mail and small freight along with passenger luggage. The passenger cars were long and box-like with seats for forty passengers on either side of a central aisle.[8] This particular train was called Thomas Jefferson, which Ramón knew as the name of the third American president, who opened up the American west with the Louisiana Purchase.

As the train left Baltimore, he was impressed by the massive stone viaduct with eight arches, carrying the tracks across the Patapsco River.[7] His eyes were busy darting from left to right all the way to Washington, where the train arrived at a depot on Pennsylvania Avenue and Second Street. They planned to spend the night and the next day in Washington before continuing on to

Charleston by boat. They stayed at the nearby Indian Queen Hotel on Pennsylvania Avenue, the city's most famous hostelry. Taking this opportunity to familiarize himself with the nation's capital, Ramón enlisted the aid of a local citizen recommended by Jesse Brown,[9] the hotel manager, to show them the sights.

First they went to the capitol building then joined a White House tour, made up mostly of women who wanted to see at least one of the four eligible sons of the new president. They also wanted to see the elegant Blue Room for which Van Buren himself was said to have selected the materials for upholstery, curtains, wallpaper, and carpeting, all in blue.

Afterwards they visited the new Treasury Department and adjoining State Department building on 15th Street just east of the White House. Little did Ramón know that he would be working there, at the State Department, fifteen years later.

The rest of the journey was by water, down the Potomac River from the port of Georgetown to the mouth of Chesapeake Bay, then down the Atlantic coast to Charleston. Immediately on arrival the boys felt balmy southern breezes and a warm southern welcome— and none too soon for Ramón. He greatly enjoyed excursions to nearby beaches to bask in the welcome sunshine after the unusually ferocious winter of 1836–7 in the northeast. It took him some time to overcome recent feelings of nearly frozen ears, nose, and fingers while dragging his thick-blooded southwestern-bred body from one classroom to another through snow-covered streets, and at day's end huddling in his rented room, trying to gain some warmth from a down comforter and a draughty fireplace.

Later he could identify with an article in the July 1838 *North American Review* on the subject of winter apparel. In criticizing American headgear, the author stated, "One great reason why Americans stoop so much is, that living in a country where high winds prevail, they are obliged to walk stooping half the time, to prevent the wind's blowing their hats off."[10] Ramón had personally experienced this problem, not only in wintry New Haven and Worcester, but also in New York on frequent visits; but he was glad to be spared the problem for a brief period in the spring of 1837 in Charleston, South Carolina.

On their way south, Hosea had told Ramón some Charleston history. Originally named Charles Town by the first English settlers in 1670, it soon became a center of wealth and culture. Charleston's distinctive architecture resulted from houses being built on long narrow lots laid out in 1680. Property was taxed on front footage, so houses were built the width of one room facing the street, with a side entrance on a long pillared porch. The porches were wide enough for a hoop skirt and usually ran almost the full length of the house and two or three stories high. Some larger houses built on two lots were the width of two rooms.

One Sunday afternoon, Ramón and his classmate attended a grand picnic at a plantation on the Ashley River upstream from Charleston. Ramón was fascinated by the strange hanging growths on the oak trees, called spanish moss, which was in drab contrast with the shiny green leaves of the magnolia trees and the brilliant red and white azaleas coming to bloom in late March.

After a sumptuous buffet of venison; chicken; ham; fish; and a wide variety of salads, cakes, and fruits, there was dancing in the ballroom of the stately mansion with its two-story Greek-styled columns and wide veranda around the front and sides. Ramón was amused by a local custom whereby a couple would take seats at opposite ends of a contraption called a "jogglin' board" and, due to its peculiar design, soon found themselves close together in the middle.[11]

In addition to visiting beaches and plantations, Ramón attended a number of Charleston social functions, notable as much for their gastronomic delicacies as for Charleston mothers promoting the southern charms of their elegantly attired and carefully groomed young daughters onto unsuspecting bachelors. In the gastronomic category, Ramón was much taken with the Charleston cuisine, including such delights as cucumber soup, shrimp "perloo" (combined with rice), crisp corn sticks, and lemon cream meringue[12]—all quite different from food in Spanish California, or the New England dishes with which he was now familiar.

In the female department, he by-passed the young ladies most obviously thrust on him, but became strongly attracted to a girl he met on his own who offered to teach him some of the local dances at a party they both attended. Ramón wrongly believed she was equally attracted to him until he learned she was serious about another man. Disappointed but undismayed, he formed a close friendship with another young lady who, like himself, was visiting in Charleston. Her name was Carla Doran, and she was from New York City, where her father was engaged in financial pursuits. Carla and Ramón exchanged addresses and planned to meet again when they returned north.

He was sorry to leave Charleston and almost reluctant to get back to the purpose of his being in the United States. It was difficult reentering the routine of concentration on studies after the pleasant, carefree time in Charleston. There was also some growing anxiety over the approaching end of his first academic year and the question of how to occupy the intervening summer months before the start of his second year of studies. While his family had financed the basic costs of his four-year education, including tuition, books, room and board, initial clothing requirements, and round-trip transportation, Ramón had planned to find employment during the three summer vacations of 1837, 1838, and 1839, which would pay for his other expenses such as excursions to New York and Charleston, additional clothing, entertainment, etc., for which he had already borrowed from funds advanced for his basic education costs. Now that the time was nigh for execution of his plan, there came the problem of how to go about it successfully.

He was advised it would not be a simple task to obtain employment in the summer of 1837 because of the financial panic and developing depression throughout the land. He was informed and believed that his best opportunities lay in the city of New York, a center of finance, commerce, and industry, where he now had some personal contacts. Through his classmate Homer Bradford's family and Carla Doran's father, Ramón obtained introductions to several New York firms that granted interviews for summer employment. Of most interest to him was the possibility of employment at one of the New York banking institutions, which he felt would broaden his knowledge and understanding of American business practices and be useful in facilitating the export of commodities from the ranch when he returned to California.

Affecting his plan was the current financial crisis whereby most banks suspended gold and silver payments, causing shortages of subsidiary coinage. The banks increased issuance of paper currency, particularly in smaller denominations, which were popularly known as "shinplasters." Many private companies, including the new railroads, followed the banks in this practice by issuing their own "shinplasters" in amounts ranging from 2¢ to $100, which achieved wide circulation and greatly complicated the monetary system. This created additional work at the banks and provided for Ramón an opening on the ground floor of the banking business.

Ramón's first interview was with the Chemical Bank, the president of which, John Mason, was one of the city's wealthiest landowners and

a personal friend of Carla Doran's father. Ramón felt a premonition
of success as he entered the bank's offices in a three-story residential
building at 216 Broadway opposite St. Paul's Chapel[13] and was ushered into the president's office. Mr. Mason appeared to be in his mid-
forties, clean shaven; with light graying hair, an angular face, and
wide, dark eyes that fixed directly on Ramón as he entered the room.
Though not as forbidding as he appeared, John Mason was direct and
business-like with few conversational amenities. At first Ramón felt he
was not measuring up to whatever Mason expected, but after a few
moments became more at ease and then almost exuberant as the president indicated approval and turned him over to the department head
for whom he would be working to receive further instruction. Ramón
congratulated himself on getting his first paying job, even a relatively
menial one of sorting "shinplasters." Because of his fluency in
Spanish, he soon was given further assignments in the bank's foreign
department, and by summer's end he felt he had a little knowledge of
the banking business as well as a lasting affection for his first employ-
er, the Chemical Bank of New York.

Through his summer employment, in addition to his academic
studies, Ramón was learning much about the fast-growing nation.
From conversations with fellow employees, college classmates and
their families, other local citizens, and from reading magazines and
newspapers, he knew there was a rivalry between residents of the
east coast and those living west of the Appalachian mountains. It
seemed to be based on distrust by western pioneers of eastern
bankers who financed them, and easterners' fears of being outvoted
by the growing western populace. Western pioneers saw easterners
as "grasping, aristocratic, snobbish, dangerous, effete, and undemo-
cratic." On the other hand, former Yale President Timothy Dwight,
known as the "Pope of Connecticut" (who considered Thomas
Jefferson an anarchist), wrote: "The pioneers cannot live in regular
society. They are too idle, too talkative, too prodigal, and too shift-
less to acquire either property or character."[14]

Ramon's reading and conversations made him aware of the ties
between northern and southern sections of the west, born of their
sharing the Mississippi River, being closer than ties between the
northwest and the northeast, separated as they were by the
Appalachian mountains, until the Erie Canal brought western access
to the port of New York in 1824.

In the fall of 1839, he came in closer touch with the issue of
slavery, which he observed first hand on his visit to Charleston two

years before. In October 1839, the Spanish ship Amisted arrived at the port of New Haven with forty-odd Africans who had revolted against their captors, been recaptured, and brought to New Haven for imprisonment pending trial. They were aided in their plight by Yale and people of the city who were predominately opposed to slavery. Ramón learned later that the Africans were freed by Supreme Court decision after nearly two years imprisonment and returned to their homes.[15]

On a personal level he was deeply hurt and disappointed by the provincialism and bigotry of some of his classmates and other Americans who equated Spanish- and Mexican-born persons such as himself with half-breeds and Indians and deserving of no better treatment. He was also disturbed by the tremendous drive for wealth, particularly in the eastern United States. This was emphasized in a *New York Sun* article of 1838, which said in part: "There is scarcely a lad of any spirit who does not, from the time he can connect the most simple ideas, picture to himself some rapid road to wealth.... He dreams of dashing into a fortune by some lucky speculation. Contentment with competence he learns to regard as a slothful vice. To become rich, and of course respected, influential, great, powerful, is his darling object."[17] This was so foreign to Ramón's own beliefs that he doubted whether he could ever be successful or happy living in the United States.

His social activities gradually expanded through contacts with his classmates' families and friends, but so far he had formed no serious romantic attachments. On one occasion he became attracted to a young widow named Jane Hodges, who was being courted clandestinely by a married uncle of his classmate Hosea. When trouble developed between her and the older man, Ramón felt and expressed sympathy for the young widow, which developed into a friendship between them. She asked him to escort her to several functions in New York, which he greatly enjoyed, but felt uncomfortable with some of her older friends, who showed amused tolerance of what they obviously considered a mismatch. He accepted this as a price for being with someone he genuinely liked and who seemed to like him as well.

Jane had two daughters, not much younger than Ramón himself, and he began to think about what it would be like to acquire a ready-made family. There came a time when Jane told him she had to go out-of-town to take care of a business matter concerning some property from her late husband's estate. It was not clear just who first suggested it, but it soon came about that Ramón would accompany her on what would be a trip of more than a day's duration to a New Jersey seaside resort. He was enthused at the prospect and Jane was too, yet she was also a bit apprehensive as to what her friends and associates might think of such a trip with a younger man, which also lent some zest to the occasion. Her daughters did not seem to disapprove, which he appreciated. But the day before they were scheduled to leave, when Ramón was at Jane's home making final arrangements, Hosea's uncle appeared unexpectedly at the door and pleaded with Jane not to go, at least for appearances sake. He finally prevailed on her to call it off, and Ramón reluctantly withdrew from the field, thus giving up his first infatuation with an older woman.

Unfortunately his frequent trips out of town and attentions to certain young ladies he met interfered with Ramón's studies during his second year to the extent that he failed to earn sufficient credits for advancement with the rest of his class to third year status. He was deeply chagrined over this development, particularly after the expense his family had incurred and the funds advanced for his education.

In order to make it up, he intensified his efforts and was able to rejoin his class the following year and to graduate with honors in June of 1840. Because of the distance, no family representatives could attend the graduation ceremonies, but he invited and was gratified by the presence of his friend Carla Doran from New York, which made him feel less alone on that significant occasion in his life—in fact it probably was more enjoyable than if someone from his family had been there.

Ramón had reserved a room for Carla at the Tontine House in New Haven. She later told him about an Englishman staying at the hotel who was used to English plumbing and complained about the lack of a "proper water closet" and of having to go outside to another structure in back of the hotel.[18] On a broader note, she described how the former rapid pace of New York City had slowed to a virtual standstill since the Panic of 1837 when bankers suspended specie payments. Ramón had been aware of this during his summer employment, but it still was hard to accept the picture of a nearly lifeless city of 300,000 with boats lying idle at the docks and building construction slowed to near standstill.

But they didn't spend all their time in such talk. Ramón showed Carla his favorite places around town and escorted her to all the commencement activities, during which he proudly introduced his

New York lady friend to envious classmates whose own activities were curtailed by visiting family members.

They attended a small gathering of classmates involved in one of his extra-curricular activities of which Ramón was exceptionally proud, development of the new *Yale Banner*, the college yearbook first published the year following his graduation.[1] He hadn't had time for many such activities and was not handy at sports, particularly American games with which he was totally unfamiliar and only embarrassed himself and probably others by attempting to participate in them. But altogether he was not displeased with his accomplishments, had few regrets, and many pleasurable experiences to recall in later years.

Finally, as the college song goes, it came time for Ramón to "bid old Yale farewell" and return home, certainly older and perhaps a bit wiser, and wondering what to do with the rest of his life. Although enjoying his studies and his exposure to the eastern United States after the relative isolation of Alta California, Ramón felt he had enough of the academic scene. He could not deny some trepidation in facing the unpredictable future with its limitless possibilities; but he was now ready to return home, possibly to manage the family ranch or take up some other occupation to begin earning his own way.

PART II
OLD AND NEW DIRECTIONS

CHAPTER 3
BACKGROUND FOR CONQUEST

To digress from the story and furnish some pertinent background information:

Don Guillermo Clemente traced his ancestry back to the ninth century in the Normandy section of what is now France. From there one branch of the family grew from a member who went with William the Conqueror to England in 1066, where the French name Clément was pronounced Clement without the accent on the first "e." Thereafter the Clements in England kept in contact with the Cléments of France, and later with the Clementes who went to Spain and the "new world," adding a final "e" to the name.

All branches of the family were proud of their name—the name taken by the first Pope in 88 A.D. and used by fourteen popes thereafter. They were also proud of an illustrious Clément who was "Maréchal de France" in 1248.[1] While all branches of the family participated in various military endeavors, they were particularly proud of the meaning of their name—clement or merciful.

In 1494 Don Guillermo's branch of the family migrated south from France into what had been the Kingdom of Granada, under Moorish rule until 1492 when it became part of what is now Spain.

From Spain Don Guillermo's ancestor accompanied the Conquistador Cortez on his conquest of Mexico in 1518 and later became part of Coronado's expedition in 1540 to what is now the American southwest. After Don Juan de Onate established a colony near the site of what is now El Paso, Texas, other colonies and missions were established further north, and the Clementes settled in Santa Fe, where they lived until moving to California.[2]

The fact that both branches of Ramón's ancestral family, which originated in Normandy, had been in the "conquering" business in spite of the meaning of their last name may have been a coincidence or just a function of the times; it also may have contributed to Ramón's later interest in the "conquest" of California by the American explorer John C. Fremont.

Not a "conqueror" by nature, Ramón was even considered by some to be passive. He did not seek out conflict or confrontation and usually conducted himself so as to avoid such if possible, without sacrificing principles or ethical considerations. If pushed too far, he had been known to fight rather well and give a fairly good account of himself against attackers, considering he had little or no training in that regard.

In spite of this aspect of his personality, the earlier background for conquest may have had its influence, along with certain other factors, on his growing interest in civics or public affairs in general and the future governance of California in particular.

One such factor was his father's response to Ramón's earliest expression of interest in learning more about ranch operations such as the disposition of hides and tallow for profit. After thinking about it for some time, at the age of nine he asked his father very seriously, "Father, how can I learn about business?"

His father seemed amused at the question and did not answer directly but laughed tolerantly. His father's actual words in reply were lost in Ramón's embarrassment and feeling of humiliation at the implied rebuke for his impertinence or precocity in asking for information on a subject he was obviously considered not old enough to comprehend. He never asked his father again for help in this area and resolved to find out on his own or from other sources what he felt he needed to know.

Another factor was the news of his distant relative Henry Clement's entrance into U.S. government employment and subsequent rapid advancement. Perhaps the chief factor in directing Ramón towards a career in public affairs was his growing awareness of the extremely loose and decadent organization that passed for government in California, as compared with that of the United States with which he was now more familiar. These experiences made him realize that some change in government was inevitable and necessary for California to reach its economic potential. While it was an extremely pleasant place in which to live an easy, uncluttered life, Alta California was considerably lacking in the cultural and economic developments that Ramón had learned to appreciate in the eastern United States.

American newspapers and journals told of the intense and growing interest of the people of the United States for westward expansion, which Ramón knew would affect directly the way of life as it had been in Alta California. He believed it would be better to have a part in whatever change took place, and perhaps play a role in helping shape it, rather than allow himself to be buffeted about by whatever developed, possibly to his subsequent disadvantage.

CHAPTER 4
WORK ETHIC AND PUBLIC SERVICE

What would a Spanish Catholic boy know about a "Protestant work ethic"? Well, Catholics had something like that too. After all both Christian faiths, Catholic and Protestant, have basically the same moral and ethical beliefs taken from the same Bible, including both Old and New Testaments.

Ramón saw first hand the New England view of the Protestant work ethic when he was in the eastern United States. But it only bore out what he already had absorbed through earlier upbringing and the examples set by his two grandfathers, although he only learned of it second hand as one grandfather had already died and the other was no longer active when he was growing up.

Unfortunately there were few living role models for this work ethic in Ramón's immediate family. His father, Don Guillermo, was ill much of the time his son was growing up and died when Ramón was sixteen years old. Several uncles, for various reasons including the easy style of living in Alta California and the munificence of Don Julio Calderon, did not set the same example as Ramón's grandfathers themselves might have. So he learned mostly from reading at home, augmented by scholastic studies and observations in the eastern United States.

Further, as he had received little practical experience or guidance in the world of business at this stage of his life, it may have been natural for him to become interested in the area of public service and to apply the inherited and acquired work ethic principles in that field of endeavor.

CHAPTER 5
TIEING IT ALL TOGETHER

So how do all these diverse elements come together to make a credible story of an actual life experience? Maybe there is no such consistency or continuity to most peoples' lives—no destiny of inherited traits driving one to some foregone conclusion. Maybe most humans inch along with day-to-day occurrences, looking for some pattern and finally realize that while there is one enormous overall plan for the universe, each person's individual plans can be overtaken and overturned by millions of unforeseen and unscheduled events.

The events that drove or led Ramón Luis Clemente into the company of John C. Fremont and his quest for California statehood were certainly not foreseen, although in hindsight one can see where they might have been predicted. Perhaps Ramón was prepositioned by chance to be in the right place at the right time for the Fremont connection.

He could just as easily have become associated with the activities in California of leaders from other nations, such as England, which made its acquisitive intentions known early on; or the Russian attempt to enlarge their base of operations at Fort Ross. After Russia laid claim to Alaska in 1784, Russian seal hunters moved south and in 1812 established a fortress near the mouth of the Russian River, about seventy miles north of San Francisco Bay. They traded with the Presidio despite Spanish opposition, prompting establishment of the two northernmost missions, San Rafael (1817) and San Francisco Solano (1823), to halt further Russian expansion.

In spite of these and other foreign incursions, Ramón's attention was directed more towards the United States effort because of his recent experiences than towards the plans of the Czars or the British monarchs which he believed had relatively less to offer in terms of developing the full potential of Alta California.

One of the things that appealed to Ramón about the Americans was their ability to poke fun at themselves and their government without losing respect for either. Such was indicated by the "Hard Times Tokens" that circulated during Ramón's early years in the United States. This unofficial coinage apparently resulted from President Andrew Jackson's removal of Federal deposits from the Second Bank of the United States in 1837, which precipitated the financial panic. This action was related to Jackson's advocacy of hard money (gold and silver) in which he was joined by Missouri Senator Thomas Hart Benton, later to become John Fremont's mentor and father-in-law.

One of the early tokens satirized Jackson's supposed egotism by depicting a Roman Emperor's draped bust on the obverse; others bore inscriptions referring to Jackson's closing of the bank. Some were a bit more ugly, bearing likenesses of pigs and jackasses, and mottos with thinly veiled criticisms of Jackson and Benton. One dated 1838, had a singularly unattractive "Miss Liberty" head on the obverse with the words "LOCO FOCO" on her headband (instead of the word LIBERTY as on regular coinage) and on the reverse was the inscription "MINT DROP—BENTON EXPERI- MENT."[1]

While there was no actual shortage of copper coinage at this time, these tokens served a purpose of releasing some of the public anger against those considered to be responsible for the current depression—the politicians in office at the time.

On a personal level, while Ramón frequently found occasion for self doubt, he tended not to look for flaws in those who became leaders at least until he became old enough to accept that all others are as human and mortal as himself. Maybe he had not yet achieved this level of wisdom when first he became associated with Fremont.

PART III
FREMONT AND THE SPANISH TRAIL (1840–1844)

CHAPTER 6
HOW PATHS CROSSED

While Ramón Clemente was pursuing his education in the eastern United States, he read in the newspapers about Senator Benton of Missouri, whose exhortations to Congress for westward expansion of the new nation to the Pacific Ocean were made in the name of "manifest destiny." One of the Senator's main arguments for this was to prevent the western part of the continent from falling into the hands of foreigners, particularly the British, who had surveyed the harbor of San Francisco Bay and indicated further intentions.

Ramón followed these developments in an abstract manner at first, if only because of a natural concern about events affecting Alta California. Later he acquired a more personal interest in Senator Benton's goals when he learned of the Senator's association with John Fremont.

Ramón Clemente had met John Fremont in 1837 while visiting friends in Fremont's home town of Charleston, South Carolina. Fremont had just returned from a tour in the U.S. Navy as an instructor in mathematics on a cruise to South America.

Though John Fremont was six years older than Ramón Clemente, they had several things in common, such as: having been dropped temporarily from their college class because of other diversions, but later reinstated; losing fathers, both of French ancestry, at an early age, and having concerns for their widowed mothers left alone; recent visits to South American seaports; and an interest in native American Indians. Even John Fremont's interest in astronomy related to Ramón Clemente's interest in geology. They had met several times at Charleston gatherings and once had a long discussion about the development of the earth in relation to other celestial bodies in space. Neither expected their paths to cross again, being from widely separated parts of the continent and pursuing different objectives at the time.

Through correspondence with his classmate Hosea Stewart, Ramón learned later of Fremont's appointment to the Army Topographical Corps and the surveying expeditions which led to his meeting Senator Benton, marrying his daughter Jessie, and going to St. Louis to prepare for the western explorations which earned him acclaim as the "Pathfinder."

By this time Alta California's population approached 25,000, including 15,000 Indians, of which one-third worked at the Missions. While the Presidio at Monterey was still the military headquarters for the area, Los Angeles was the civilian capital with close to 1,500 population.

For the first three years after returning home, Ramón occupied himself principally with details of running the family ranch, assisted by the aging Antonio Morales. Ramón's favorite horse Bolivar was now seven years old, and while still ridden frequently, needed replacement for the more demanding aspects of ranch work. For this purpose, Ramón selected a two-year-old bay he named Cristobal and broke him to the bit as he had Bolivar six years before.

Doña Caterina, who continued to mourn for Don Guillermo, was at no loss for eligible escorts to social functions, or other opportunities for male companionship, but found none to compare with her deceased mate; so she turned more toward her son. Ramón wanted to do all he could for his mother but felt somewhat constrained in efforts to expand his own horizons.

However, along with his ranch duties and trying to help his widowed mother, Ramón found time for courting a variety of señoritas from neighboring haciendas and the town of Los Angeles. While most of these relationships remained within customary bounds, he became more than casually involved on several occasions. Once was with a young American girl of Scandinavian descent named Hedda Pringle, who came west with her aunt from Michigan, apparently to seek a husband. Hedda seemed to be friendly with many young men, and Ramón should have known better, but his brief involvement was such that he was later named, along with several others, in connection with a scandal that developed when Hedda became pregnant. Eventually one of the others was determined to be the father and assumed responsibility. Ramón was relieved of considerable anxiety and embarrassment over the attention the incident received in the community.

A more serious involvement was with another American, Margaret Heath, a widow with a young daughter who had come with her husband from Illinois to settle in California. Though a few years older than Ramón, she seemed to genuinely care for him as he did for her, and they had many good times together. One evening when he was waiting for Margaret in her parlor to escort her to a party, her young daughter Lenore, who was very precocious, asked him point-blank, "Are you and my mother going to get married?"

Somewhat flustered, Ramón replied, "Well, we haven't really talked about it yet."

He realized that although he had thought about it, he had not admitted to himself the proximity of his need to make a choice in the matter. Now he knew, from his reaction to the young girl's question, that much as he cared for Margaret and enjoyed being with her, he was not yet ready to make such a commitment.

Of all the young women he had met thus far, he most fancied Señorita Juanita Gutierrez-Delgado. Her father was an English sea captain who fell in love with California, decided to stay, and married a local woman who bore Juanita. The captain died when Juanita was fifteen. Her mother remarried a Mexican, and Juanita took the names of her mother and stepfather.

Ramón and Juanita had in common the loss of their fathers at an early age. They enjoyed talking together in English—Juanita to keep from forgetting the language of her father, and Ramón to practice what he had learned in the United States. He became very fond of Juanita, and their relationship might have gone further had he remained in California, but fate had other things in store for each of them.

Ramón particularly enjoyed summer seaside "meriandas," or picnics at ranchos Sausal Redondo, San Vicente y Santa Monica, and Topanga Malibu Sequit, which bordered on the Pacific Ocean. Even getting there was pleasurable for him. The climate around his ranch and the Mission San Gabriel was hot and dry in the summer, and about the same in the pueblo of Los Angeles, but riding west from there he turned off El Camino Real onto El Camino Viejo which followed an ancient Indian trail from the former village of Yang-Na past the tar pits to the Chumash seaside fishing villages, now absorbed by the Spanish land grant ranchos.[8]

The scenery changed after the tar pits. There were fewer pepper trees which the padres had planted for shade and more live oaks which flourished on the coastal hillsides. He thought of the Gabrielenos taking this same trail to visit and trade with their seaside counterparts and recalled their naive belief that the porpoises offshore were guarding the land from celestial dangers.[9]

A few miles further, before the ocean came in sight, the air changed from hot and dry to cool and damp, which Ramón enjoyed all the way to Don Francisco Sepulveda's Rancho San Vicente y Santa Monica, or further north to Don José Tapia's Rancho Topanga Malibu Sequit.[10] This simple enjoyment was augmented by the excitement of arriving at the ranch and joining the other guests for the occasion. After appropriate greetings, they would proceed to the seashore picnic area and consume large quantities of roast chicken, barbecued beef, tamales, and enchiladas, washed down with wine from the rancho vineyards. This was followed by siesta and sometimes a cooling dip into the surf by unclad younger male guests at a discreet distance from the others. Much later there was dinner with music and dancing at the hacienda, usually until early morning.

Sometimes Ramón would ride Cristobal a short way south of Los Angeles to attend a party at Rancho Los Alamitos, which bordered the south coast. This ranch was acquired in 1842 by Don Abel Stearns, originally from Massachusetts, who at age forty had married fourteen-year-old Arcadia Bandini, daughter of a prominent Californio. Stearns, called "Cara de Caballo" (horse-face) by the natives, was given to entertaining in a grand fashion. He built an elegant adobe in Los Angeles named El Palacio, where he and his young bride also entertained frequently.[11]

One of Ramón's favorite trips when he wanted to get away by himself for a while was to ride down El Camino Real about sixty miles south from Mission San Gabriel to a spot four miles past Mission San Juan Capistrano and camp out on the cliffs above the ocean. Most of this area, which lay about half way between the pueblos of Los Angeles and San Diego, had been divided into six land grants awarded to favored leaders of Capt. Pedro Fages' "Soldades de Cuero" (Leather Jacket Guard) that subdued the original Indian inhabitants. Because of its rugged terrain, the particular location Ramón selected for his campsite was not a part of any of the official land grants, although cattle from the nearby ranchos grazed on the surrounding hills.

After the long ride he slept soundly under the stars, lulled by the sound of the surf pounding on the shore below. In the morning he would ride down to the beach through a secluded canyon which was said to be the site of the first Christian Baptism in Alta California. The story was that Baja California Governor Gaspar de Portolá took an expedition north from San Diego, after leaving Father Junipero Serra to found the first mission, and camped in this location. Two padres who were members of the group observed two Indian women outside a nearby village carrying children who appeared very ill and near death. Although the mothers would not allow their children to be examined, they did permit the priests to sprinkle the babies' heads with water so that if they died the babies would go to heaven.[2]

Upon arriving at the beach, Ramón would ride Cristobal along the wet, hard-packed sand where the incoming surf rolled across, sending up a spray of cool sea water before the wave receded. Then he would dismount and dash into the surf himself, diving into the waves and sometimes letting them carry him back to the shore. Often when the waves were high he would be rolled underneath the water and nearly lose his breath, which was momentarily frightening but otherwise exhilarating. Afterwards he would stretch out on the sand and dry off under the sun, while Cristobal grazed nearby, snatching isolated clumps of grass and seaside plants from outcroppings of rock and the cliffs surrounding the beach.

Some days when it was very clear, he could see offshore the two southernmost of the chain of Channel Islands. The nearest one, to the north just off the point of land where author Richard Henry Dana landed in 1830,[11] was named Santa Catalina. The farthest one, directly ahead of where he stood, was named San Clemente which Ramón looked upon with great warmth as if there were a personal connection between him and the island which bore his name.

On his way home after such an outing, Ramón rode past the Rancho Santa Margarita, nearest of the Spanish land grants. Its adobe ranch house, built in 1837 by Governor Pio Pico, was later sold, so it was said, to pay his gambling debts. This brought Ramón back to reality after enjoying his brief respite from normal daily life.

Richard Henry Dana's *Two Years Before the Mast*, which was published in 1840, had reached California, and Ramón was interested in seeing his native land through the eyes of an American, just the reverse of his own recent experience in the United States. The author's name reminded him of Richard Henry Woodward, his fellow passenger aboard the Valiant around Cape Horn in 1836. Since then he had tried to contact Woodward many times without success and often wondered what had become of him.

Dana wrote of smuggling hides, which he called "California banknotes," down cliffs at night to his waiting ship; of riding fast horses on California ranchos; and of attending lively fandangos where he danced with lovely señoritas. But Ramón was particularly struck by Dana's description of "the average lazy Californian as a man blighted by a curse, which deprived him of all good qualities but pride, a fine manner, and a cultivated voice."[3] Dana's writing reflected what Ramón recognized as American Protestant contempt for the Spanish Catholic way of life and a belief that Californios were unworthy of the beautiful land they inhabited. Ramón recalled his own possibly too-harsh judgements of life in eastern American cities, such as fast-paced, money-chasing, self-centered New Yorkers, and wondered if perhaps visitors might be overly biased on their first trips to new lands and needed more time to realize that most people have more in common than they have differences.

While involved in many activities, Ramón noticed that the political climate of Alta California was changing. With the unstable conditions in Mexico, many government officials were underpaid and resorted to graft and corruption. Administrative chaos followed, foreign debts grew, and disintegrating forces were felt throughout Alta California.

Secularization of the mission system in 1835, while indirectly stimulating the growth of Los Angeles as a city, led directly to the plundering of mission lands. Mission San Gabriel had 16,500 head of livestock when the first civil administrator took over, but nine years later, when management was restored to the Franciscans under Padre Estenega, there were less than 800 animals to be turned over.[4] Disorder in the local government and the military establishment resulted in general dissatisfaction and strained relations between California and the rest of Mexico.

The system of land grands was widely abused. During forty years before Mexican independence, less than twenty large concessions of land were authorized in Alta California by the Spanish government. For the next eleven years until the Mexican government secularized mission property, there were only twelve to fifteen land grants. But after secularization, during the thirteen years before

American occupation, there were more than 500 land concessions, averaging nearly 50,000 acres apiece, to private individuals without any compensation. This tremendous increase, under the leadership of Ignacio del Valle, who was appointed by Governor Jose Figueroa as commissioner for secularization of the missions, was said to be justified as an economic stimulus to the area.[5]

Del Valle almost benefitted from discoveries of small quantities of gold on his property in San Fernando Valley. Mineral experts came from Sonora to inspect the finding and del Valle planned to charge a rental fee to prospective placer miners, but the amount of gold turned out to be not worth the cost.[14]

American settlers coming into California took advantage of the situation to acquire more land. In 1841 a Scotsman, Hugo Reid, who married an Indian woman, was granted the 13,000 acre Rancho Santa Anita east of Mission San Gabriel.[12] The same year John Rowland and William Workman came from New Mexico over the Spanish trail. They already had Mexican citizenship and Mexican wives and were able to buy the Puente ranch in San Bernardino valley.[13] The rapid progress of such newcomers earned the respect of many Californios, who became more closely bound to them than to Mexico.

General Micheltorena, who replaced Juan Bautista Alvarado as Governor, brought thirty-five "soldiers" to help defend Alta California from outsiders such as Commodore Jones, who attempted to claim Monterey for the United States. The general/governor's men, mostly convicts, were poorly clothed, ill-fed, and lived off the land, which angered the Californios.[15] Thus Alta California was ripe for the next stage, which was heralded by the arrival of John C. Fremont.

Ramón had not given much thought to John Fremont after their brief acquaintance in Charleston until April 1844, when he talked with Miguel Olivas, a vaquero from a ranch near Mission San Fernando. Olivas had been visiting relatives near the Sierras and, on his return, met Fremont's expedition coming down the San Joaquin valley. They had recently crossed the Rocky Mountains in mid-winter, which everyone including the Indians said could not be done. Then they crossed the desert and the Sierra Nevada and now were looking for the Spanish trail leading east to Santa Fe.[6] They wanted a guide who was familiar with the area so Olivas had volunteered and was on his way back to join them. He passed on to Ramón what he had picked up concerning Fremont's not-so-secret agenda which was aimed at opening up the west, including California, for U.S. emigration and possible later acquisition.

With his former interest in this subject rekindled and his earlier acquaintance with Fremont recalled, Ramón decided to accompany Olivas on his return trip to Fremont's camp. After a ride of two long days, they reached the camp at the base of the Tehachapi mountains on land now known as part of the vast Tejon Ranch. Fremont was surprised to see Ramón after so long a time and greeted him warmly.

Fremont appeared shorter than Ramón remembered, a full head shorter than himself, and now leaner and harder from his pioneering exploits. He had the same deep voice that compensated for his short stature; the same dark hair, now with full beard and moustache; and the same dark, brooding eyes, with almost a sad expression, inconsistent with his outwardly optimistic demeanor.[16] Expecting more of a military group, given Fremont's status with the Army Topographic Corps, Ramón was surprised by the somewhat bizarre appearance of Fremont's followers who seemed to represent many different races and nationalities, with clothing and language to match. They wore no uniforms, but all were armed, typically with muskets and long knives.

Fremont described his current mission as an extension of his first in 1842, which had been aimed at mapping a route to Oregon. The present expedition was to survey the Oregon trail west to the Pacific coast, connecting with a recent survey by Navy Lt. Charles Walker; then to continue south into the Mexican territory of California, picking up the Spanish trail on the return trip, all in the interest of western expansion of the United States, and to demonstrate the feasibility for travel by American settlers.[7]

Ramón expressed his interest and was encouraged to join the expedition on its return to St. Louis. It was also suggested that he might go on with Fremont to Washington to participate, as an interested Californian, in further developments for the westward expansion. Without hesitation Ramón agreed.

CHAPTER 7
OLD TRAILS AND NEW BEGINNINGS

After returning to the ranch to pack a few things and say farewells, Ramón rejoined Fremont. For what he expected to be an arduous journey over difficult terrain, Ramón had selected for his mount the horse Cristobal, as best suited by size and temperament to meet the unknown challenges ahead.

Ramón kept a journal of the trip from April 14, 1844, through July 31, 1844, which is reproduced in its entirety as follows:

"April 14, 1844: We join Fremont party near Tehachapi Pass. He introduces me to his principal assistants—Alexis Godey, a tall dark-haired Frenchman from St. Louis, and scout Kit Carson, a rough-hewn American also from Missouri. I first saw Carson when he came to San Gabriel Mission in 1830. He was 21 then and hasn't changed a lot, but I was only 11 so he doesn't recognize me. Maybe I'll tell him later.

"The group is a mixture of American, French, German and Indian, speaking all languages and with equally varied dress and equipment. One of the members is Prussian cartographer Charles Preuss, who charts the route taken by Fremont, as basis for maps to be used for later emigration west from the United States. He also functions as an artist who records significant events and features of the landscape we traverse. There are about 100 horses and mules, half wild. When on the move with scouts ahead and on both sides, and pack animals and horned cattle in the center, the entire group stretches out about one quarter mile.[1]

"We descend into grassy country, pass spot where Olivas says a refugee Christian Indian was killed by soldiers. Now in semi-desert region with many yucca trees. Make camp next to creek surrounded by black oak, with good grass for animals. I wonder what kind of food a party like this eats on the trail. They acquired beef from ranchos passed along the way, and now pan-fry steaks which they first pound to make tender, then cover with batter of egg and flour, which is delicious. With this we have beans, excellent cornbread with bacon, and much strong coffee, which helps keep me from falling asleep right away, as my head is full with thoughts of my new adventure.

"April 15–16, 1844: Leave grassy country, travel south, skirting desert. Pass through yucca forest into field of orange poppies, which greatly impresses Fremont party. I tell them how Mission Indians use poppies to make paints for their art works at San Gabriel Mission. Made camp by spring at foot of ridge. Many antelope and hare about. Fremont sends men back along trail to look for missing pack mule.

"April 17, 1844: Cross ridge near trail leading to Missions San Fernando and San Buenaventura, north of Los Angeles. Miguel Olivas, who brought me to Fremont's party three days ago and has guided the party thus far, points out the Spanish Trail ahead and leaves to return to Mission San Fernando. We continue through more flower fields and yucca forests, and make camp near stream without any nearby grass. Animals searching for range will have to be rounded up tomorrow morning.

"April 18–19, 1844: One day spent rounding up scattered animals. Continue eastward close to mountains south of desert. Make camp in rocky, sandy area with a few pine trees but little grass.

"April 20, 1844: A few miles further east, we reach Spanish Trail going north and south. Fremont party jubilant at being on homeward route. I am enthusiastic about starting my second trip from Alta California to the United States and my first by land. We make better time now on trail than over rocks and bushes encountered in getting here. We camp by river with considerable grass.

"April 21, 1844: We stay here all day to allow animals food and rest, making up for past deprivation and preparing for hardships ahead. My horse Cristobal is doing well so far. Reviewing notes of past week, find no entry for social activity in evening when work is done—like story-telling or singing and guitar playing around the campfire after eating, as California vaqueros would do. Fremont does not linger after meals, but retires early, probably to work on notes and reports relative to the purpose of his expedition. Some smaller groups form according to ethnic origin, particularly among the Indian members, and drift away from the others. I usually stay with Godey and Carson who speak mostly of serious matters concerning the expedition, and in lighter moments, speculate on the possibility of U.S. annexation of Texas after the November Presidential election and what form it might take, as to one or more states, free or slave, etc.[1] When such speculation takes place concerning California, should it become independent of Mexico, I join actively in the conversation, thinking in terms of two states, northern and southern California, both free of slavery. I recall similar conversation with my geology classmates after Texas became independent.

"As to the lack of more light-hearted activities among the group, possibly because of the many hazards encountered before my arrival, I'll keep looking for an answer."

(Author's note: This is one of Ramón's few expressions of interest in such personal subjects up to this time of his life, perhaps due to his father's warning that he was "too analytical" as a child.)

"April 22, 1844: Travelling beside river bed surrounded by willows and cottonwood trees. River disappears into sand. We locate old camping place used by annual caravans from Los Angeles to Santa Fe, and stop for night.

"April 23, 1844: Continue following dry river bed. Water reappears from time to time. Meet party of six Mojave Indians, one of whom speaks English. He had lived at Mission San Gabriel and left when Mission secularized. He joined Mojaves who live near Rio Colorado, raise melons, and trade blankets and other goods with Cahuila tribes in California. Warns of danger with Paiute Indians in mountains near Rio Virgen further east.

"April 24, 1844: Continue down dry stream bed. Cattle weak; three killed for meat—occasion for feast, and for making beef "jerky" for future use, from what we do not eat now. For this the remaining beef is cut into 1/8 inch strips, pulled or "jerked" into long thin sheets, and dried on sticks in the hot desert sun.

"We are joined by a Mexican named Andres Fuentes and a boy named Pablo Hernandez who escaped from Indian attack. They were part of a group of six with thirty horses, led by Pablo's father. The party left Los Angeles ahead of the annual caravan to travel more leisurely and get better grass for their animals. They were approached by Indians who seemed friendly at first, then attacked, apparently intending to capture horses. Fuentes and Pablo, on horse guard, drove the animals through the assailants to a water hole where they left them, and were going back to meet the caravan when they met us. Fremont gives them food and offers any help he can give. They continue on with us.[2]

"April 25, 1844: Trail continues northeast. Now mostly desert—black rocky ridges and sandy basins with large stones, hard on horses hooves. Little water and burning sun. Fremont keeps note of flora and fauna, discovering new species even in this barren spot. We arrive at spring called Agua Tomaso where Fuentes and Pablo left horses, but none were there, apparently driven off by Indians. Kit Carson and Alex Godey volunteer to go with Fuentes in pursuit. Fuentes' horse failed and he returns to camp. Fremont uses chronometer regularly to plot our bearings on map, attesting to his skill as navigator and topographer.

"April 26, 1844: Carson and Godey return with Mexican horses and two bloody scalps, announcing victory over the marauding Indians.[3] Their gory tale of pursuit and defeat of a much larger Indian band, encompassing about 100 miles and thirty hours, rivals any feats of western adventure I have ever heard. It is not reassuring to me, however, in looking ahead towards the rest of the trip. We travel all night to avoid excessive heat. Clear moon shine shows skeletons of animals who had perished along route before reaching water. A few hours before daybreak, we find water at a canyon entrance and make camp.

"April 27, 1844: We find camp ground not as good as expected, with salty water and poor grass, and surrounded by animal skeletons. We move on and stop at another place not much better.

"April 28, 1844: Travel north across bare ridges and sandy plains to camping place where Hernandez group was attacked. Find corpses of naked and horribly mutilated men. No trace of women, apparently carried off by Indians. Pablo is frantic with grief, as the little dog who belonged to Pablo's mother and remained with the dead bodies, rushes to greet him. I can better understand the scalps taken by Carson and Godey after viewing this brutal, loathsome scene. After burying the dead, it is too late to move on so we stay for the night.

"April 30, 1844: We leave a large marker to notify the approaching caravan of the fate of their advance group, and name the place Hernandez Springs for the group's slain leader.[3] Continue across same landscape for 24 miles, reaching at evening a campground, again with little grass or water.

"May 1, 1844: Weather clear and cold. Abundance of cactus and wildflowers as we cross plain and approach foot of mountain. Make camp in pass at site of old village, with good grass but little water. Fremont notes types of trees and shrubs in this wooded mountain area with over-looking snow capped peaks. Many rocks and shortage of grass and water has been hard on horses and mules. Fremont says he was misled as to nature of trail in this regard, and that some animals that would have been shod had he known how it would be, are now suffering from crippled feet. My horse Cristobal having been shod in California does not yet have this problem, but I share in concern over the potential loss to the entire group.

"May 2, 1844: Descend through rugged terrain into small valley with good grass and water for camp site. Digger Indian tracks around, but no Indians visible.

"May 3, 1844: Travel northeast 18 miles to campground in broad valley surrounded by mountain ranges called Las Vegas (fertile plains). The name recalls a story I heard at the age of 10, about a trading party from New Mexico looking for a shorter route to Los Angeles, and being nearly out of water when they came upon this oasis.[9] Now as then, it is a welcome sight. There are streams of clear water, including two from warm springs of more than 70 degrees which provide ideal opportunity for much needed bath.

"May 4, 1844: Travel northeast, leaving snowy ridge behind, and reenter oppressive desert heat. Reappearance of animal skeletons, warning of another dry journada—perhaps to be the longest yet without water. We continue on until midnight before reaching a running stream to make camp. It is the Rio de Los Angeles, not the one near my home, but a tributary of the Rio Virgen.

"May 5, 1844: We stay in camp all day on account of the animals. I feared Cristobal might be a bit lame, but he seems alright now. We are surrounded by Indians, haranguing us from nearby bluffs and harassing our horses. They seem to be Utes, judging from their dialect as interpreted by our guides, and apparently of the same tribe whose members murdered the Mexican party from which Fuentes and Pablo escaped. One who appears to be chief, forces his way into camp and speaks threateningly. Fremont restrains our people to keep peace, at least temporarily, in face of overwhelming odds. He dissipates some of the Indians' animosity by giving them a worn out horse which some of the Indians butcher to eat, but refuse to share with others who complain loudly. Some of these Indians have long hooked sticks with which they pry lizards and other small animals from holes in the ground, hence the name 'Diggers.' I recall that the same name is applied in a derogatory fashion to certain California tribes who subsist to a large extent on seeds, berries and plant tubers in addition to small game. Carson compares 'Diggers' with other more sophisticated Indian tribes, such as the Pueblo Indians near Santa Fe who mulch their gardens with small pebbles to retain soil moisture for growing healthier plants.

"May 6, 1844: We leave the Rio de Los Angeles and continue 20 miles through desolate countryside to reach a deep rapid stream with wooded banks. We cross and make camp, killing for meat three remaining steers that have given out. Fremont calculates the altitude at over 4,000 feet, judging from the boiling point of water. The stream appears to be the Rio Virgen, a tributary of the Colorado. Again the camp is surrounded by Indians, but none come in. I begin to understand the lack of evening socializing around the campfire, questioned in earlier notes.

"May 7–8, 1844: We continue up the Rio Virgen, followed by Indians who pick off any straggling animals. We lose the caravan trail and follow an Indian trail further up the river, bounded by high, rocky mountains. Make camp on small grassy plateau with cool water spring.

"May 9, 1844: We move camp further upstream for better grass. Scouts relocate Spanish Trail across river. One of our men who went to recover a lame mule, is missing. Smoke signal nearby indicates his fate at hands of Indians. Carson takes some men to search but returns with news only of the mule, mortally wounded by an arrow and left to be butchered.

"May 10, 1844: At daylight Fremont goes with a few others to search for the missing man. They find only blood on leaves and beaten down bushes indicating a fight for his life. Fremont at first wanted to avenge the man's death then and there, but realized the party was too small for an attack.[5] The Indians do not reappear. We follow the Spanish Trail north to a gap in the mountains. Trail increasingly rocky and difficult for unshod animals. Crossing the ridge, we find the terrain is wooded and green, completely the opposite of the desert we just left. Our spirits are lifted as we find an excellent camping place with good grass and clear water, on the Santa Clara Fork of the Rio Virgen.

"May 11, 1844: Morning cool with rain shower—first since entering desert after joining party 27 days ago. Fremont says it is like climate of Rocky Mountains. Laborious travel over rough ground. Stream flanked by cottonwood trees and frequent grass; pine trees on surrounding hills. Cool wind at night makes campfires welcome.

"May 12, 1844: We ascend towards summit of snow capped peaks on right. Camp at mountain meadow with abundant grass and water. This location considered end of desert, where annual caravan from Los Angeles to Santa Fe halts to rest and recuperate. We do the same. By preceding the caravan we have more grass, but also more danger from marauding Indians, requiring constant vigilance with all-night guards. Sometimes the whole party is on guard at once. We are joined by Joseph Walker, an experienced guide, who left the caravan after seeing signs of our party ahead, and came to find us. He too had run-ins with desert robbers, killing two Indians and getting some of his horses wounded.

"Walker, originally a trapper from Tennessee, is a tall, handsome man in his early thirties, with a long narrow nose, dark brown beard and moustache, and deep-set brown eyes. Fremont tells us Walker had served with Captain de Bonneville's expedition in 1832 seeking a westward route from Salt Lake to the Pacific.[14]

"May 13–16, 1844: We remain one day at rest. After supper we gather around the campfire and Walker talks of earlier mountaineering experiences, such as his first view of the Yosemite valley in the central Sierra Nevada, between the Merced and Tuolomne rivers. He says he and de Bonneville had never before seen anything to match the magnificent falls and chasms of this valley, or the giant Sequoia trees they passed descending into the San Joaquin valley. I vow to see it for myself some day.

"Continuing northeast, we sight snow-capped Wahsatch mountain range on right with Sevier Lake on left. Meet mounted Utah Indians watching for approaching caravan. There is no trouble with them, but we remain vigilant. Reach small lake at base of Wahsatch range and make camp.

"May 17–19, 1844: Leaving Spanish Trail, which goes southeast to Santa Fe, we continue northeast along foot of range on right, with Sevier Lake on left. Area rich with grass and fertile soil which Fremont notes as very promising for future agricultural development.

"May 20–22, 1844: Meet band of Utah Indians, mounted and armed with rifles. Their chief had taken the name Walker, same as our newly acquired guide. They are on way to meet caravan and levy usual tribute, a higher form of robbery than that of the desert marauders. They eschew murder and theft, but affect trade by taking horses and giving something nominal in return. The chief named Walker knows our Walker, and also knows of Fremont's earlier expedition in 1842. There is an exchange of gifts (blankets) as tokens of friendship.

"May 23, 1844: Reach Sevier River which is 8–12 feet deep. Make rafts of bullrushes, bound in bundles and tied down on poles, which are pulled with ropes by swimmers to ferry our supplies across. The horses swim across, a new experience for Cristobal, which he performs well. A member of the party is killed accidentally, pulling a gun towards him by the muzzle. The hammer catches and fires the gun into his head, a lesson I will never forget. He is buried on the river bank.

"May 24–25, 1844: We cross mountain ridge, descend and continue along river into valley heading towards snowy peak above Utah Lake. Meet party of Utah Indians—no trouble. We sight Utah Lake and descend to Spanish Fork. Three Utah Indians approach on horseback and stay near our camp.

"May 26, 1844: Indians appear troublesome. We move camp further away to remain a day in peace. Fremont compiles information about local plants and geographic features. Visit nearby Indian village and obtain some salmon-trout, which Fremont finds inferior to those in California mountain waters. One of his objectives is to reach Utah Lake and compile data about the surrounding territory. He deems it an 'excellent locality for stock farms.'[10] He says Utah Lake, with fresh water, is actually a southern branch of the Great Salt Lake further north. It is fed by many streams, the principal one called by the Indian name Impanogo, meaning rock river. His investigative task includes demarcation and description of the 'Great Basin' between the Wahsatch range and the California Sierras, enclosing a succession of lakes and rivers with no outlet to the sea, requiring further examination by a subsequent expedition. Confirmation of this interior basin proves there is no 'Rio Buena Ventura,' the mythical river from San Francisco Bay to the Rocky Mountains, as had been thought previously.[13] Having completed this part of his task, Fremont is now ready to recross the Rocky Mountains and return home.

"May 27–28, 1844: We ascend the Spanish Fork in a narrow valley between rugged mountains, well wooded and with frequent grassy areas. Our camp, near the head of one of the stream branches we ascend, displays strata of bituminous limestone containing a variety of fossil shells, of great interest to me as a former student of geology.

"May 29, 1844: We cross the dividing ridge separating the waters of the great Basin from those of the Rio Colorado. We cross the White River and the Uintah and approach the Bear River range. We stop at an altitude of 6900 feet.

"May 30–31, 1844: Descend along river to point of three forks; one we call Red River from its color, which we follow for a while, then cross a highland to camp at another Uintah tributary called Duquesne Fork. Travel further down river and after about 16 miles, camp on left bank.

"June 1–3, 1844: Leave Duquesne Fork, and by noon reach Lake Fork, a river of great velocity, too deep and swift to be forded. We spend a day constructing a bridge for the crossing, which is accomplished with the loss of only one animal. After a half day journey, we reach Uintah Fort, a trading post belonging to Mr. A. Roubideau of St. Louis. Roubideau enthusiastically promotes travel to California, citing an advertisement in the St. Louis *Argus* for participants in an emigrant train, generated with his encouragement.[15] His fort is located on a principal fork of the Uintah River which is also very swift and too wide to be bridged. With help from the fort, we ford the river and camp nearby.

"June 4, 1844: We obtain needed supplies and a skin boat from the fort, which is peopled with Canadians, Spanish, American hunters and Indian women. Fremont recruits another man to reinforce our party, helping to replace the two lost so far.

"June 5–6, 1844: Travel 25 miles to Ashley Fork; delayed a day finding ford. Travel 15 miles further to make camp high on mountain side, 7300 feet above sea level, with view of the Colorado River below. Abundant supply of grass—a species not seen before we reached Fort Uintah. Unfortunately it has a purgative effect which weakens the animals.

"June 7–9, 1844: A long journey through beautiful valleys and high mountains, finally descending into "Brown's Hole," where the Colorado canyon forms a narrow valley about 16 miles long. The river is swollen to the top of its banks, several hundred yards wide and 15–20 feet deep in places. Using the skin boat, we make the crossing after a day delay, and camp near the remains of an old fort on the left bank. We surprise a flock of mountain goat, and the hunters kill several for meat. Continue through canyons and make camp by Vermillion Creek.

"June 10, 1844: Ugly, barren country; hot sun and bad water. Camp at Elk Head River, tributary of Bear River. Make corral and fort to guard against Sioux war parties considered a danger in area. Fortunately none appear.

"June 11, 1844: Continuing up river, Fremont records varieties of plants. Countryside sandy and lightly wooded with good pasture. Hunters kill three antelopes. Camp at St. Vrain's Fork.

"June 12, 1844: Moving east towards Rocky Mountains that divide the continent. First view of buffalos not only pleases me, having never seen any before, but also gladdens Fremont's men who seem to have missed them since the trip west. But that doesn't keep hunters from killing two for meat. Fresh entrails seen in river indicate Indians upstream, according to Fremont, so we move camp higher up and make fort. Indians do not appear. Bands of antelope and elk roam hills and buffalo herds raise dust in plains below. Fremont says this area has more game than any area of Rockies he has visited.

"June 13, 1844: Morning cool from snow near camp. At noon we cross 8,000 foot summit ridge dividing the continent—cause for great exultation as we behold a stream coursing east called Pulliam's Creek, which runs into the Platte River, a Mississippi tributary. The creek is named for a trapper killed by three Gros Ventre Indians. Coming down and out of the pines, we can see the Platte River valley. To explore new ground, Fremont turns south, up the Platte River valley towards three mountain coves called parks, where the headwaters of the Platte and Arkansas Rivers (going east) and the Colorado (going west) have their beginnings. Make fortified camp in beautiful country with bountiful water, grass and game.

"June 14, 1844: Continue up broad Platte valley, crossing several clear mountain streams. See many buffalo, antelope and elk. Stop at noon at Potter's Fork. Make camp at evening by stream with several trees recently cut by beavers, which Fremont names Beaver Tree Creek.

"June 15–16, 1844: Continue up creek. Fuentes tries to lasso a grizzly bear, who escapes. In afternoon we enter, through a gorge, the north park where we camp. It is a circular valley surrounded by snowy mountains, with much grass and water. This beautiful spot, at an elevation of 7,700 feet, is the source of the Platte River. We expect to see herds of buffalo but there are none because, as we learn later, we were preceded by an Arapahoe Indian party. Continue across park and camp near upper end.

"June 17, 1844: Pass over border of park, following buffalo trail. Recross Rocky Mountain summit and descend to edge of second mountain valley called middle park, in which headwaters of Grand River branch of Colorado is formed, coursing west into Gulf of California. We travel cautiously to avoid Arapahoes who apparently passed ahead of us. We camp at a tributary of the Grand River.

"June 18, 1844: We meet a party of 30 Arapahoes—men and women. Fremont gives them usual presents but they still seem unfriendly on leaving. We stop at a defensible spot and soon about 200 Indians appear, including 20 Sioux, all mounted, painted and armed. After a short parley and more presents, a truce is arranged due partly to the presence of an old Sioux chief who is friendly to whites. We camp near their village and keep careful watch, but some supplies are stolen.

"June 19, 1844: Although the Indians had told us the river by their village was fordable, we have to descend about eight miles before finding a spot we could ferry. We travel another six miles and make camp.

"June 20, 1844: Proceeding further south, we find the river is increasingly swollen and the valley increasingly narrow. We make a strong fort at the evening campsite, alert for possible Arapahoe attack.

"June 21, 1844: River not yet fordable. Appearance of many buffalo indicates presence of Indians in south park, who had driven the animals out, according to Fremont's surmise. Hunters kill seven buffalo cows for meat. At a place where the river forks in three directions, Fremont selects the fork he expects will lead to a pass from which the head of the Arkansas River will be found, which he intends to follow home. His selection is based on the fact that buffalo tracks are plentiful up the other two forks which probably lead to lower passes. But no tracks go up the third fork which apparently leads to the higher spot, probably behind the Arkansas head-waters. At night we camp among pine trees, fields of mountain flowers, and wild strawberries which we enjoy eating. After dark we see fires across the valley. Fearing attack we put our fires out and the others go out too. We keep vigilant guard throughout the night.

"This is as close as we have come to a festive mood after dinner around the campfire, but how quickly it can stop! This relates to my earlier question at the beginning of the trip. I enjoy the sound of wind in the pine trees and the smell of fresh mountain air punctuated with flicks of pungent aroma from the freshly extinguished fires. I think about the extremes of exhilaration and trepidation that one experiences on a journey such as this.

"June 22, 1844: Party across valley turns out to be six trappers hunting beaver. They tell us two of their original number were killed by Arapahoes. While they prepare to join us, an Arapahoe party arrives with news of a large Utah Indian war party coming from south park. We continue on, reaching summit of dividing ridge at 11,200 feet without further incident. Small stream below believed to be beginning of tributary to either Arkansas River or south fork of Platte. We camp in grassy bottom separated by one ridge from head of main Arkansas River. At dusk a herd of buffalo creates excitement by charging through camp.

"June 23, 1844: Descending into valley, we sight mounted party believed to be Arapahoes, and halt in defensible spot. Turns out to be a party of Utah Indian women escaping Arapahoes who attacked their village. We see signs of fighting as we pass at safe distance. Make camp, strongly fortified, 15 miles further south, expecting attack from either side. Fremont points out Pike's Peak ahead, a familiar landmark from their earlier trip. He explains that it was named for Army Lieutenant Zebulon Pike who headed an exploratory mapping mission in 1806. This massive snow-covered mountain peaks at over 14,000 feet above sea-level, and punctuates the long, winding Rocky Mountain ridge dividing the continent. It signals the start of the many eastward flowing streams that pass through the central plains into the Mississippi River and the Gulf of Mexico.

"June 24–28, 1844: Laborious travel southeast through steep rocky foothills. We finally descend from mountains and camp near main Arkansas River.

"June 29, 1844: Continuing along Arkansas, we meet and leave party of Arapahoes without incident. Arrive before sunset at small pueblo near mouth of Fontaine-qui-bouit (Boiling Spring River) which has its source near Pike's Peak. Fremont meets several old acquaintances at pueblo.

"June 30–July 4, 1844: We move rapidly along broad road down Arkansas River, arriving July 1 at Bent's Fort, a large adobe bastion[3] about 70 miles below mouth of Fontaine-qui-bouit, where we spend next three days. We are greeted on arrival by flag display, gun salutes, and warm reception by Mr. George Bent.[6] Carson tells us later how the Fort, built in 1833, was established by Bent brothers William and Charles, to supply caravans travelling on the Santa Fe trail.[11, 12] As dangers and difficulties of road are now considered over, four experienced mountaineers, including Carson and Walker, leave Fremont's party to remain at Bent's Fort, ready for next journey into the mountains.

"July 5, 1844: Leave Fort by same broad road along Arkansas River which is a part of the Santa Fe Trail. Encounter large band of Sioux and Arapahoes returning from meeting with Kiowa and Comanche Indians. They tell of having recently massacred a party of 15 Delaware Indians, and they expect retaliation. They request we carry a peace message for them to the Delawares at the frontier.

"July 6–8, 1844: Fremont decides to leave the Santa Fe Trail to explore new territory. We travel three days northeast towards the Platte River, crossing prairies without timber, and using for fire 'bois de vache' (dried cattle excrement) and buffalo dung. We camp at Smoky Hill Fork of Kansas River.

"July 9, 1844: Meet advance members of Arapahoe war party returning from expedition against Pawnees. By evening we camp at site where river widens to 80 yards, with cottonwood and buffalo grass.

"July 10–16, 1844: We are in heart of buffalo range, with many animals around. Halt for day while hunters replenish meat supply with enough to reach frontier. For evening meal we enjoy buffalo steaks pan-fried in batter, as were the beef steaks I enjoyed my first night with the expedition. We also have beans with bacon, and skillet bread, a dish to which I have become accustomed in spite of an initial dislike. Some of the remaining buffalo meat I am told will be used for stew in the next days, cooked with wild onions and potatoes and dried corn acquired along the way. This will be a welcome change from the rabbits, birds and occasional fish we have had most of the past two weeks. The rest of the buffalo meat will be made into 'jerky' for future consumption as described earlier, but dried over the fire instead of in the desert sun.

"We continue eastward and camp on high river prairie near stream about 100 yards wide. During night heavy rain and thunderstorms cause stream to overflow and ruin all our perishables. We are grateful for the one good meal we had the night before.

"July 17, 1844: We come to large Pawnee village. We expect friendly reception from these people who receive regular payment from U.S. Government, but are rebuffed with rudeness and insolence. Fremont distributes remaining supplies among them without effecting change in their attitude. Indicates once again that gifts do not buy friendship. We leave and camp 15 miles down river.

"July 18–30, 1844: Country gradually changes from flat prairie to more hilly, wooded regions along Kansas River, which Fremont describes as comparable to northwestern part of the State of Missouri, which we are approaching. The unrelieved flatness of seemingly endless plains we passed through was new to me; I wouldn't care to settle in such a place, given other choices. As we were leaving buffalo country, Alex Godey describes an incident on a previous trip when a prairie fire stampeded a nearby herd of buffalo, causing an awesome spectacle: a long line of blazing fire and smoke along the flat horizon, and the deafening sound of hundreds of crazed, galloping animals trying to escape the approaching danger.

"Today one of the party has accidentally shot himself in the leg, reinforcing my earlier resolve to be particularly careful with firearms.

"On reaching intersection with wagon road from Santa Fe to Independence, Missouri, I am reminded of my earlier wish to visit Santa Fe, where my father's family lived before moving to California. I recall my father and Aunt Isabel discussing the area's history.

"Beginning with Coronado's 1540 expedition, and by 1776 when de Portola reached San Francisco Bay, Spanish expeditions penetrated the heart of the Rocky Mountains as far as Utah Lake, crossed the plains to the French outpost of St. Louis, and established a string of missions on the California coast. To them, according to my father, this west was 'the rim of Christendom' with the vast plains and the Rockies protecting them from unwelcome intruders and European rivals.[7]

"Since its settlement by Spaniards in 1609, the community of Santa Fe on the western side of the Rocky Mountain rim, has reflected this philosophy of discouraging visitors for more than two centuries.[4] After Mexico gained its independence from Spain, I understand the area has become more hospitable to traders from the United States outposts to the east, and that trade is now expanding.

"July 31, 1844: We continue on the wagon road to Independence and camp outside the town of Kansas on the banks of the Missouri River, on the present western frontier of the United States of America."

Here Ramón's journal ends. The Fremont party spent the next five days crossing the State of Missouri on board a steamship travelling downriver to St. Louis. The animals of the expedition were left in pasture at the frontier to be ready for the next expedition. Ramón arranged for Cristobal to be transported with him, not knowing what the future might hold. Fremont had admired Cristobal, as he did his own saddle horse named "Sacramento," a beautiful iron-gray about four years old, which he had brought from California. Knowing he would be leaving soon for Washington, Fremont arranged for two Indian boys who were members of his expedition to take Sacramento to spend the winter on property near Lexington, Kentucky, belonging to his father-in-law, Senator Benton.

It had been agreed previously that Andres Fuentes and Pablo Hernandez were to be taken in by the family of Senator Benton while arrangements were made for Fuentes' employment and Pablo's education in St. Louis where the boy preferred to stay after the murder of his parents.[8]

John Fremont was a compassionate man, as indicated by the many things that happened during the trip just ended. He spoke later of trying to keep up with developments concerning Pablo Hernandez, who later left St. Louis. Apparently Pablo did not fare so well after returning west and was said by some to have become a notorious bandit known as Joaquin who terrorized parts of California for many years.[8] There were several desperados known by the same first name, the most famous being Joaquin Murieta. Most were young Mexican-Californios who had been displaced or abused by immigrating Americans and who then took to the hills as outlaws to gain revenge or restitution of what they felt to be rightfully theirs. While Pablo Hernandez did not fit this category, his experiences at the hands of Indian raiders might have led him to the same end. If true it was not a happy result either for Pablo or for those who tried to help him, but perhaps to be expected considering the emotional injury he sustained.

In spite of his personal knowledge of the outrageous and brutal acts of which some Indians were capable, Ramón recognized that it was because the Americans were invading the Indians' country. It seemed to him that Americans were damning Indians for defending themselves the only way they knew, as Americans had done themselves against lesser foreign provocation.

Although he was an experienced horseman and trail rider, Ramón had not been prepared for all the difficulties and hardships encountered over the past four months, which were normal occurrences for others on Fremont's expedition. He had crossed half the continent under trying conditions and had many fascinating, exciting, and sometimes terrifying experiences. He wouldn't have missed it but wouldn't want to repeat it. He often recalled it in later years, particularly when crossing the plains, mountains, and deserts under the more comfortable circumstances of the newer modes of travel which resulted to a large extent from Fremont's earlier efforts.

The steamship with the Fremont party aboard, docked in St. Louis after midnight August 6, 1844. Most members of the expedition went immediately to their homes and families, if they lived in St. Louis, or to other quarters. John Fremont, who did not want to awaken his family at such an early hour, took Ramón on a predawn walk downtown, past the city's spired cathedral, the domed courthouse, and a stone mansion with portholes from which to shoot at attacking Indians. About 3:00 A.M. they approached the Benton home, south of the business district, on a rise overlooking the river. Fremont awakened one of the servants who lived above the coachhouse and said he would be back at dawn. As the sun rose, they entered the house and Ramón waited in the entrance hall while Fremont went to greet his wife, who had been expecting him for the past four months.

This gave Ramón a chance to observe more of the Benton home. It was built in "creole" style, around a central courtyard not unlike the Spanish homes to which he was accustomed. But instead of tiles, the floors were of waxed black walnut, and instead of oaks and pepper trees, the Benton house was shaded by acacias.[16] He was beginning to feel even more of a stranger in this land when Fremont returned with his wife.

Even at this early hour, Jessie Benton Fremont could make a favorable impression on even an unexpected visitor such as Ramón. Senator Benton's daughter was wise and witty, as could be expected from regular association with prominent persons in the nation's capital and among her father's St. Louis supporters. Her large, round, dark eyes were set deep and wide apart under perfectly curved eyebrows in a heart-shaped face. Her dark hair pulled straight back gave full effect to her shapely neck and shoulders. Her gracious manner and friendly warmth soon made Ramón feel less of an outsider.

Soon guests began arriving, and from 8:00 A.M. until noon there was a large gathering of friends and family to welcome Fremont home.[17] The Bentons had many Spanish friends, and both the Senator and his daughter spoke Spanish, which made Ramón feel less alien. Thus he became involved in a series of social activities where he made new friends and met someone who changed his entire life.

Illustration No. 1: Mission San Gabriel Archangel. 1832 painting by Ferdinand Deppe.

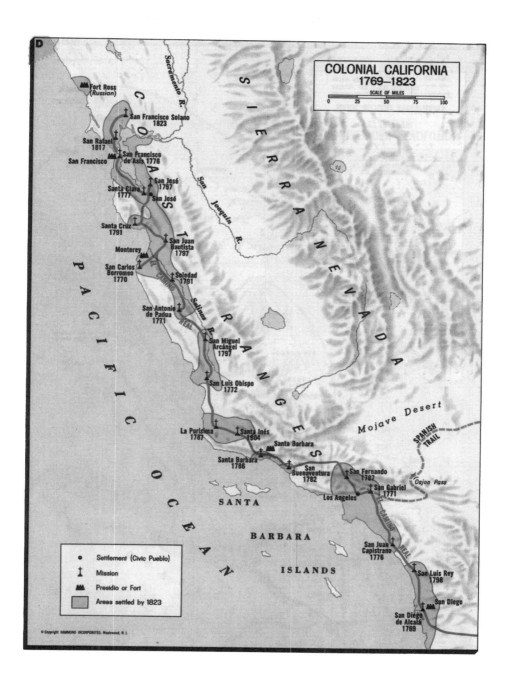

Illustration No. 2: Spanish Missions in Alta California.

Illustration No. 3: The Founders of Los Angeles, Woodcut 1883

Illustration No. 4: New Haven from Ferry Hill, engraving about 1832

Illustration No. 5: Brown's Indian Queen Hotel, Washington City, Lithograph about 1832

Illustration No. 6: The Department of State, Washington, about 1830

Illustration No. 7: City of Charleston, South Carolina, about 1840

Illustration No. 8: Harbor and City of Monterey, California, 1842, Lithograph 1850

Illustration No. 9: Portrait of John C. Fremont

Illustration No.10: Tejon Canyon, near route of Fremont's 1844 Expedition. (1989 photograph)

Illustration No. 11: Carson's Men, Oil on canvas by Charles Russell, 1913

Illustration No. 12: Domes of Yosemite by Alfred Bierstadt, chrome Lithograph about 1868

Illustration No. 13: Portrait of Jessie B. Fremont

Part IV
St. Louis to Washington, DC via Mexico
(1845–1854)

CHAPTER 8
ST. LOUIS AND THE CALIFORNIA CONNECTION

Ramón was on his own again for the first time since leaving college. His first priority was to find a place to stay and plan his next move. He had heard from fellow travellers on the river boat that the most elegant hotel in St. Louis was the Planter's House. Feeling lonely after the close associations of the past four months, he decided a little elegance would help lift his spirits, even though it might be beyond his means for any extended period.

First opened in 1817 and recently rebuilt on Fourth Street between Chestnut and Pine, the Planter's House met his expectations. While rooms were $1.25 a day, there was a fine dining room in which breakfast was served from 7:00 to 11:00, dinner at 1:30, tea at 5:30, and supper from 9:00 to 12:00.[33]

As soon as he checked in and was shown his room, he returned for a hearty breakfast of ham steak, grits baked with orange honey, and hot chocolate. Later in the day he visited the bar, where he had a mint julep, reminiscent of Charleston. On another occasion he tried the Planter's Punch, a house specialty made with rum, which he particularly enjoyed.

While getting settled in his new surroundings, Ramón was pleased to receive an invitation to a party for the Fremonts given by the Larkins. He learned that Thomas and Susan Larkin had come to St. Louis from Delaware in 1837 and that Thomas became successful in the grocery business and expanded into real estate.[1] Having just spent four months on the trail, Ramón needed to obtain suitable attire for the occasion and the hotel manager directed him accordingly.

It was at this, his first St. Louis party, that Ramón was introduced to Leann Richards, who would become his wife, his partner, and the love of his life. He was taken immediately by her striking good looks, with dark hair, large brown eyes, and warm smile which often blended into a faraway look, as if savoring some cherished private thought. Her natural exuberance and joy of living was catching, and when in her company Ramón lost his feeling of being an outsider.

After their initial meeting in October 1844, he saw Leann again at a ball given for the Fremonts and tried shamelessly to monopolize her dance card, which was virtually impossible in view of the many young men with the same thought in mind. But she did save him a few dances, saying she would call him by his middle name, "Luis," after her native city of St. Louis, and thereafter his heart was lost to her.

Leann Richards was born in St. Louis on June 23, 1816, to parents of French and German ancestry, Randolph and Dorothy Richards. Belonging to the Lutheran Church but accustomed to the large French Catholic population of the area, her family welcomed Ramón with customary St. Louis warmth yet seemed to view the possible acquisition of a Spanish Catholic son-in-law with some reservations.

Following a brief off-and-on again courtship, during which they sorted out the differences between their backgrounds, they decided there was more to keep them together than apart. Ramón asked Leann to become his wife, and she accepted.

A few days before the date scheduled for their wedding, Leann's mother took her daughter aside for a last private talk. Mrs. Richards told Leann she liked Ramón, or Luis, as Leann called him, but feared that with his foreign background he wouldn't have the requisite social graces to fit into their St. Louis circle of friends and provide the kind of surroundings she believed her daughter should have. Leann told her mother she was not concerned about that and was sure Ramón/Luis could learn or acquire whatever knowledge or skills he needed to provide the surroundings and type of life they both wanted. Her mother said she would never again mention her misgivings and would counsel the other family members to do likewise.

Leann did not tell Ramón of her mother's misgivings at the time for fear of hurting his feelings and perhaps losing him. When she did tell him many years later, a serious argument ensued on the merits of openness, followed by a temporary but hurtful separation. For the present, however, Cupid pursued his course, bringing the couple together for better or worse, till death would they part.

Leann and Ramón were married July 17, 1845, at the new Trinity Lutheran Church.[34] Leann's family and friends were present but none of Ramón's family could come from such a distance, although he did notify them. After a few twinges of nerves on such a momentous occasion, Ramón experienced feelings of great pride and joy as he watched Leann coming down the aisle on her father's arm, in a slow measured gait. She carried a white Bible with a cascade of lilies-of-the-valley. She wore a wedding dress of white satin that was trimmed with seed pearls, as she later described it to him.

After the wedding, there was a reception at the Richards' home. The table was filled with many St. Louis delicacies which Ramón would have assessed in greater detail had he not been preoccupied with the excitement of the moment. He did remark on the "syllabub," a drink made of rum, sugar, and warm milk, which some of the ladies enjoyed while men consumed stronger libations. As soon as the wedding cake was cut and toasts were made, the newlyweds prepared to leave for their honeymoon by steamboat to New Orleans. Each of them had long wanted to visit this city but for different reasons—Leann because of her parents' earlier trip, which they often spoke of with great enthusiasm, and Ramón because of curiosity about the effects of Spanish occupation and later American influences on its French background.

In preparation for the trip, Ramón had taken time before their wedding to read up on New Orleans history, drawing from, among other sources, Stahl's *New Orleans Sketch Book*, published in 1843, and also an article titled "A Description of New Orleans" in the July 1805 issue of *Liberty Magazine and American Register*, which Leann's parents had kept to commemorate their trip.

Founded in 1718 by Governor Bienville, New Orleans was French territory, except when ceded to Spain from 1762 to 1800, until it became part of the United States with the Louisiana Purchase of 1803. Governor Bienville laid out the original town by the river as a fortified city, in a rectangle of 4,000 by 1,800 feet bounded by ramparts. This became known as the "Vieux Carré" or Old Square as the city grew larger, and later was called the French Quarter, bounded by Canal Street, North Rampart Street, Esplanade Avenue, and the Mississippi River.

Original colonists were drawn from jails, hospitals, and the dregs of Paris with promises of free land. Levees were built to protect the area from floods, but as late as the 1840s New Orleans was still called "wet grave" because of river infiltration into cemeteries. All who could afford it were entombed above ground.[3]

In 1743, Bienville was replaced by Governor de Vandreuil, who tried to establish French court life in New Orleans, with elaborate balls and banquets that seemed incongruous given the town's raw frontier status. But some of it took hold and became the basis for many of the current social customs.

When Spain took over, New Orleans had a population of 3,190, including 1,225 negro slaves and 60 Indians. Ramón noted that Spanish law forbade counting Indians as slaves. After a fire destroyed most of the old town in 1794, it was rebuilt with Spanish design and architecture, providing its distinctive French/Spanish flavor.

After retrocession by Spain to France under Napoleon I in 1800, the city lacked a strong central government for three years until the Louisiana Purchase. This lapse contributed to the already high degree of criminality and loose law enforcement in New Orleans and reminded Ramón of the similar period in California history before it joined the United States.

When the Americans came in 1803, they established above Canal Street what was almost a separate city from the old French Quarter and attempted to restore order throughout the town. The Americans were looked down upon at first by the Creole descendants of the original French and Spanish settlers, but that changed when they all fought together against the British in the War of 1812.[4]

In preparing for their honeymoon, Ramón had made reservations in advance at the St. Charles Hotel, considered by many to be one of the grandest hotels in the country. The St. Charles, with its huge dome and Corinthian portico, occupied an entire city block on Charles Street in the American Quarter. Visited by many celebrities, including British author Charles Dickens on his American tour, it was very elegant and most impressive.

Unfortunately, the hotel's recordkeeping was less impressive, as the newlyweds learned upon arrival, when they were told there had been some mixup and their reservation was lost. As the St. Charles was completely full, they were directed to the St. Louis Hotel in the French Quarter. Originally the City Exchange, the building destroyed by fire in 1841 was rebuilt and reopened the following year as the St. Louis Hotel. James Hewlett, first owner and manager of the City Exchange and afterwards the St. Louis Hotel, had introduced a series of subscription balls at the hotel which became the social center for the Creoles.[5] Thus Ramón and Leann got more of the essence of old New Orleans than if they had stayed at the St. Charles, and what seemed like a loss became a gain.

They had excellent meals in the dining rooms of both hotels and also enjoyed a variety of other restaurants which typified the cuisine for which New Orleans was becoming famous. They sampled not only traditional French items but also unique Louisiana "creole" dishes such as gumbo filé (with chicken, ham, and oysters), red beans and rice, sweet potato bread, sugared pecans, and watermelon ice.[6]

They visited cafes on Royal and Charles Streets, the Cafe des Améliorations at Rampart and Toulouse, and the Absinthe House at Bienville and Bourbon Streets. The latter was in one of the oldest buildings in the French Quarter, built in 1798 as a private residence and turned into a saloon in 1826. Most of the bars served a "free lunch," which might include soup, a piece of beef or ham with potatoes, meat pie, and oyster patties. It was sometimes given to a customer with a drink order but mostly served at a separate counter. The custom was introduced at the bar of the City Exchange and soon spread to other bars in New Orleans and to other cities in America.[7]

The Clemente's outside activities were not limited to eating. They attended performances at the Théatre d'Orleans which had four operas a week, two "grande" and two "comique," which were great social occasions. At other times there was vaudeville for the "hoi polloi." The most fashionable opera performances were on Tuesday and Saturday when full dress was required except in the "Parquet," the only area open to non-subscribers. Even there gentlemen were expected to wear white gloves and a full dress coat over trousers and boots of their own choosing. The best location was the "dress circle," where the Clementes sat one evening as guests of friends of Leann's parents.

In a separate wing adjacent to the Theatre d'Orleans was the Orleans ballroom, scene of the annual Quadroon Ball, which the Clementes were told was to introduce carefully brought-up negro girls with the highest degree of white ancestry to white gentlemen for selection as mistresses.[8]

Ramón and Leann enjoyed browsing around the streets of the French Quarter, but only in the daytime, as evenings could be dangerous because of thieves and hoodlums. They also had to be careful where they walked because of the city's inadequate sewer system consisting of open gutters, which made New Orleans possibly the unhealthiest U.S. city and caused a cholera and yellow fever epidemic in 1832–33.

One day they shopped at the French Market on the riverfront and then visited the nearby branch of the U.S. Mint. They learned that the New Orleans Mint was established in 1838 primarily to produce gold coinage, often from Spanish-American pieces that were melted and remade into U.S. coins. The Mint also struck silver coins, and Leann, who began collecting with a large cent from her father, obtained for her collection an 1844–0 half-dime, an 1845–0 dime; an 1844–0 quarter; and two half dollars, 1844–0 and 1845–0. This renewed Ramón's interest in numismatics, and he got three 1845 gold coins with the "O" mintmark—the quarter eagle ($2 1/2), half eagle ($5), and eagle ($10).[9] He also saved one of the New Orleans $10 banknotes which were printed in French and English. The French word "dix" for ten printed thereon earned for them the name "dixie," which also became a term applied to the entire south, although for other reasons as well.

From the French Market it was only a few blocks walk to the Cabildo, seat of government during the Spanish administration, and the adjacent Catholic Church, which was being rebuilt as a much grander cathedral. Facing the Cabildo on Chartres Street were pillories, long banned as punishment for white lawbreakers but still used for negroes.

In walking about the streets Ramón noted the Spanish influence—houses mostly of stucco over wood, some of brick with slate or tile roofs, usually of three stories built around courtyards or patios. Many had wrought iron balconies and galleries screened with lattice work. While looking for interesting sights, they avoided areas such as Gallatin and Girod Streets with their dance halls, gambling dens, bordellos, and barrel houses offering "all the whiskey you can drink for 5¢." They were warned such places were populated with thieves and prostitutes, giving New Orleans its "City of Sin" label.

They learned about the "filibusters"—gangs of adventurers, plotters, and soldiers-of-fortune who met at certain coffee houses such as the Banks Arcade on Magazine Street near Gravier.[10] It seems the filibusters were interested in supporting any sort of revolutionary movement, especially against Spanish/Mexican territory, so Ramón thought it best to avoid them.

They did visit St. Cyr's on Chartres Street, one of the better gambling places, where they ventured a few "dixies" on roulette and "vingt-et-un" or blackjack. They decided against faro, the other most popular game, not having enough knowledge of its intricacies. One form of gambling they enjoyed was "keno" at a hall on Royal Street owned by John Quinn, who also owned keno halls in St. Louis. A keno player buys one or more cards, each with three horizontal rows of five random numbers from one to ninety-nine, and receives a supply of buttons. On a table at the front of the hall is a globe containing ninety-nine balls that drop one at a time at random, the number of each called aloud by a "roller." The player places a button on any number called that appears on his card, and yells "keno" if he gets five in a row. The game stops for the winner's card to be inspected, and if confirmed the player receives all the money paid by the other players less 15 percent for the "house." Leann won one game, but the Clementes became less enthusiastic on becoming aware of the possibilities for cheating. They were told that the "roller" sometimes palms legitimate balls, substituting others with numbers matching those on cards previously issued to selected players called "cappers."[11]

Leann wanted to visit a Voodoo doctor for a reading. She was told of a negro with a tattooed face called Doctor John who dealt in mind reading and astrology. After learning the unsavory details and activities of certain of his clients, they decided against it and sought safer pursuits. There were always new places and things to explore in New Orleans and what with learning more about each other, they almost lost track of time in this unusual town, so much like being in a foreign country. After an idyllic fortnight, they decided it was time to return to St. Louis and begin planning the rest of their lives together.

This time they paid more attention to the boat ride on the return journey up-river. The paddle wheel steamboat was quite luxurious, with such amenities as berths with feather beds and down pillows, thick rugs, an individual gilded spittoon for each gentleman, and excellent cuisine. The saloon extended the entire length of the vessel—about two hundred feet, with elegant furnishings including a grand piano. There was an impromptu race with another vessel going upstream from New Orleans to Natchez. Such contests had become regular sporting events with much wagering on board, as well as in towns on both sides of the river.

Another popular activity was riverboat gambling, about which Leann's father had warned them before they left on their honeymoon.

Thus they were not surprised to meet aboard ship a Missourian named John Powell, charming and distinguished in his upper thirties, who had turned down a nomination to Congress in order to pursue his career as a professional gambler.[12] He was well dressed but not overly flashy, in soft black hat, black broadcloth suit, black high-heeled boots, white frilled shirt with black tie, and black embroidered vest with pearl buttons. With gambling aboard ship not only condoned but apparently expected, Powell set up his gaming in a cabin on the "texas," the name given to a structure on the upper deck where the officers quarters and pilot house are located. As Powell was reputed to be the most daring and expert poker player on the river, and the most consistent winner among the presumably honest riverboat gamblers, Ramón thought better about getting into a game; Leann was tempted but settled for watching the players.

After five days on the river they reached St. Louis and were just as glad as their enjoyment of the relative luxury of their "floating hotel" was beginning to wear thin. Upon returning to land, they learned, among other things, that the Fremonts had gone to Washington DC to report through Senator Benton on the results of the last expedition and to draw up maps of the western regions. Now they were back in St. Louis planning the next expedition, with instructions from the United States Government to include plans, or one might say schemes, for the acquisition of California from Mexico.

Although just married and wanting to settle down with his new bride, Ramón still felt an urge to participate in some way in this new venture, which would affect directly his homeland and family property in which he had interest.

In spite of his "background for conquest" described in a previous chapter, Ramón was reluctant to embark on a full-scale expedition with all the harrowing experiences of Fremont's earlier trips, now with more military overtones. After his brief participation in the last leg of Fremont's second western expedition, though it had been a most fascinating adventure, Ramón freely admitted his preference for more creature comforts than usually are available on such an endeavor and preferred to make whatever contribution he could in more comfortable circumstances. He felt that perhaps "blessed are they" who admit their own shortcomings or weaknesses, without pretending to others contrary to their own feelings and beliefs. He never claimed to be a hero or a physical activist for a "cause" but did admire those who were, such as Fremont.

Thus recognizing that he was not an explorer or adventurer by nature, and not eager to be separated from his new bride for an indefinite period, or perhaps forever if worst came to worst, Ramón decided he could still participate by assisting in logistical plans and arrangements for Fremont's third expedition while remaining in the more comfortable surroundings of St. Louis, which he was beginning to appreciate.

Though still a frontier town in a sense, St. Louis had a rich heritage from the earlier French colonization, now further enriched with European flavor by the increasing German immigration. This old world atmosphere blended with the excitement of America moving west gave St. Louis a unique aura. It was the major gateway to the west, the last large city before crossing the United States border. It was a part time home to fur trappers and traders, guides and suppliers of caravans, riverboatmen travelling north and south, and for easterners waiting to go further west. In addition to being Leann's home, St. Louis had much to fascinate and hold the Clementes while they planned their future.

Mostly through newspaper articles, Ramón learned the details of Fremont's third western expedition which merged with the Mexican War and resulted eventually in statehood for California. It also resulted temporarily, and Ramón believed undeservedly, in disgrace for Fremont, who got caught in bureaucratic crossfire between the War and Navy Departments in Washington. Ramón was surprised to read an anonymous letter in the St. Louis *Republican* critical of Fremont's role in the California conquest as reflecting adversely on the Army.[38]

Although Ramón had not directly participated in events leading to California statehood, he felt satisfaction in the outcome and was glad to have been a small part of its indirect support and to have known some of the principal players.

He also felt that this period was now behind him, although he always would be interested in Fremont's future endeavors. He was now ready to start a new life with Leann and pursue interests of their own.

When first married, Ramón wanted to take his wife to California, but land travel was difficult at that time, as he had learned from his recent journey with the Fremont expedition. Travel by sea took too long and was too expensive. He had no paying job and little money available, although he had inherited from his father a potentially valuable interest in California property.

Therefore the Clementes lived for a while with the Richards, who were very courteous and obliging, yet Ramón felt not fully accepting of him. He was a foreigner to them with an accent and strange ways, unlike their friends and neighbors. Leann's two older brothers, Arthur and Randolph, Jr., were polite but distant. They joined with their father in trying to include Ramón in various activities, which he appreciated, but always felt like an outsider.

Perhaps it was expecting too much to be accepted immediately and unquestioningly as a family member in full standing. Ramón could understand how difficult it would be for Leann had their positions been reversed and she were trying to fit in with his family and their Spanish style of living in California.

Ramón came to find out that Leann's family were disappointed that she had not married a close family friend who had been courting her for several years. They frequently called Ramón by this other man's name, always followed by profuse apologies. Ramón was extra-sensitive about this situation which recalled to him the negative attitude towards persons of Spanish/Mexican heritage that he had encountered in the east. Although this attitude was not so prevalent here in the Mississippi valley, some St. Louisians still referred to such persons as "greasers."[35]

For the first time Ramón began to take stock of himself as a person—an adult male starting a new life, in new surroundings among comparative strangers. He was twenty-six years old, slightly less than six feet tall, of medium build, clean shaven with brown hair and gray/green eyes. He did not have the dark, swarthy appearance frequently associated with persons of Mexican descent nor the smooth continental appearance and demeanor of many Spaniards. His physical appearance stemmed back, perhaps, to his early Norman ancestry.

He believed himself to be friendly and responsive to others, neither very shy nor overly outgoing. Not overly energetic either, he nevertheless worked hard at whatever he undertook, using, he hoped, at least average intelligence. He usually maintained a good sense of humor, tried to be considerate of others, and believed honesty and integrity to be of utmost importance in all relationships. He knew he did not make a strong first impression but thought people tended to like him if they got to know him better. He also knew there was at least one count against him and possibly more as far as his in-laws were concerned. He tried to retain his self-confidence while realizing that his shortcomings in their eyes always would remain as such.

Now that he was married, and since Leann started calling him by his middle name, he had begun to feel differently about himself—not so much as Ramón, living alone with his own thoughts, but as Luis, who shared his life and thoughts with another person by his side. The new Luis was perhaps more acceptable than the old Ramón, or so he thought. He suggested to Leann that they drop the final "e" from Clemente and make the change complete by becoming Mr. and Mrs. Louis Clement. Donning one of her faraway looks, Leann replied, "Let's think about that for a while." There is no record of the subject having come up again.

One of the brightest spots for the young couple during this period was visiting Leann's maternal grandmother, Minerva Breuer, whose house was high on a bluff overlooking the Mississippi River. Fabulous afternoons were spent there, usually after a picnic on the lawn, sitting under the grape arbor behind her house, sipping her homemade wines and listening to her tales of the "old country," which is known as Alsace. She was loved and respected by all family members, young and old, and paid particular attention to the needs of the younger members. While teaching the girls culinary and other feminine arts, she also taught the boys to bake potatoes over smoldering coals in their own caves on the river bank. She seemed to know instinctively what young people needed and how to provide it.

Leann had a younger sister, Elena, who died unexpectedly at the age of three. It was a great shock to the entire family and a special blow to little Leann, who lived at her grandmother's house for a brief period thereafter. Leann could recall herself as a small child, following her grandmother about, holding onto her long calico skirts that smelled of lavender, and felt a strong attachment to her grandmother ever after.

Following is an excerpt from a school paper Leann wrote illustrating a part of her childhood in St. Louis on the Mississippi River, and her family's closeness and affection for her maternal grandmother:

"For the first outing during summer vacation from school, my mother, my two aunts and their offspring all went on a Mississippi riverboat excursion. Each child was allowed to bring one friend, totaling eighteen children and three adults. We always got the same table facing the dance floor to enjoy the music.

We all wore our new summer outfits. Each of the three mothers brought a basket of food and tried to outdo each other. My mother always won with her spectacular creations. One time it was a 'watermelon cake' that was such a hit people still talk about it. I wasn't interested in dancing, but was curious to see how the boat was made and run. The captain took me on a tour and patiently answered my myriad of questions. My favorite place was over the paddle-wheel, which I'd watch as if in a hypnotic spell.

"When the boat reached the first stop below St. Louis, we got off and boarded another going back upstream. As it approached St. Louis, its newly installed whistle blew in a succession of toots, the band played in a final frenzy, and family and friends rushed to one side of the boat to wave to my grand-mother who was waving to us from the top of the bluff in back of her house, just opposite where the riverboat sounded its approach. When we got back, husbands/fathers met us at grandmother's house for dinner, games and conversation about the outing."

While in St. Louis, Ramón became a United States citizen with encouragement from Leann. She helped him learn American history to pass the necessary tests. In preparing for the examinations, he learned perhaps more about American history and geography than the average citizen knows. In any event, from that experience he developed a strong interest in both subjects and ever after derived great pleasure from perusing maps of all sorts.

While at the Courthouse for the citizenship proceedings, the Clementes listened to a portion of the hearings on the case of Dred Scott and his wife, both slaves who claimed freedom based on pre-vious residence in a free territory. Ramón was interested that a case of this sort was tried in an American court while instances of injus-tices to Indians seemed to receive less consideration.

Ramón intended to keep his horse Cristobal after the trip with Fremont's expedition was over but found stable and feed costs in St. Louis excessive in view of his having little or no income. With the growing infrequency of his riding Cristobal, he reluctantly decided to sell his horse to a local landowner for use by his growing son, believing Cristobal would thereby receive the care and attention he deserved.

To earn some income, he tried teaching Spanish to persons planning to go west into Mexican territory, but there were few takers. Most Americans arriving from the east were of the opinion that everyone should speak English and had little patience with the idea of learning anything, including the language, of countries they planned to visit.

After a few months living with the Richards, Leann and Ramón decided a home of their own would be best for all concerned. They first stayed at a boarding house run by Andrew Jackson Grayson and his wife Frances, who were recent arrivals from Louisiana.[13] Being close to the same age, the two couples enjoyed visiting together in the evenings and comparing their experiences. Ramón seemed to have impressed Andrew with stories about California and the Fremont expedition, for soon Andrew was planning to move there with his wife and two-year-old son Ned.[1] Leann and Ramón wished them well, agreed to keep in touch, and started looking for another place.

They were fortunate in obtaining a flat of two rooms on the second floor of an old house in the French section near the Sisters of the Sacred Heart school. The Sisters had been brought from Paris to establish the school by Bishop deBourg, who was a friend of the Fremonts. Through the Bishop, Ramón got a part-time job tutoring the few students who wanted to learn Spanish, but he soon realized further occupation was required to earn more income.

He could see that there was almost unlimited export and import business opportunity in this gateway city with the Mississippi River on its doorstep. The boom in trade and city growth followed the increase of river steam boats or packet boats, which the Indians called "big thunder canoe."[36] These double-decked side wheelers with their tall stacks were soon joined by the larger more luxurious stern-wheelers that became known as "floating palaces."

St. Louis was becoming a distribution center for eastern goods in the Mississippi Valley and for western products to the east and abroad through the port of New Orleans. One drawback of the rapid population growth was housing shortages which resulted in overcrowding and epidemics of various illnesses. Many who considered moving further west to avoid these plagues were encouraged by Josiah Gregg's new book *Commerce of the Prairies*, which described the benefits of the "prairie cure" for eastern and mid-western ailments.[14]

Ramón noted that a number of young men from Santa Fe had come to St. Louis for their education to learn American ways, much as he had done in going east from California in 1836. He also noted that the young men from Santa Fe concentrated more on learning American business methods, and Ramón decided to do the same. With Leann's encouragement and assistance, he set about to learn and practice American aspects of foreign trade in combination with his Chemical Bank experience and his familiarity with the exporting of hides and tallow from the Clemente ranch in California. Soon, working out of their small flat, they developed several clients in Central and South American port cities, and even some in California which Ramón felt might provide an opportunity for them to visit his former homeland.

Further growth of the Clemente export-import business was interrupted by the outbreak of war with Mexico in 1846. The beginning of the war was followed shortly by formation of the California Republic, when the Bear Flag was raised at Sonoma on June 14, 1846. Ramón derived considerable satisfaction from the news, particularly when he learned more about Fremont's part in the activities. The war ended in February 1848, when the Treaty of Guadeloupe-Hidalgo ceded to the United States, Mexico's former holdings in the southwest including California.

After his court-martial, Fremont resigned from the Army and returned to St. Louis with Jessie, who was expecting their second child. When Congress adjourned in the spring, Senator Benton also returned to St. Louis and was arranging another expedition for his son-in-law to find a new railroad route west.[39]

By this time, Ramón was becoming drawn towards the idea of working for the government of the United States and perhaps playing a role in the western expansion movement. Because of his former association with Fremont, Ramón decided to approach Fremont's father-in-law, Senator Benton, with his aspirations. He made an appointment and arrived at the Senator's office with high hopes.

At age sixty-four, Benton was still an impressive figure who seemed perhaps larger than he actually was because of his rolling rhetoric, voiced in stentorian tones normally used to address the U.S. Senate, but which reappeared at times in his normal speech. Ramón had been reluctant at first to approach this "great man" on such slight acquaintance but proceeded nonetheless with considerable prodding from Leann. He was pleasantly surprised at the Senator's patently sincere if slightly strained interest in Ramón's plans. The Senator couched his interest in terms of his early advocacy of "manifest destiny" as discussed in his speeches and writings, on which Leann had coached Ramón before the meeting. Senator Benton graciously offered to give him a letter of introduction to Secretary of State James Buchanan, to whom Ramón could apply, stating his intentions and what he believed to be his qualifications.

Ramón did so and within a few weeks was tentatively offered a position as commercial attache with the U.S. Embassy in Mexico City which was to be reactivated in October 1848. The Chief of Mission Nathan Clifford of Maine had been appointed in July and was building a new staff for the post-war period.[15] As a prerequisite to his appointment, Ramón was called to Washington for an interview at the State Department. He went by steamboat up the Ohio River to Wheeling, Virginia (now West Virginia), then by stagecoach 200 miles over the National Road to Cumberland, Maryland. From there he took the Baltimore & Ohio Railroad to Washington, which cost $8.60 for the twelve-hour trip. The entire journey required twelve days.[16]

He stayed overnight at the Indian Queen Hotel, in which he had stopped in 1837 on the way from New Haven to Charleston, South Carolina. As soon as he saw the identifying bright red sign of Pocahantas swinging above the entrance, Ramón recalled why this hotel had been such a pleasant place to stay. It was because of the personal attention given to guests by its warm, engaging manager, Jesse Brown, in such ways as meeting them on arrival and describing their assigned accommodations; remembering their favorite portions of the principal dish of the day, which he carved; and inviting guests to partake of a foaming eggnog he concocted in a mammoth punch bowl once owned by George Washington.[17] Ramón was glad to find him still there and that Jesse still remembered him, or at least said he did, after a ten-year time lapse.

Ramón had arrived a day early to be fresh and ready for the all-important interview. The next morning he ate lightly and walked the few blocks down Pennsylvania Avenue to the State Department, recalling his earlier visit as a tourist. Ushered into the secretary's waiting room, he did not meet the secretary himself but, after a brief delay, was escorted to a nearby conference room in which an assistant to Mr. Nathan Clifford and two other foreign service officers were gathered to interview him. Ramón felt as he imagined a defendant before a court of justice might feel, sitting alone at a small table facing a large curved desk on a raised dias where the three interrogators were seated. After brief introductions, which Ramón promptly forgot in his nervousness, the three men began questioning him on his background, education, work experience, knowledge of U.S. and Mexican history, geography, economy, and the war just ended. He felt the questions were fair and he responded honestly when he did not know an answer but said he would find out. He felt it went well and was told he would be notified promptly of the outcome. As it was the Clementes' first separation since their marriage, Ramón did not linger in Washington but returned to St. Louis as soon as he could after the interview and told Leann all about it. They waited expectantly, and not long thereafter an affirmative answer was received.

This was his first real job and his first connection with the United States Government. Leann and Ramón were both tremendously excited at the prospect of moving to and living in a foreign land, albeit one with which the United States was recently at war. With transportation and living accommodations to be provided by the government, there was little else to worry about or keep them from enjoying this new adventure in their lives—assuming Ramón performed his new duties satisfactorily.

The thought crossed his mind that as an American, although of Spanish/Mexican descent, he would be entering Mexico as a representative of a "conquering" nation and might encounter some resentment on the part of the "vanquished" Mexican citizenry. Ramón felt he might become even more of a target as a former Mexican citizen, possibly perceived as a "turncoat." It could hardly be expected that any American envoys would be warmly welcomed little more than a year after General Winfield Scott, with 12,000 American troops, had entered and captured Mexico City.[3]

Ramón could not help but wonder privately at the apparent double standard of the United States Government in criticizing other nations for their "imperialism" while themselves taking over lands of other nations (including that of the native North American Indians) in the name of "manifest destiny." He would learn later on in Washington that ambivalence often is the handmaiden of political counterpoint (to mix a few metaphors in Ramón's newly acquired English language).

He approached his new job with some trepidation, being without experience in the workings of a government office, but his superiors and co-workers were understanding and helpful in putting him at ease and showing him what to do. His job required local travel to report on business opportunities for U.S. importers and exporters, reporting on economic conditions in Mexico, and participating in the development and negotiation of trade agreements between the United States and Mexico.

The fact that Spanish was his native tongue, plus his export and import experience, were advantages in the job and apparently also were the reasons for Ramón's appointment to this post. After mastering the basic aspects of his assignment, there was opportunity for him and Leann to see and learn more of the fascinating area in which they were living.

The Federal District of Mexico, like the District of Columbia, is by definition the seat of government. Unlike the District of Columbia, which includes the relatively young and somewhat provincial city of Washington, the Federal District includes the far older and much more cosmopolitan metropolis of Mexico City, sometimes referred to as the Paris of the western hemisphere.

With a long history going back to the fourteenth century as part of the Aztec empire, the city is colorful and diverse, from the National Palace on the Plaza Zocalo to the hilltop Castle of Chapultepec, to the Basilica of Guadeloupe on the outskirts, and along the wide boulevards in between. Quite disturbing, however, was the stark contrast between the extremes of wealth and poverty existing side by side.

The Clementes noticed this contrast in their travels about the city and surrounding countryside. It was exemplified by the daily spectacle of poor Mexican peasants donating their meagre savings at the gilded statue of the Virgin of Guadeloupe in its ornate gold encrusted basilica, a scene not duplicated at any of the California missions. Nowhere was the contrast more apparent than in the elegant social activities of the wealthy aristocrats, carried on in the midst of the grinding poverty of their fellow citizens who often hadn't enough to eat.

One similarity with Washington DC is that both cities are built partially over marshland. The Mexican capital is in a basin of 120 miles circumference, once covered by water, now with three lakes remaining—Texcoco, Chalco, and Xochimilco. A portion of the city is on land that is slowly sinking, particularly evident at the Plaza Zocalo in the city's center. There apparently is little that can be or is being done to slow or reverse the process.

Major differences exist between the two capitals in climate and terrain. Mexico City is in rarified atmosphere over 7,300 feet above sea level, with dry cool nights and surrounded by towering mountain peaks, such as the smoldering volcanoes of Popocatepetl and Iztaccihuatl; whereas Washington DC is practically at sea level with low surrounding hills and often unbearably oppressive summer heat and humidity, causing British diplomats to classify it as a "hardship post."[18]

Living in Mexico at the time were Ramón's sister Cristina and her new family. In 1845 her husband Raimundo Carillo had accepted a position with the Mexican government and moved his family to Mexico City before the war began between Mexico and the United States. Characteristically Doña Caterina claimed credit for getting her son-in-law his new position although quite the opposite was true. Raimundo was related to the former Commandantes of the Presidios at Monterey and Santa Barbara and thus had his own direct connections with the central government.

Leann and Ramón visited the Carillos at their home in Cuernavaca, not far from Mexico City. The Carillos took them on a scenic tour which included the remains of the precolumbian city of Teotihuacan, one of the world's largest cities prior to its destruction in 750 A.D. They were impressed with its Temple of Quetzalcoatl and Pyramids of the Sun and Moon, said to rival the pyramids of Egypt.

The Clementes enjoyed their time in this foreign capital and considered making it their home, but their American roots tended to hold them back from doing so. There was a very unfortunate occurrence during this period when Leann had a miscarriage which, complicated by a doctor's mistake, rendered her unable to bear children. Being in a foreign country didn't help in considering and dealing with the options available. This was something Leann and Ramón learned to live with in spite of the disappointment felt by both, perhaps bringing them closer together as a result.

When they finally did leave Mexico, they brought with them two tiny dogs of a breed named for the Mexican state of Chihuahua. Leann and Ramón admired their miniature size, trim lines, and keen intelligence, and looked forward to breeding them on returning to the United States.

In the fall of 1849 Mr. Clifford was recalled to Washington, to be replaced as Chief of Mission by Robert Letcher of Kentucky.[15] Soon thereafter Ramón was informed of a new assignment for himself. He was to proceed to the State Department in Washington by way of California, a rather unusual and out-of-the-way routing.

It was explained to him that Mr. Larkin, the former U.S. Consul at Monterey, was still in California as a member of the Constitutional Convention for the new state; and that he had information, including some confidential papers, to transmit to Washington; and that, although not of an urgent nature, it required someone employed by the government who was familiar with the situation, to meet with Larkin, receive the information, and deliver it to Washington. Ramón would then be assigned to the State Department to work initially, at least, on matters pertaining to the information he would receive from Larkin.

As the matter was not of extreme urgency, Ramón requested and was granted time to visit his former home in southern California before travelling to Washington, with the proviso that he ascertain and report on the attitudes of Californians in the south towards the acquisition of the former Mexican territory by the United States. It was beginning to dawn on him, as would be revealed after his meeting with former Consul Larkin, that there were additional reasons, beyond what he had originally thought, for his being chosen for the job at the Embassy in Mexico and for this current reassignment.

Ramón was briefed on the background of Thomas O. Larkin (no relation to the St. Louis Larkins), who was the first and only American Consul in California and served from 1844 to 1848.[19] He had arrived from New England in 1832 and soon become a leading merchant and prominent local figure. His services as interpreter and mediator during the temporary seizure of Monterey by the American Commodore Jones in 1842 brought him to the attention of the State Department. Larkin remained on good terms with the Californians, including Mexican government officials. He reported continuously to the State Department on political and social currents in California, including any foreign influences, and noted the lack of sympathy between California and the rest of Mexico.

As Ramón would learn later in Washington, it was important for the United States Government to know if there were any feelings of dissatisfaction or counter-revolutionary activities that might reverse the recent acquisition. For example, any possibility of a secession movement, like the "Bear Flag" revolt from Mexico, would require advance political and military planning and would be dealt with accordingly. This would be something which a native Californian with "grass roots" connections might be able to ascertain more readily than a transplanted Yankee.

As such information seemed to have had some influence on U.S. policy with respect to California, it was logical to conclude that Ramón's presence on the scene, and his observations as a native Californian, could be helpful in dealing with the aftermath of the war, not only in Mexico but also in Washington, after having shared Larkin's confidence. Ramón's observations could also be helpful in monitoring the activities of persons who were engaged in events leading to California statehood, such as Larkin and Fremont, particularly in view of the latter's court-martial.

Ramón was more than willing to undertake the assignment in view of his earlier friendship with Fremont and his own participation in the second Fremont expedition. Larkin's role in the tense situation that developed between Fremont and Mexican officials before war broke out apparently was as a moderator, trying to get each side to see the other's viewpoint and not act rashly through misunderstanding of the other's motives. Ramón Clemente could understand and relate to this and hoped to be able to convey to Washington the information made available to him in just those terms.

It probably was much to Larkin's credit that there was not more trouble between Americans and Californians, and that the acquisition of California, in which he as a confidential government agent participated with Fremont, was not more violent than it turned out to be—a by-product of the larger war with Mexico.[20]

The Clementes' arrived in Monterey in the midst of the tremendous wave of emigration from the east after the discovery of gold in California. Thus the scene was new to both—for Leann a first visit, and for Ramón—seeing his former homeland as it had never been before.

Because of the gold rush, settlement of California differed from other American frontier areas which had been colonized by agriculturalists after the first stage of hunters and trappers. All types of easterners came to California seeking immediate wealth through gold acquisition or related activities. The sleepy Spanish town of Yerba Buena on San Francisco Bay grew from a few houses to a city of 20,000 people in months. Less than 2 percent were women, and most men didn't intend to stay.[21]

Over the next decade nearly 300,000 people would move overland to California, plus the many who came by other means. There was a proposed "aerial locomotive"—a 1,000-foot long propeller-driven balloon, powered by two steam engines, that would take passengers from New York to San Francisco in three days, but this project never "got off the ground," so to speak.[22] The rush to the gold fields nearly depopulated the newly named city of San Francisco itself, so that newspapers and other businesses sometimes closed for lack of help.

Ships from all over the world came to San Francisco and often their crews deserted ship to join passengers in the gold rush. Many ships were abandoned in the harbor and some were beached for use as hotels where errant sailors often were "shanghaied" back to sea duty. A great fire slowed activity for a while but not for long. An emigrant from South Africa named Norton, who had made and lost a fortune, declared himself "Emperor," issued 50¢ "bonds," and ate at "free lunch" counters. The amused citizens accepted him as a symbol of their illusions of sudden wealth.[23]

Southern Californians participated in the gold rush in a different way—by selling cattle and wine to meet needs of the growing population in the north and watching their own herds and vineyards increase in value.[32]

With all these people coming to California and many of them mining gold, there soon was a huge demand for goods and services met by a growing amount of gold dust and ore which could be exchanged only in its raw form. Raw gold trading for $16 an ounce would bring $18 an ounce at the Philadelphia Mint, but the cost of getting it there was a strong deterrent. Colonel Mason, California's military governor, recommended establishment of a branch mint which was delayed nearly four years in Washington because Senator Benton, hoping to expedite the measure, connected it with a similar request for New York, which caused unexpected complications.[28]

Meanwhile enterprising citizens were establishing private minting facilities, some such as Moffat & Co. of San Francisco, with temporary government sanction to fill the urgent need. Ramón obtained, and retained for many years, a sample of their first issuance—a small rectangular ingot with a stamp bearing the company name, the designation "20–3/4 carat" and the value "$16.00."[29] In later years this became the most valuable item in his collection.

But getting back to the Clementes' arrival in Monterey, they were delighted to cross paths again with old friends. Jesse Fremont was in town awaiting results of the constitutional convention, which was expected to nominate her husband as one of California's first two senators. He was away on business resulting from newly discovered gold on his land in Mariposa. Jessie and her daughter Elizabeth, whom she called "Lilly," were staying in rented rooms at the home of the wife of Mexican General Castro, who had been exiled to Mexico City. The Clementes were fascinated by the way Jessie had decorated their limited space with a variety of Oriental, European, and American furnishings John had sent from San Francisco, set off by two grizzly bear skins on the floor. She described entertaining delegates to the California Convention as she had done before in more elegant quarters for her father's guests in St. Louis and Washington.[40]

Then Ramón and Leann were delighted to see the Graysons, who came to Monterey on business from their home in San Francisco. Andrew and Frances looked much the same as when they had the boarding house in St. Louis in which Ramón and Leann stayed three years earlier. Andrew, of medium height and slight build with long dark hair, moustache, and small beard, did not present the typical pioneer image. Frances, with stronger facial features and reddish brown hair pulled back into a bun, appeared more the pioneer woman. Their son Ned, now almost a young man, had lighter hair than either parent, but the same wide-set large liquid-blue eyes.

Andrew related how they first settled near Sutter's Fort where he looked up John Fremont and became active in recruiting Californians for the cause of independence from Mexico. In 1847 they moved to Yerba Buena, now San Francisco, where Andrew engaged in various commercial enterprises and also served in the local government. He tried gold-mining but achieved greater success with real estate and eventually founded a town bearing his name.[13]

Thomas Larkin also was involved in real estate, building a city on the bay called Benecia, named after the wife of Colonel Mariano Vallejo, former Commander of Mexican forces in the north, who favored annexation of California by the United States.[31] Larkin's town, where one of the private mints was established,[29] was expected to rival Yerba Buena.[24] Thus Larkin and Grayson had something in common although they had never met. The Clementes and Graysons enjoyed visiting together and were sorry that business pressures on both sides prevented them from spending more time in each others company.

Ramón met with Larkin at the latter's home on Monterey's Calle Principal. He was struck by the innovative style of the house which Larkin built in 1835 at a cost of $5,000. It was a pleasing combination of California adobe with New England two-story frame, which was becoming known as "Monterey colonial."[26] Its hip roof extended over a second floor gallery across the front and two sides of the house. A wide central hall ran from the street entrance to a central courtyard. There were two large rooms on both sides of the hall and a stairway leading to the upstairs bedrooms.

As Ramón entered, Larkin pointed out the largest room on the right which was used as a commercial trading station where local rancheros exchanged hides and tallow for household furnishings, clothing, and firearms that Larkin imported from Boston. He described the two doors on the left as leading into his family living quarters and took Ramón to the second room on the right, which was his office. It was here, Larkin related, that he had received Lt. Archibald Gillespie, who brought messages from President Polk and Navy Secretary Bancroft for Larkin and Fremont in 1846, leading to the American conquest of California, during which time his house became their headquarters.[30]

At this initial meeting with Larkin, Ramón found the former U.S. Consul to be shrewd yet even-tempered and amiable. He was meticulously attired in black with a white shirt more appropriate to New England than California. Not physically robust, Larkin had light eyes, thin lips, and a thin nose. At age forty-seven he was not only rich in experience but had acquired considerable wealth as a merchant and landowner. They talked easily and openly about the changes taking place in California and about Larkin's plans to withdraw from active public life and devote full time to his business interests. Ramón explained the purpose of his trip, and they arranged to meet further after his visit to southern California which would combine business with a few days at the Clemente ranch.

As Ramón had taken no extended vacation since beginning his government service, he and Leann were pleased to have some time to themselves. He was looking forward to showing her his former home, but they both felt some apprehension about meeting his family. After a long dusty stagecoach ride down the central valley, Ramón found his former surroundings just as he remembered. Leann was entranced by the beauty of the countryside, especially where the mountains met the sea. She said they must seriously consider making their home there on a later visit.

Their enthusiasm was dampened after spending time with Ramón's family. Leann's experience was worse than he had imagined when staying with her family in St. Louis, and he had tried to consider how it would be if their situations were reversed. Doña

Caterina Clemente-Calderon, herself an immigrant into California, seemed more provincial and elitist than Ramón remembered as he began to see his family through Leann's eyes. He began to realize that his mother had always tended that way, to which he had sometimes objected as he grew older, but usually ignored or passed off as a private family joke between himself and his sister, and later his cousins. Doña Caterina complained about newcomers, particularly Americans, spoiling the area. Her latest complaint was that the Rancho Topanga Malibu Sequit, where Ramón had attended beach parties as a young man, and which was originally owned by the Tapia family who came to California in 1775 with de Anza on orders from the King of Spain, had been sold for a mere 800 pesos to a French man who married one of the Tapia granddaughters. While admitting it wasn't as bad as selling to an American, Doña Caterina still looked askance at any newcomers or foreigners displacing those she considered to be "our kind."

Although Leann and Ramón received traditional California hospitality and were treated with courtesy by friends and family, there was an air of condescension on the part of Doña Caterina and others towards the "outsider" who married her son. Ramón was very disappointed that their apprehension over Leann's meeting his family proved well founded. The fact that his mother's patronizing attitude towards his wife was concealed ever so slightly by conventional Spanish manners made it all the more difficult to deal with openly.

After valiant efforts by Leann to establish a good relationship, which she truly wanted, and ineffective attempts by Ramón to maintain a pleasant face on things that were not going well, they realized that their marriage would not thrive, and perhaps not even survive, under such conditions. Thus they were not sorry when it came time to return north and carry on with Ramón's assignment.

During their brief visit, he picked up some information from talking with friends and relatives that would be useful in Washington. It seemed there was a growing movement to separate from northern California among southern Californios such as Don Juan Bandini and the brothers Pico, Andrés, and Pio, who felt they would be better off as a territory under the Federal government than neglected by the legislature of the new state.[27] Ramón thought it best to keep this information to himself for the time being and not mention it to Larkin before discussing it with his superiors in the State Department.

While Ramón was meeting with Larkin, Leann received word of her father's serious illness and the advisability of her going to St. Louis. This was particularly worrisome because of the cholera epidemic spreading through the midwest. They arranged travel by ship to Panama, where they would cross the isthmus and pick up another ship that would let Leann off at New Orleans to go to St. Louis and take Ramón to the east coast. The trans-isthmian portion was said to offer less danger from hostile natives than when Jessie and Elizabeth Fremont made it seven months earlier[25] but still bore the risks of contracting malaria and yellow fever. However the entire trip could take only a few weeks, depending on the wait for a ship at Chagres, instead of five months to go around Cape Horn.

The Clementes boarded the S.S. California in Monterey Bay which required being rowed out from shore and climbing the ship's rope ladder. Although they had done that before when they arrived in Monterey, it was still somewhat of an ordeal, particularly for Leann, who was glad when they finally got all their belongings, including the two dogs, into their cabin. Then they could enjoy sitting in wicker lounge chairs on deck, watching the California coastline slip by.

After the sea voyage from Monterey to Panama, the passengers moved across the isthmus to the port of Chagres on the east coast by a combination of transportation modes including small river craft, mule trains, and Indian bearers. In this tropical land, mostly without any roads, they went from extremes of dense jungles to high mountain gorges and swift water streams, with extremes of temperature to match. It took six days and was a harrowing experience even for the two small dogs, Cherubino and Violetta, that Ramón carried in a wicker hamper separated into two compartments by a wooden divider with wire fasteners. All were so relieved when they finally boarded the S.S. Panama for the rest of the journey that they didn't even mind climbing up the rope ladder.

Tension mounted as the ship approached New Orleans, for this would be the Clementes' first lengthy separation since their marriage. After a tearful farewell, Leann disembarked to travel by riverboat up the Mississippi to St. Louis in the company of friends they met aboard ship. Ramón and the two little dogs continued on by sea to Georgetown, a thriving Potomac River tobacco port adjacent to Washington DC.

As this foreign service phase of their lives drew to a close, Ramón knew they would look back on it in years to come as one of the more interesting and enjoyable times of their lives, providing many rich memories on which to draw as they grew older together.

Fortunately Leann's father was in much better health by the time she arrived in St. Louis. After a brief visit she was able to meet Ramón in DC within a few weeks of his own arrival. Rather than travel alone, Leann joined friends who were going the same way. The eastern railroads were working their way west, but were not yet through to St. Louis, so they travelled approximately the same route as Ramón had taken in 1848—a combination of steamboat and stagecoach to Cumberland, Maryland, then the B&O Railroad to Washington.

Ramón was never so glad to see anyone in his life. The dogs were glad to see her too when he brought her to their temporary quarters—but first, let us return to Ramón's arrival in Georgetown.

CHAPTER 9
LIFE IN GEORGETOWN DC

Ramón heard about Georgetown from Jessie Fremont, who attended Miss Lydia English's Seminary there.[1] He first sought lodging at the Union Hotel on Bridge Street at Washington Street, a block south of Miss English's Seminary. The Union would not accept dogs, so he took a room at the more accommodating Georgetown Hotel, formerly the City Tavern, on Falls Street at the corner of Water.

Constructed in 1796, this hotel had been run since 1834 by Mrs. Eleanor Lang and her son, John. As the City Tavern, it had been used by President Adams as his headquarters when he came from Philadelphia in 1800 to inspect the new buildings being constructed for the nation's capital. Ramón often thought of that while eating dinner in the "long room" in which President Adams had been given a banquet on his visit more than fifty years before.[2] Ramón also enjoyed an occasional meal at nearby Suter's Tavern, which was popular with visitors to the capital as being better than what was available in Washington City.

He was quite comfortable living at the hotel while getting settled in his new position at the State Department. Although as a native Californian he was used to riding even short distances on horseback, Ramón soon became accustomed to, and almost enjoyed, walking to work, except in inclement weather. His route was east on Falls Street, which became Bridge Street a block past the hotel. After four more blocks and across the creek, Bridge Street turned into Pennsylvania Avenue, which was lined with Federal townhouses, and led directly to the State Department, next door to the White House.

After such a walk Ramón sometimes took breakfast at the Willard Hotel about two blocks from his office. The Willard's menu included hearty delicacies such as fried oysters and steak with onions—rather too heavy for the beginning of a day's work. He soon thought better of this and saved the Willard for special occasions.

One may wonder what had become of the little dogs, Cherubino and Violetta, that accompanied Ramón to Georgetown and how they fared while he was at work. The Langs were very understanding and helpful, allowing him to keep the dogs in his room and arranging to have the room made up and cleaned each day before he left for work. He took the dogs out for a brief walk in the early morning and put food and water out for them before leaving. The Langs agreed that no one was to enter the room while he was gone, which might have frightened the dogs and allowed them to run out the door and possibly outside the building before anyone could stop them; then they might be gone forever, one of his recurring fears. The Langs also agreed to have someone keep an "ear" out for any unusual sounds indicating the dogs might be in trouble and necessitating emergency entrance to extricate them from any harmful situation that might have developed.

Sometimes after work Ramón stopped by Rhodes Tavern at 15th and F Streets for a drink with his colleagues before returning to his room at the Georgetown Hotel. They would speculate on conversations that might have occurred in 1814 when British officers dined at Rhodes Tavern the night they burned the White House and set fires in the Capitol after defeating the American Army at Bladensburg, Maryland. Apparently the only thing that saved Washington from further devastation or capture was a severe rainstorm with prolonged thunder, lightning, and hurricane winds that caused the British to retreat.

On one occasion, the group at Rhodes Tavern was joined by a Scottish lass named Deborah Cass, cousin of one of Ramón's colleagues, who was visiting Washington for a few days before returning home. After the second round of drinks, she said she had to leave because she was dining with friends in Georgetown but wasn't sure how to get there. Ramón offered to show her on his way back to the hotel. As they walked, they talked of their experiences before coming to Washington. Ramón mentioned the two dogs and Deborah Cass said, "Oh, I'd just love to see them!"

Ramón replied impulsively, "Why not stop by my hotel on the way and you shall?"

As they approached the Georgetown Hotel, he felt that an attraction was developing between them, but when they arrived at his room the sight of Cherubino and Violetta with eyes like four warning beacons so forcibly reminded him of Leann that he rather too brusquely terminated the visit and quickly escorted his erstwhile guest to her friends' nearby home.

On another occasion during this first lengthy separation of their marriage, Ramón was again tempted to break one of his sacred marriage vows, this time with a secretary he met at a State Department office party. After imbibing too much he offered to escort her home, she invited him in, and they were on the verge of indiscretion when Ramón recovered his senses, excused himself, and left before things went too far.

When it came time for Leann's arrival from St. Louis, Ramón arranged for a larger room at the hotel so they could stay on more comfortably while looking for a permanent home. On his way to meet Leann at the B&O station, which was then a converted house at the corner of Pennsylvania Avenue and Second Street, NW, he recalled the conditions, still unchanged, surrounding his 1848 arrival for the State Department interview. As Congress did not allow steam engines within the city limits until 1852, the railroad cars were drawn into the city by horses at three miles an hour, preceded by a man on horseback carrying a red flag to warn pedestrians and vehicular traffic of the approaching danger.[3] Leann was both amused and annoyed by this procedure, which delayed her arrival after so long a journey, but seemed as pleased to see Ramón as he was to see her. She was not displeased with the hotel room but vowed to begin search immediately for an alternative.

The next day when she had unpacked, gotten the dogs taken care of and Ramón off to work, Leann set forth to find their new home. Within a few days she found what seemed just right—an early Federal-style town house about four blocks from the hotel on West Street between Congress and Washington Streets facing south. The house was about forty years old and occupied by the original owners, now elderly and moving to smaller quarters. It needed considerable repair and upgrading, which the Clementes felt they could do themselves while living there. After moving in, they continued making improvements during most of the fifteen years they were there and loved every minute of it.

A few weeks after the move a letter arrived from Deborah Cass in Scotland thanking Ramón for his kindness during her visit to

Washington. He told Leann of his experiences with Miss Cass and also with the secretary from the State Department that had stopped short of more serious impropriety. Leann was hurt by his revelations and Ramón always regretted these lapses which, fortunately for their marriage, never were repeated.

They saw briefly the new California Senator John Fremont who was in Washington with his wife and daughter for the Congressional debate over California's statehood which was finally resolved October 18, 1850, with much celebration by all concerned.[32] The Clementes attended a reception at Senator Benton's home on C Street but did not get much chance to talk with the Fremonts, who were now "darlings of Washington society," what with gold wealth from their California property added to Senatorial status and full removal of the previous court-martial stain.

Jessie at twenty-six was still very attractive. Her brown hair, now slightly thinning, was still worn pulled back over her ears and gathered at the back of her neck. Leann noted her Empire gown of blue brocade reportedly worn at a dinner for the Fremonts given by James Buchanan.[33] John Fremont, now thirty-seven, looked older with grey hair and weather-beaten face. Unfortunately, he had drawn by lot the shorter of the first two Senatorial terms, so when Congress adjourned he would have to stand for reelection or find something else to do.[34]

One of the three bedrooms on the second floor of their new home was reserved for the dogs which they intended to breed after getting settled. Unfortunately, Violetta died before that was possible. While grieving her loss, they began looking for a suitable mate for Cherubino. The Langs told them of a Richmond man who raised small dogs that might be of the same breed. An exchange of correspondence confirmed the breed and that the man had a female for sale. They travelled to Richmond, boarding the train in Alexandria for the 113-mile ride. Leann was skeptical at first but Ramón was enthusiastic and convinced Leann they should take the dog with them to Washington. Cherubino liked her too and after the appropriate interaction and passage of time there were four tiny offspring. The Clementes assisted in their birth, with Ramón actually breathing life into the smallest one who was not breathing at first. Thus began a bonding process and before long, contrary to plan, the Clementes could not give up any of the dogs for any price.

After settling into their new home, the Clementes sometimes attended services at Christ Church on the southwest corner of

Congress and Beall Streets. Although neither were Episcopalian, they wanted to participate in the life of their new neighborhood. Ramón was interested in the history of this church, built just a year before he was born. It was founded two years before that, in 1817, at a meeting at the nearby house of Thomas Corcoran, former mayor of Georgetown, whose son William later joined with George Riggs to form the banking institution that helped finance the Mexican and Civil Wars. The firm benefitted from Corcoran's close connection with the Jacksonian Democrats, resulting in the Federal Government depositing in the new institution funds that were withdrawn from the Second Bank of the United States in Philadelphia by President Jackson preceding the panic of 1837. The successor firm, Riggs & Co., later absorbed the Farmers & Mechanics Bank in Georgetown where the Clementes opened their first bank account.

One of the Clementes' new neighbors was Commander Cassin, a decorated veteran of the battle of Lake Champlain in the War of 1812. He and his wife, daughter of an English Army officer, lived a block south on Beall Street in a large free-standing mansion built around 1816. They entertained frequently and everyone in the neighborhood was saddened by his death in 1857.[4]

Another neighbor, Alderman Francis Wheatley, who lived two blocks south on Gay Street, built "two first class brick buildings" on lots adjoining his property, as reported in the Georgetown column of the *Evening Star* on April 15, 1859.[5]

Dr. Grafton Tyler lived at the corner of Gay and Washington Streets, where he also had his office for private medical practice. He was a Professor of Medicine at the Columbia Medical School and Washington Infirmary, President of the Georgetown Board of Council, a director of the Children's Hospital, and Vice President of the American Medical Association. He resigned his professional duties in 1859 and later built the double mid-Victorian town houses on Washington Street between Gay and Dumbarton.[6]

Neighbor Reuben Daw, two blocks east on the northwest corner of West and Montgomery Streets, built around his property a fence made of used musket barrels from the War with Mexico, which was the talk of the neighborhood.[9]

Another more controversial neighbor was author Emma Dorothy Eliza Nevitt (E.D.E.N.) Southworth, whose 1849 novel *Retribution* was serialized in Washington's only abolitionist newspaper, *National Era*. EDEN Southworth used proceeds from book sales to acquire the fourteen-room Prospect Cottage on a bluff overlooking the Potomac River on the southwest corner of Prospect and Gay Streets.[7] Here she befriended and housed another controversial author, Harriet Beecher Stowe, who came to Washington in 1852 for publication of her book, *Uncle Tom's Cabin*, which drew attention to and encouraged sympathy for the plight of blacks in the United States.

Through all these neighbors the Clementes developed interest in and knowledge of other Georgetown dwellings, complementing the enthusiasm they both felt in upgrading their own home. In this latter endeavor they received assistance from two other neighbors— William Knowles, a carpenter, who lived at 123 Washington Street, and Samuel Fearson, also a carpenter who lived further south on Washington Street between Bridge and Olive.[8]

In 1851, the Clementes attended one of the first gatherings of Georgetown citizens at the new High Street meeting hall built by Bladen Forrest, Georgetown's wealthiest citizen. The meeting was to discuss the proposed retrocession of Georgetown to the State of Maryland, which many favored over absorption into Washington City.[10] Being new to the area, the Clementes were surprised at the heights of emotion reached by the citizens of Georgetown over the question of losing their separate identity.

From his familiarity with California water projects, Ramón was fascinated by the Aqueduct Bridge and the reservoir system. The bridge, completed in 1843, included a canal channel to carry barges across the Potomac from the Chesapeake and Ohio canal in Georgetown to the Alexandria canal in Virginia, allowing Alexandria to compete with Georgetown as a shipping port.[11]

The reservoir system was developed after the water supply for Georgetown and Washington became critical in 1850. Army Engineer Meigs' plan, which was adopted in 1852, consisted of conduits from the source at Great Falls to nearby reservoirs for receipt and distribution, reminiscent of the system worked out by the San Gabriel Mission padres and Ramón's father thirty years earlier. In the Washington system, water flowed by gravity through pipes laid under Falls and Bridge Streets in lower Georgetown and along Pennsylvania Avenue to serve Washington City. As most of Georgetown's residents were above this level, a high service reservoir was built at High and Road Streets to which water would be pumped so as to flow by gravity to Georgetown recipients.[12]

Although the entire system was not in full operation until 1865, an earlier benefit was the Public Pump installed in 1858 at the northwest corner of High and Bridge Streets. The pump had two dolphin head spouts—the upper to fill buckets with drinking water for domestic use and the lower to service the adjacent horse trough.[13] Other civic improvements were: the installation in 1855 of new gas street lamps with tapered square glass lanterns on which were painted street names to replace less visible signs on buildings at intersections; and in 1862 the first horse-drawn streetcars on metal rails from Georgetown down Pennsylvania Avenue to Washington City.[1]

The Clementes often attended lectures and exhibits at the Smithsonian Institution which, in 1853, accepted custody of the "National Cabinet of Curiosities" from the U.S. Patent Office. They also enjoyed exhibits of American artists at the Smithsonian by the newly formed Washington Art Association.

When news came that the "Swedish Nightingale," Jenny Lind, would perform at the National Theater in December 1850, they planned to attend. Leann was shocked by the price of $14 for two tickets, plus $4 for hack hire,[14] in addition to an expensive dinner at the Willard Hotel dining room. Ramón felt the evening well worth the cost as it was not something they did often. They were surprised to learn later that Phineas T. Barnum, who promoted and managed Jenny Lind's US tour, made over half a million dollars on the venture while the Swedish Nightingale netted only $176,000.

The Clementes' visits to the National Theater were infrequent not only because of high prices but also because of the unruly audiences whose spitting, cursing, and failure to remove tall hats made it unpleasant. Also there was the constant danger of fire, which actually destroyed the theater on several occasions, causing it to be rebuilt six times by 1855.

Sometimes the National Theater didn't seem so bad, as when the Clementes read of audience excesses in New York, when two rival productions of "Macbeth" appeared at the same time, one with an English actor and one with an American. The English actor met with hostile crowds chanting "three groans for the codfish aristocracy" accompanied by throwing of food and furniture. This precipitated the "Astor Place Riots" in which more than 20 people died and 150 were injured.[8]

More pleasant and safer diversions were visiting the Botanic Gardens near the Capitol and the public resort at Analostan on Mason's Island in the Potomac, reached by ferry from Georgetown. Mostly they enjoyed evenings together at home playing backgammon, chess, or dominos while watching the antics of their four new puppies.

At the national level, the Army Appropriation Act of 1853 directed Secretary Jefferson Davis to survey possible railroad routes west to the Pacific, of which there were five under consideration. The one farthest north, between the 47th and 49th parallels, was opposed by Senator Benton, who wanted the route to originate further south in St. Louis. The second route, between the 38th and 39th parallels, was favored by Senator Benton, but he failed to get John Fremont appointed to head the survey expedition. The Senator then promoted two privately funded expeditions, one headed by Fremont, and the other by Lt. Edward Beale. Fremont departed in November 1853.

The Fremonts had rented a house in Washington next door to Senator Benton, in which Jessie and her family lived while John Fremont was away on his expeditions. Mrs. Fremont did not go out much socially during her husband's absence but sometimes had guests for dinner. On one occasion, when the Clementes were present, Jessie's younger sister Susie entertained the guests by playing selections from Beethoven's compositions on Jessie's Viennese Pleyel piano.[16]

The winter of 1853–54 was particularly bad not only in Washington but in the west as well. Jessie had strong forebodings that her husband was in trouble, but on the night of February 6, 1854, she felt a hand on her shoulder and heard her husband's voice calling her name.[17] Later, when he returned and they compared notes, she learned that on that date his group arrived safely at a Mormon settlement after nearly starving and Fremont himself physically collapsing from exhaustion as a result of heavy mountain snows which caused a lack of game for food and lack of grass for horses.

The Fremonts' son Charles was born on Easter Day, 1854. Prior to that time, Jessie had arranged with the Epiphany Church, which they attended, to have the font decorated with flowers on Easter Day. Although this was a first for Protestant Churches in America, it was so well received that the custom spread to other churches throughout the country.[18]

An 1854 newspaper report on the clipper ship Flying Cloud recalled Ramón's first sea voyage in 1836 from Monterey around Cape Horn to New York, which lasted three months. The Flying Cloud set a record of less than thirty days for the 14,000 mile journey from New York to San Francisco via Cape Horn.[19] Clipper ships like the Flying Cloud were able to brave the sometimes eighty-knot blizzards around Cape Horn and cut through heavy seas at great speed. They carried eastern fortune hunters to California for the "gold rush" and brought back much of their produce. Between 1847 and 1855 U.S. gold production rose from 43,000 to 2.9 million ounces a year, which was about 45 percent of world output, and clipper ships carried a good part of it.[20]

The Clementes' tenth wedding anniversary was July 17, 1855, and for the occasion they bought a set of Gorham silver flatware in the Chantilly pattern, which Leann greatly admired. They could now afford the lower price of about $1 per piece, which was considerably less than the formerly handmade coin silver pieces, because of a new manufacturing process using a drop-press that Gorham recently acquired from England.[21] They first used the new silver service to entertain the Fremonts at dinner.

In 1856 Leann's parents wrote her about the "Great Fair" sponsored by the Agricultural and Mechanical Association in St. Louis to show the latest in tools, machines, and agricultural methods. They also had news of the Larkins, at whose party for the Fremonts Ramón and Leann had first met. The Larkins' son James, now twenty-five years old, had been promoted to junior partner in his father's business and was occupied with collecting rents from the many tenants of Larkin-owned buildings. His chronic poor health and his mother's urging led James to seek the "prairie cure" by joining one of William Bent's caravans over the Santa Fe trail.[22] The Richards were waiting to hear how it turned out but thought the Clementes might be interested in view of Ramón's trip with Fremont in 1844.

Leann said, "How thoughtful of them, don't you think so, Luis?"

"Yes, of course," he replied, "but the Santa Fe trail now is much more civilized than the route we took in 1844. Furthermore, my trip with Fremont was part of an exploratory expedition, not like joining a routine caravan for health reasons."

"Well that's really a minor difference. It's the thought that counts."

"Yes, dear, of course." Ramón felt a bit guilty that he had not been more appreciative of her parents' thoughtfulness.

Leann had become an expert in house remodelling and restoration from working on their own home and was branching out into similar endeavors with other Georgetown houses. Although there were other women engaged in business activities, usually managing enterprises left by deceased husbands or fathers and with help from experienced employees, few women of the time evidenced the ability to venture out on their own in a new business, particularly one such as this. Leann was indeed a pioneer and an innovator in this respect.

Her initial appearances at government offices to obtain necessary permits, licenses, and approvals were met with thinly disguised amusement and even disdain by the generally all-male staff members. Through sheer persistence and thorough knowledge of what she was doing, she soon turned the situation around, earning the respect and admiration of all with whom she came in contact, and thereafter was greeted with enthusiasm on her arrival.

While Ramón was occupied with his government job, Leann conducted her own business with great success. She acquired old houses that needed restoration, researched the earlier period to assure authenticity of her work, and gave each her full attention and careful consideration until it was completed to her discriminating satisfaction. She then rented or sold it and started another.

It was by no means easy going, however, and could sometimes be threatening, as Leann experienced on several occasions. One was with an overly attentive real estate agent who had designs on Leann personally—entreating her to leave Ramón and go off with him. When she rejected his pleas, he threatened to tell Ramón they were having an affair, but as she had already apprised Ramón of the situation, she was able to call his bluff.

Another time was when a contractor who had not completed his work demanded full payment. He arrived unexpectedly while Leann was alone in the house in which the work was being done. With him was a large negro who plopped himself down in a chair while the contractor, approaching Leann, said, "If you don't pay me the full amount now, it will go badly for you."

The burly negro in the chair pushed his fists together and announced ominously, "Yeah, that's what I'm here for!"

Fortunately for Leann, her other workmen appeared at that moment so she was no longer at the mercy of the intruders and could ask them to leave without danger to her personal safety.

When she reported this incident to the police, Leann was shocked to learn they would do nothing unless she were physically harmed. The police captain's only advice was, "Get a gun!"

Ramón was also shocked at the news and thereafter viewed his wife's activities in a completely different light. He didn't ask her to give it up, as he knew she wouldn't, but was apprehensive for her safety from that time on as she continued working full pace.

Each evening when he came home, after assuring there had been no untoward incidents, he enjoyed seeing what changes had taken place in their home or the house on which she was currently working. In the evenings and on weekends he helped with the work and enjoyed it immensely. Fortunately Leann was able to find capable craftsmen in the area, such as their neighbors Mr. Knowles and Mr. Fearson, to perform most of the work under her supervision, but there were frequent problems requiring her constant and careful attention.

Leann respected the distinction between restoration to original condition and remodelling to meet current tastes. She accomplished both either separately or blended together as required to meet the needs of a particular situation.

Remodelling in the sense of "Victorianizing" became popular in the more opulent 1860s, as many wanted to get away from the chasteness of the early 1800s architecture. This was done in such ways as embellishing flat front facades with wooden bays and adding dark wood panelling and corner cupboards to the bare white walls of dining rooms and libraries.

In restorations Leann rapidly became an expert in many fields or had to obtain expert advice. One needed to know architectural history and do some detective work with regard to both exterior and interior, grounds, and furnishings to perform faithful restorations. Paint analysis was important to restore original colors. Sometimes scraps of old wallpaper from behind mantels provided evidence of earlier decor. Exposing original lath under plaster showed where original doors and stairs were located. Dimensions of missing mantels and chair rails were often revealed by traces in plaster.

The Clementes took such interest in each property Leann did that they often considered moving in themselves. She put into each property things she liked and knew they both would enjoy so, when it came time to sell, even a financial gain became something of a personal loss.

In addition to her house remodelling and restoration business, Leann became active in Georgetown civic matters. She was a leader in several legal battles to protect the neighborhood from unwelcome encroachments by greedy land speculators. She evidenced a natural proclivity for the law, which earned her the respect and admiration of all members of the legal profession with whom she came in contact. Undoubtedly she would have made a fine lawyer herself.

One problem Leann and Ramón had was with certain lawyers getting too friendly. A lawyer with whom Leann had a business meeting admired her beyond her technical abilities and began to chase her around his desk. As her protests were to no avail, she had to leave to escape his amorous advances. She did not mention this to Ramón until much later so as not to generate an angry confrontation between him and the lawyer.

When the Clementes were dining at the home of another lawyer and his wife, the latter, also a lawyer, began chasing Ramón around the kitchen table after he helped remove some plates from the dining room. She later remarked to Ramón, in the presence of her husband and Leann, "I think you and I married the wrong people!"

Ramón tried to pass it off as a joke rather than object and possibly cause an unpleasant scene with their host and hostess, which probably was a mistake on his part. Later at home, he told Leann about the kitchen incident, and she was not amused. While they could not avoid lawyers entirely they became more aware of the need to keep business and social encounters from becoming too personal.

But the problem wasn't confined to lawyers. There was an accountant handling some of their business matters who wanted Leann to go away with him; and two women friends who asked Leann, on separate occasions, if they could have an affair with Ramón, quite unbeknownst to him. These incidents seemed ridiculous at first, even slightly amusing on the surface, but later led to some uneasy feelings and concerns.

It occurred to Leann and Ramón that some people might be envious of them and thus try, perhaps unconsciously, to cause them trouble. Single or widowed people, or couples with unhappy marriages, might be envious of a happily married couple which did not engage in affairs on the side. Through Leann's efforts, they had a lovely home and entertained beautifully on a relatively low budget, which caused resentment in some people. The Clementes didn't spend extravagantly on themselves and did not gamble heavily or incur large debts. By savings from Ramón's salary plus Leann's business profits and income from investments and some inherited property, they were able to live at least as well or better than many of their contemporaries.

Leann had an excellent knowledge of antique furniture and furnishings and had acquired some excellent examples from foreign diplomats and other sources both in Washington and during their tour in Mexico City. She had a flair for interior decorating and a knack for locating and acquiring good buys at local auctions and house sales. As a result, in spite of a limited budget, the Clemente home was well furnished in excellent taste, which drew the admiration of all their guests and visitors.

It became so attractive and desirable that their idyllic existence with their family of five little dogs (by this time they had lost Cherubino, the father of the brood) was frequently invaded by house guests visiting Washington from various parts of the world. All were welcomed at first as the friends or relatives they were, but after a few years of such visits Leann and Ramón felt they were running a hotel, which began to wear a bit thin.

On one occasion his mother, who was uninvited and hadn't asked to visit, used the installation of the first transcontinental telegraph[13] to announce she would arrive on a certain date for an indefinite period, having already made arrangements for the lengthy Cape Horn voyage. Doña Caterina apparently believed it her maternal right and privilege to visit her children at any time of her choosing for as long as she chose, as she had done often with her daughter Cristina's family in Mexico. Ramón could understand how his sister must have felt and the strain it must have been on her marriage. He also realized that his mother's loneliness after his father's death made her more emotionally reliant on her children without recognizing the problems it caused for them.

Doña Caterina's attitude of condescension was even more apparent than when they last saw her. She looked down on most things American and complained about foreigners taking over California. She was especially bitter about the Rancho Malibu being sold by the Frenchman, who bought it in 1848 from the Tapias, to an Irishman in 1857 for 10¢ an acre. Aside from the land price, Ramón tried to explain the "melting pot" theory of American society to his mother, but to no avail.

Leann went to great lengths to make the visit as pleasurable as possible for her mother-in-law, with special appointments installed for Doña Caterina's own private room during her stay; planning special meals, shopping, and sightseeing tours; arranging gatherings of friends and neighbors in her honor; and hiring a new maid to take care of her mother-in-law's personal needs. Ramón couldn't say these efforts weren't noticed or appreciated at all, but in Doña Caterina's grand Spanish colonial manner, blended with mother-in-law undertones, there were frequent instances of "damning with faint praise" which caused strains and tensions, particularly for Leann.

One of the most difficult times for the Clementes in their new home came after Ramón's sister left her husband of fifteen years for a deposed French count in Mexico. Ramón was particularly saddened by the news as he had always felt his brother-in-law Raimundo Carillo to be the real brother he never had. He recalled Doña Caterina telling him not long after his sister's marriage to Raimundo that Cristina asked her mother: "Do you think I married beneath me?" Ramón had thought at the time that such a statement was not only in bad taste but grossly inappropriate considering some of Raimundo's more illustrious forbears and the Clementes' relative lack of pretension in that regard. He did not let Doña Caterina know how he felt at the time as it would only have led to arguments, and he had become accustomed to such remarks from her. But now he wondered if his sister had really asked the question with the meaning inferred by their mother or if Cristina was only questioning her mother's elitist attitude. He suspected his sister's latest action was perhaps a belated declaration of independence against maternal domination and interference.

But the saddest part of all was the five Carillo children being left without a mother. Raimundo brought them to Washington for a visit and to plan their future. Leann and Ramón were very happy to see them all; opened their hearts and their home to them; and offered to join with Raimundo in the children's care and upbringing, at least until he made other arrangements. But these warm, compassionate feelings were dealt a cruel setback by Doña Caterina's expressing her belief that Ramón and Leann were not suitably situated to bring up "her" grandchildren—stated in terms that the Clementes did not have friends with children the same age. This dampened their enthusiasm for closer involvement in the lives of their nieces and nephews whom they loved dearly or for further involvement in any other family activities.

A further blow came when Leann's mother died in St. Louis after a lingering illness. Leann knew that her parents wanted her to come back to help care for her mother but believed her place to be in her own home. The Clementes invited Leann's parents to come to their Georgetown home where Leann could do more for her mother and obtain medical attention for her. The Richards declined the offer, apparently preferring to remain in familiar surroundings, unbeholden to anyone else. When the end came, the Clementes went to St.

Louis for the funeral and burial at Bellefontaine cemetery. This was Ramón's first visit in nearly fifteen years and Leann's second.

Leann planned to spend time with her widowed father to help him readjust, but this was not welcomed by her family. Therefore she accompanied Ramón back to Georgetown, but not until after further rejection from Doña Caterina. Ramón had suggested to his mother a possible visit to California as long as they were part-way there. Doña Caterina's reply, indicating her anticipation of a visit from him alone, with no appreciation of Leann's loss of her own mother, was selfish and unkind. This, on top of previous experiences, firmed up the Clementes' conclusion to lead their own lives from that time forward, without further attempts at family contacts.

In order to gain some relief from these tensions, Leann and Ramón began reading Herman Melville's *Moby Dick*, first published in 1851.[13] Ramón also reread Richard Henry Dana's *Two Years Before the Mast* and showed Leann Dana's description of "the average lazy Californian as a man blighted by a curse, which deprived him of all good qualities but pride, a fine manner and a cultivated voice."[14] Ramón told Leann that he hoped he had evaded such a curse by leaving California at an early age and marrying an American girl from St. Louis. Leann smiled enigmatically but did not reply.

Further in the literary field, the Clementes obtained a copy of Thoreau's *Walden* when it arrived at Taylor and Maury's bookstore on Pennsylvania Avenue.[1] They noted that the book was not well received by the public at first, as indicated by the uncomplimentary review in *Knickerbocker Magazine*, comparing it to promoter P.T. Barnum's autobiography, and referring to both as "humbug."[24]

A welcome letter arrived from the Graysons, whom the Clementes last saw in California. It brought good and bad news—the bad news being that they had lost almost everything in the "bad times" of 1851. The good news was that Andrew had begun a new career in ornithology after Frances showed him a copy of *Audobon's Birds of America*, borrowed from the library where she worked, which rekindled his earlier interest in drawing and painting birds when a boy in Louisiana.

The Graysons had moved to Mexico hoping for better opportunities. They were in touch with Assistant Secretary Baird of the Smithsonian Institution, who was interested in Andrew's drawings and descriptions of Mexican birds. Being on the scene in Washington, Ramón offered to be of any assistance he could in their new endeavors. Andrew replied suggesting Ramón call on Professor Baird to make his acquaintance in case any need for intervention arose and also to provide an opinion of the man with whom Andrew had been corresponding.

Baird's office at the Smithsonian was not grand but business-like and cluttered with a variety of objects apparently being considered for, or in process of being included in, the Smithsonian collection. He had a serious yet kindly face, dark hair and heavy slightly graying beard, and appeared to be in his early forties. He was well-groomed, wore a dark business suit with a blue polka-dot bow tie over a starched white collar, and a gold watch chain hung from the top button of his lapelled vest. Their brief yet friendly conversation revealed Baird to be a selfless scientist whose main interest was recruiting and guiding others in advancing the cause of natural science and the Smithsonian Institution. Ramón could see that Baird employed ingenuity and perseverance to achieve these goals yet seemed to maintain good personal relations with all those with whom he came in contact.[25]

Ramón conveyed these observations to the Graysons, who indicated their encouragement therefrom.

For Ramón's thirty-fifth birthday, Leann had given him a $1 gold piece for the first year of issue—1849. He then augmented his collection with a $20 gold "double eagle" for its first year of issue—1850. He had a special interest in such coins issued just after discovery of gold in California, knowing of the miner's difficulties in getting their produce assayed and turned into coinage, at first done mostly by private mints. He particularly wanted an 1848 "California Gold" quarter eagle, of which less than 1,400 were made by the U.S. Mint with the letters "CAL." on the reverse. This indicated they were minted from gold sent by Col. Richard Mason, military governor of California, by Army messenger to Secretary of War Marcy.[26]

At about the same time, Navy Lieutenant Edward Beale was bringing samples of California gold to Washington on orders of Commodore Jones in Monterey, reflecting the depth of interservice rivalry in the American military establishment. Beale arrived in Washington two months before the Army messenger (who rode cross-country) by taking a ship to the Mexican west coast, riding horseback 1,000 miles to the east coast port of Vera Cruz, from which he took a ship to Mobile, then a stage to Washington. Some were skeptical of his gold discovery news until it was corroborated by the later arrival of Col. Mason's Army messenger.[27]

After receiving specimens from both sources, President Polk officially proclaimed to Congress that gold had been discovered in great quantities in California. Horace Greeley's *New York Tribune* picked up the news, claiming that gold available in California was worth "a thousand million."[28] This confirmed what became known as the "Eldorado vision" of California and the end of the "pastoral paradise" depicted in earlier writings.

The ensuing "gold rush" developed a newer breed of westerners with different ideas about California. For example, William Stewart and George Hearst, drawn from the east and midwest to the goldfields of California, later turned up in high places in Washington DC, where they built large mansions reflecting the results of their participation in the "twaining of America."

William Stewart, from New York and Ohio, went to Yale in 1848 and left for California in 1850, where he made a fortune mining gold. He studied mining law and became Attorney General of California in 1854 at age twenty-seven. In 1859 he moved to Nevada, attracted by the silver deposits of the Comstock Lode. He was instrumental in separating Nevada from western Utah Territory in 1861 and sponsored Nevada's 1864 statehood, which secured rich gold and silver deposits for the Union. As U.S. Senator from Nevada he built his Washington "castle" on Pacific Circle (now DuPont Circle), completing it in 1873.[29] Stewart earlier attracted to Washington author Mark Twain, who worked on the Senator's staff for a brief period before becoming disenchanted with Washington politics.[31]

George Hearst left Missouri in 1849 to join the gold rush. He didn't do as well in California as Stewart, but, like Stewart, struck it rich with the Comstock Lode in 1859. He continued mining in the west with mixed fortune, having best results with the Homestake gold mine in South Dakota and with copper mining near Anaconda, Montana. In 1882 he tried for nomination as Governor of California but lost. In 1886 he was appointed U.S. Senator to fill a vacancy and built his mansion at 14th Street and New Hampshire Avenue, not far from Stewart's castle.[30]

Thus grew Washington after the Civil War. But now let us see how the Clementes were faring in the years leading up to and during that war.

PART V
WINDS OF CHANGE
(1854–1870)

CHAPTER 10
POLITICS AND THE CIVIL WAR

In 1854 the Republican Party was formed in Ripon, Wisconsin, and John Fremont was their first nominee for president in the 1856 election. The Democrat nominee was James Buchanan, the former secretary of state through whom Ramón obtained his first position and began his career in government.

When the campaign started, Ramón was torn between conflicting demands on his loyalties, requiring resolution in his mind as to who would best serve the needs of the country as president. While greatly admiring Fremont's unique capabilities in many fields, Ramón was less sure of how he would carry out the duties of the highest office in the land. He also admired the more meticulous, though less daring former secretary of state, of whose executive abilities he had direct knowledge.

On the question of slavery, Buchanan was believed to favor popular sovereignty and election by state constitution, yet he denied the right of states to secede. To Ramón the idea of slavery was repugnant in any form, even as seen during visits to the south in 1836–40, where it was said that "benevolent" plantation owners did not abuse their slaves and were even loved by them.

He compared slavery with treatment of Indians in Spanish/Mexican California, who were required to work hard for little if any pay at the ranches and missions, were expected to convert to Christianity, but were not treated as someone's private property to be bought and sold as livestock. However, if they left the ranch or mission grounds, they could be and were pursued and brought back, punished sometimes very cruelly, and when penitent allowed to go back to work.

Some believed the mission padres had degraded the Indians into dependency as virtual slaves. Many were unable to shift for themselves when the Mexican government broke the mission system land monopoly with secularization decrees of 1833–34 and the Indians were suddenly freed.[3] If not actual slavery, this was something like it, and Ramón had seen its sad results. Even though the Indians were granted citizenship rights and half of all mission lands, livestock, and farm tools, many had become too dependent to work their own lands, much of which was lost to crooked administrators. Such Indians turned to working at private ranches under conditions often resembling slavery or medieval peonage, with little if any pay.

As Americans acquired the Mexican land grants, they drove off the ranch Indians. With their former hunting lands confiscated, these Indians were left to starve. Those who worked in towns were paid half the wages of whites and were weakened by disease and drink.

In spite of conditions approaching slavery, California had come into the Union as a free state although there were those who would have had it otherwise. Fremont, whose candidacy was supported by speeches of Abraham Lincoln and Yale Professor Silliman, had been California's first acting governor and was chosen as one of the state's first two senators, attesting to his popularity as a hero in the events which led to statehood.

As the new Republican Party was shaping itself with the slogan "No Compromise with Slavery," Ramón found himself increasingly drawn towards their banner, while still favoring Buchanan for his managerial ability and expertise in foreign as well as domestic matters.

It was painful to hear Fremont, whom Ramón knew as a fair and decent man of great integrity, being scourged not only by the southern press and pro-slavery Democrats but also by northern abolitionists for not being more of an anti-slavery extremist. It was worst when Fremont was called a "French bastard," referring to his long-rumored and undenied illegitimate birth, having nothing to do with his ability to govern, although possibly motivating some of his more daring exploits to overcome this blot on his family name.[30]

All of this toughened Ramón's resolve never to go into politics himself, to Leann's relief. He knew he could never become so thick-skinned as to suffer "slings and arrows" from both sides of an issue he might try to resolve in what he believed was the country's best interest.

Sadly for Fremont, California cast her four electoral votes for the Democrat Buchanan. The Republicans carried only New York and ten other states, not enough to catch Buchanan, who was backed by the more powerful Democratic machine.[4]

Ramón had finally decided to vote for Fremont, of which he made no secret, and soon thereafter found his services no longer required at the State Department, formerly run by the new president. Ramón never knew if his openly expressed preference had anything to do with his enforced departure. He only knew he needed another job.

Matters were not helped by the financial panic of 1857, which though not as severe as that of 1837, spread faster by use of the telegraph.[1] The panic increased westward movement, repeating historical tendencies under similar conditions. Ramón could see how American sympathy for the underdog developed as an instinctive reaction in support of the oppressed or underprivileged, except where such feelings conflicted with their own needs, as in the case of Indians or southern slaves. It was interesting that northern abolitionists would fight against slavery, and the new Republican party was formed to prohibit slavery and Mormon polygamy, but neither group pushed for the rights of Indians. For example, the Kansas-Nebraska Act of 1854 facilitated the building of transcontinental railroads, but broke a treaty with the Indians leaving them only the territory known later as Oklahoma.

With Ramón now unemployed, the Clementes considered moving to California, which seemed a desirable alternative to the hectic life in and around the nation's capital, not to mention the cold winters and hot, humid summers. They went so far as to put their house on the market for sale, but received few offers. This could be expected during a post-election year when the same party stayed in power. The slow real estate market may have been exacerbated by the war clouds gathering over the District of Columbia, located as it was, midway between north and south.

However, the same war clouds caused a stir in the War Department, which increased hiring of civilians, drawing Ramón once again into the government fold. So the Clementes stayed on and were relieved to remove their house from the real estate market and continue the way of life to which they had become accustomed.

The move to the War Department was simple, being practically next door to State, in an almost identical building on the opposite side of the White House.[2] The qualities that made Ramón valuable to the State Department, while useful to the War Department, needed some augmentation for him to contribute fully in the area of logistical planning and reporting where he was assigned.

His superiors suggested further training at a local college while he continued at his job. Ramón readily acceded, feeling that he could now make better use of such education in relation to his work than when he first attended college and nearly failed because of outside distractions.

The two principal institutions of learning which were readily accessible were Columbian College, founded in 1821, and Georgetown College, founded in 1789. As a Catholic, Ramón was drawn to Georgetown, a great Jesuit center of learning located on a site selected in 1788 by Bishop John Carroll of Baltimore that was near the Clementes' home. However, the newer Columbian College, originally intended to provide theological training to Baptist ministers, now offered more courses such as mathematics and accounting which related to Ramón's field of work. Therefore he chose the latter, although its more distant location opposite Meridian Hill Park on Boundary Avenue between 14th and 15th Streets required more travel time.[3]

At first he planned only to audit those classes he specifically needed. Leann convinced him to take them for credit with additional courses leading towards an advanced academic degree. Once again Ramón congratulated himself for marrying a woman with such good sense. With hard work and financial assistance from the War Department, he graduated from Columbian College in 1859, this time with his wife by his side.

One result of his new training was that Ramón was placed in charge of the group in which he formerly was a member, the previous leader having received another assignment. Ramón saw his new supervisory role as helping his employees to do the best job they could rather than just issuing orders and judging results. He also believed those doing the work should contribute to decision-making.

These ideas were considered unusual, particularly in a military department where the philosophy of discipline and control were predominant. Ramón's managerial methods were sometimes viewed disdainfully by his more traditional colleagues and military superiors who often likened their non-combat work goals to the "taking of a hill" on the battlefield. Although his views and practices in this regard may have restricted his advancement in the military establishment, Ramón was encouraged in later years to note the development at certain private industrial companies of similar philosophies and practices for helping employees to do better work and encouraging their participation in management.

While employed at the War Department, Ramón was gratified to be able to make a small contribution from a segment of his work in which he was especially interested—that of developing and presenting funding requirements in terms of planned operations and objectives together with a means of keeping track of accomplishments in relation to cost.

Sometimes this sort of thing wasn't too well received, particularly where officials responsible for carrying out programs didn't want higher-ups or Congress to know what, or perhaps how badly they were doing; and when they wanted to use funds appropriated for one purpose on something different. There came to be a dual tracking system—one for the official record which kept track of appropriations and expenditures in terms of things paid for, such as salaries, supplies, and equipment; and another internal system such as Ramón devised, to keep track of what the agency planned to do with these funds and how well they did it.

Ramón began working on this system in the State Department under Secretary Everett in the Fillmore administration. Being from Massachusetts and more business oriented than some of his predecessors, former Senator Everett[18] was receptive to at least trying Ramón's approach. He realized that the existing system was not satisfactory and that with information such as Ramón would provide, agency heads could better plan and justify their funding needs.

Although Secretary Everett understood and wanted this system, it was hard to sell to some of his department heads and members of the Foreign Service. The traditional diplomatic corps did not consider that planning and execution of foreign policy lent itself to the kind of quantification Ramón proposed in terms of cost and program goals. He tried to convince them that even if they could not cost some of their non-routine activities in terms of measurable work units, at least costs could be arranged by geographic areas of foreign policy concern, so that program priorities could be weighed in terms of relative cost.

He hadn't much opportunity to develop and promote this system before the election of President Buchanan which preceded his termination at State. At the War Department Ramón found a more receptive clientele and programs that lent themselves more to the system he developed.

By 1857 Ramón achieved recognition when Secretary of War Floyd of Virginia[1] became so dissatisfied with the existing budget system that he asked if anyone in the department could come up with something more useful. Ramón was able to step in with the right thing at the right time. With his new program performance budgeting system, he was called on to participate in budget presentations at Cabinet meetings and before Congressional Committees. He received considerable acclaim and commendation, for which he was justifiably proud.

The new system was appreciated even more as the War Department expenditures rose from about $170,000 per day just before the war, to $1.5 million per day soon after and $2 million per day in 1864.[28] However Ramón's part in it soon faded into the background as higher-ups sought credit for having encouraged, approved, and directed its full use throughout the department.

There was another aspect to the matter which caused him more concern. His assigned duties included supervision of a small group of people preparing reports on the status of plans and programs. As existing information was inadequate for this purpose, Ramón's original objective was to work out a better system for his group to carry out their assigned task. To accomplish this, he had to leave them without enough to do for several months while he went off to develop and install the new system. Along the way he garnered credit for himself, which he hoped would enure to his staff's benefit in the long run.

He had mixed feelings at seeing his people just "keeping busy" while he was involved in an intensely interesting special assignment. It was something like the way he had felt at first about being placed in charge of people who were more experienced than he, because of his educational qualifications. Now that his staff could better perform their jobs, Ramón felt somewhat relieved about his earlier concerns.

Outside his office, Ramón was aware that the financial panic of 1857 had developed into a major economic depression. Contributing thereto was the sinking of one of the "Panama Packets" laden with gold from California. Since completion of the trans-isthmian Panama Railroad in 1855, U.S. Mail steamships had been transporting gold seekers and finders between New York and the Panama Isthmus on an average of two voyages a month. One such vessel, the 300-foot paddle steamer Central America, with 500 passengers and three tons of gold, sank in a hurricane off the Carolina coast on September 12, 1857. Women and children were saved by a passing vessel and a few male survivors were picked up in open seas in days following.

One of the female survivors, "the notorious Jenny French," as described by the newspapers, escaped with her pet parakeet tucked in her bosom. Captain Herndon, who went down with his ship, was honored by citizens of Fairfax County, Virginia, who named a town after him; and by the U.S. Naval Academy at Annapolis, Maryland, where stands the only memorial for a Navy man who never served in a war.[4]

This was not only a major human tragedy but also a financial disaster because of the huge quantities of gold bars and coins aboard belonging to the passengers who made fortunes in California. The failure of many eastern banks which were awaiting arrival of the gold to pay debts and meet payrolls led directly to the financial panic that ensued.

A recurring effect of the financial panics, Ramón noted, was rekindled antagonism of east against west—of town against country, of industry against agriculture. Westerners feared what they perceived to be the greedy mercenary easterners causing financial panics, and withheld the Republican nomination from New York Governor Seward. This opened the way for nomination of a westerner, Abraham Lincoln of Illinois, which some say led to the Civil War.

In 1859, Leann's brother Randolph wrote that James Larkin, who took the "prairie cure" on the Santa Fe trail three years earlier, had married a St. Louis widow two years younger than himself, and they left for a honeymoon in Europe. Randolph passed on some local comments to the effect that James had been a "momma's boy" who could have travelled to Santa Fe faster and cheaper on the monthly stage from Independence but chose the more rigorous route by freight caravan with William Bent not only for health reasons but also to become more self-reliant.[5]

Randolph wrote that James spoke of meeting Kit Carson, who described a joint ranching venture with Lucien Bonaparte Maxwell, a fellow trapper. Maxwell had access to a land grant along the Rio Vermejo in northeastern New Mexico, through his Mexican bride, daughter of the owner of the original land grant.[6] Later Ramón learned how Carson joined with Edward Beale in experimenting with use of camels for western freighting and to replace Army mules. They had seventy-five of the animals shipped from Egypt to Texas, and brought them to Fort Tejon in California.[7] The camels were used in surveys of transcontinental wagon roads but were never accepted by the Army or by local horsemen, so Beale kept the remainder on the Tejon Ranch, which he had recently acquired.

Meanwhile the threat of war was moving closer to actuality. The Supreme Court decision in the Dred Scott case, reversing the St. Louis court decision in Scott's favor, aroused a storm of protest in the north. The Scotts' master freed them himself, but Dred Scott died the following year.[7] These events gained support for abolitionist John Brown's "Provisional Constitution" for "people degraded by laws."[8]

On October 17, 1859, President Garrett of the Baltimore and Ohio Railroad wired Secretary of War Floyd that armed abolitionists had stopped the B&O train at Harper's Ferry, Virginia, and seized the U.S. Arsenal there.[9] Floyd sent a detachment of Marines led by Col. Robert E. Lee, who overcame the raiders led by John Brown. These warlike events were moving closer to Washington, and there was fear of more trouble with rumors that buildings near the Georgetown waterfront were being used as refuges in escape routes for slaves coming up from the south. The Clementes thought such might occur with two buildings Leann had restored on Copperthwaite Lane, below Peter von Essen's Brickyard Hill house on South Street.[10] This was never confirmed, but they later learned that one of the buildings was used as a hospital for Union troops.

They also learned that the burial vault next to the cemetery, and the meeting house on Greene Street in Georgetown, were used as part of the "underground railroad" for escaping slaves headed north to freedom.[29]

When Lincoln arrived in Washington after the 1860 election, he was met by citizens with mixed feelings in this border city. His inaugural address before the half-finished new capitol dome received only light applause, after which he returned to his headquarters at the Willard Hotel. There was much tension in the streets, with mutterings from groups of secessionists and southern sympathizers, arousing open opposition from groups of abolitionists. Federal troops were close at hand to prevent violence or hostile demonstrations. Suddenly an unidentified man stepped out on a balcony from a room at the Ebbit House and began to sing the "Star Spangled Banner" in a loud voice. Gradually the street crowds joined in and the tension was broken.[11]

After Lincoln took office, it soon became apparent that war was inevitable. This was a discomfiting prospect for the Clementes, with their home at the southern edge of Maryland facing Virginia, squarely between the opposing sides.

On February 8, 1861, seceding southern states proclaimed themselves the Confederate States of America with Jefferson Davis as President. After the Confederates attacked Fort Sumter April 14, 1861, Lincoln called for volunteers, blockaded southern ports, and the long dreaded Civil War became reality.

At the age of forty-two, being without military training or experience and with some understanding of both sides, Ramón was not anxious to join the military forces of either. Leann, from the state identified with the "Missouri compromise" in the debate over its statehood, had grown up with friends on both sides of the issue, had no fondness for the military, and was against Ramón getting into uniform.

Although many men hired surrogates to take their place in military service, Ramón had neither the income nor the inclination to do so. It seemed to him a distasteful if not a cowardly practice, and he would rather have taken the criticism, if any were forthcoming, for not joining up than pay someone to go to war in his name. Perhaps that view was unduly critical of those who did, considering that mercenaries were used in many wars, like the Hessians sent from Germany to help with the American Revolutionary War, but that was an augmentation on a governmental level, not a personal substitution for individual American citizens.

At the Clementes' home in Georgetown, there were many evenings of usually friendly discussions with neighbors and colleagues on these topics which sometimes flared into outbreaks of temper on the parts of those who did hold strong feelings. As this point was reached more frequently, Ramón and Leann decided to stop having such social gatherings and spend more time with their little canine family, which had no strong positions other than that they be fed regularly and receive a certain amount of stroking.

On these "at home" nights, in addition to their regular bouts of backgammon, chess, and dominos, Ramón and Leann also enjoyed playing the new "bagatelle" game from France. It had been popularized by an 1863 newspaper cartoon of President Lincoln playing the new game on a tabletop board in which pins were stuck and balls maneuvered into holes with cue sticks.[12] They also read the latest books available from French and Richardson's Bookstore (formerly Taylor and Maury's) on Pennsylvania Avenue, such as Dickens' *Great Expectations* and Oliver Wendell Holmes' *Elsie Venner*.[13]

As Ramón became more involved in his work at the War Department, the question of getting into uniform gradually faded into the background. He continued to feel some discomfiture in gatherings where men in uniform predominated and those in civilian clothes might be regarded as lacking in courage or conviction.

He was not surprised when Secretary of War Floyd resigned to join the Confederate Army. Floyd had been an advocate of states rights and was at odds with General Meigs, developer of Washington's aqueduct system, who was promoted to Quartermaster General.

Many facilities were taken over by the Army for official use, such as the Corcoran Gallery for the Quartermaster; Forrest Hall for the Provost Marshall as a drill hall and military prison; and the Union Hotel in Georgetown as an Army hospital. It was here that Louisa May Alcott of Concord, Massachusetts, served as a nurse and reflected her experiences in her book *Little Women*, published in 1868. Another writer, Walt Whitman, whose brother was killed during the Civil War, took part time government jobs and was a frequent visitor to military hospitals where he comforted wounded soldiers.

Certain sections of the city were especially affected by the war effort, such as the block between 13th and 14th Streets south of Pennsylvania Avenue, that was used by General Joseph Hooker to bivouac troops defending the capital. Prostitutes were attracted to the area in large numbers and became known as "hookers." One newspaper described it as "the plague spot of Washington, a center of vice, liquor selling and prostitution." The section was said to contain over 100 brothels and 50 saloons, as well as the city's four newspapers.[14]

Among other excesses that took place during the Civil War was the system of "sutlers"—purveyors of a wide array of groceries and dry goods to soldiers of both sides, usually at exorbitant prices, according to anecdotes of returning troops. A necessary service, sometimes performed by retired army officers, the sutlerships were three-year appointments and often obtained through political influence and bribery. In their defense, it must be said that the sutler's work was more dangerous and subject to greater expenses and possibilities of loss than that of other civilian merchants. There were few complaints when the sutler system was replaced after the war by post traders, and finally, in 1890, by the non-profit post exchange.[15]

Although the tide of battle turned in favor of the Union in 1863 at Gettysburg, Washington and Georgetown residents were mindful of the proximity of Confederate troops early in the war. One such instance was the first battle of Manassas, which took place at Bull

Run near Chantilly, Virginia, twenty-five miles south of Washington on July 21, 1861. As full-scale warfare was not anticipated, many curious civilians, including Congressmen and their families, travelled by carriage from the Federal City to observe the encounter and enjoy a picnic in the Virginia countryside. Unfortunately the unseasoned Union troops, repelled by equally unseasoned Confederates, retreated in panic amid the spectators' carriages, creating havoc on the road back to Washington.[14]

Another such instance occurred in July 1864 when General Jubal Early's Confederate troops, retreating from the battle at Monocacy River near Frederick, Maryland, came within shooting distance of Georgetown and Washington DC. While Grant's troops were many miles south attacking Lee at Petersburg, Early's troops were only six miles northeast of Washington near Fort Stevens. Washington citizens had always felt safe, surrounded by thirty-seven miles of fortifications normally manned by 18,000 men; however all but 4,000 were with Grant, and Early's actions indicated his intentions of taking the Federal Capitol, the Treasury, and anything else he wanted. The citizens became extremely fearful. President Lincoln himself appeared on the Fort Stevens battlements and was warned to keep down. The Army Quartermaster, General Meigs, mobilized the civilians in his office to defend the city, and Grant sent troops back to Washington when he heard what was happening. General Early, whose troops were exhausted after the battle at Monocacy, commandeered publisher Francis Blair's mansion "Silver Spring" as his headquarters and planned to attack the next day.

At dawn Early noted the arrival of fresh Federal troops, some of which were deployed west towards Tenleytown Road above Georgetown, to attack his flank. After several hours of fighting, Early's troops retreated to Virginia and the crisis passed. More than one hundred men died, mostly Confederate, but some Federal as well. A national cemetery was erected nearby, marking how close Washington came to being captured. It was soon forgotten, however, and in 1875 an order had to be issued prohibiting picnicking on the site.[16]

These were terrifying times, made worse by blood-curdling tales of brutal warfare brought back by the press reporters and artists, and by men who were wounded or on leave from the battlefront. Hardly a home was spared the loss of a friend or relative because of this Civil War, which many southerners still call the "war between the states." Certainly no one was every really happy about it except when it was over.

The joy of peace in 1865 was shattered almost immediately by the news of President Lincoln's assassination, only five days after Lee's surrender at Appomattox, Virginia.

As reported later by Walt Whitman in his *Memoranda During the War*,[17] the real drama of the assassination far exceeded the stage performance of "Our American Cousin" at the Ford Theater April 14, 1865. The Washington *Evening Star* had announced "the President and his Lady will be at the Theater this evening." The Ford Theater was crowded with prominent citizens and military officers. Exhilaration over the recent Union victory pervaded the air. During a pause between scenes of the play, there was a hum in the audience, then the muffled sound of a pistol shot, not even noticed by much of the audience. Then a man jumped from the railing of the president's flag-bedecked box, catching his boot heel on one of the draped flags, so that he fell on one knee on the stage. He rose shouting "Sic semper tyrannus" and disappeared off stage.[12]

In the hush following his exit, came Mrs. Lincoln's cry, "Murder!" and "He has killed the president!" There was immediate terror and confusion as the crowd became unmanageable. Some two hundred soldiers of the Presidential Guard burst into the theater with fixed bayonets and roughly cleared out the shocked and frightened theater patrons. An infuriated crowd outside nearly killed a suspected culprit who was rescued by police with billy-clubs and later released.[12]

Lincoln died the following morning. The real assassin, actor John Wilkes Booth, fled south through Maryland with a co-conspirator but was captured and reported dead April 26, 1865.

It was said that Lincoln, a deeply religious man, was not technically a Christian until his later years, towards the end of the Civil War, when he came to believe that his beloved son, whose early death was one of Lincoln's personal tragedies, had achieved eternal life through Jesus Christ. Lincoln's own belief in Christ was then evidenced by his statement to an Illinois clergyman; by his letter to the New York Avenue Presbyterian Church in Washington requesting to make a public profession of his faith; and in proclamations signed shortly before his death, among them one forbidding any recriminations against the south—in effect granting full pardon and complete acceptance of former enemies as full partners, in accordance with Christ's teachings.[18]

No matter how one felt about Lincoln's politics, there were few who did not feel revulsion at this cowardly act of assassination against one who felt he was doing his duty for the long-term benefit of his country and its citizens. Ramón thought there must be better ways to settle disputes. Legal or constitutionally declared war was bad enough, he felt, but cold-blooded murder to settle a difference of views he believed to be the ultimate in moral depravity and degradation.

There was little realization in the north of another Civil War that took place within the south and helped bring about the Confederate defeat. While it was known that many southerners were against secession, it was not generally understood that the longer the Confederacy fought, the more divided it became, particularly as between the plantation owners in the lowlands and the farmers in the hill country. In 1860 a majority of southern whites lived in the hills and owned few if any slaves. It had been predicted before the war that southerners without slaves would not fight long to save the institution of slavery. Non-slaveholding men made up the majority of the Confederate Army as well as the majority of deserters and draft resisters who suffered great persecution in the south.

Such opposition to the Confederacy was so strong that the western mountain region of Virginia seceded from the Confederacy in 1861 and became a separate state two years later. Disloyalty in other areas was such that the mountain region of east Tennessee was under martial law in 1862; and in an Appalachian province of North Carolina, Union sympathizers were imprisoned and murdered in 1863.

Much of the anti-confederate feeling stemmed from a belief that the plantation people were not bearing their fair share of the war. Many plantation owners refused to shift from growing cotton to planting food, so that the hill farmers suffered disproportionate losses in giving up food and animals to the Army. It was considered "a rich man's war and a poor man's fight." This feeling grew after the Confederacy enacted the first conscription law, including a provision that a draftee could avoid service by producing a substitute, and that one able-bodied white male could be exempted for every twenty slaves. The hill people without slaves deeply resented this provision.

Desertion of soldiers from the hill country grew, as did robbery of families of soldiers remaining in the Confederate Army, which seriously disrupted the soldiers' morale. There were many examples of southern Union sympathizers advising Federal authorities of Confederate military movements, which directly affected the war's outcome. Subsequently these southern Unionists who resisted the Confederacy became the backbone of the Republican Party in the south during the reconstruction period.[19]

Woven into the end of this conflict between north and south was a continuation of the friction between east and west, which erupted in the planning for a "grand review" of the victorious troops marching down Pennsylvania Avenue in May 1865. The Union Army consisted of two major parts—the Army of the Potomac under Major General George G. Meade, which had won the war in the east, and the Army of Tennessee under Major General William Tecumseh Sherman, which had won the war in the west and south. Complicating the situation was the attitude of Secretary of War Stanton, who suspected General Sherman's western forces of planning to overthrow the Federal government and of being too lenient on the south after his devastating march through Georgia. Sherman's followers believed he was carrying out Lincoln's policy of reconciliation and resented Stanton's outspoken criticism. On the other hand many easterners, and Washingtonians in particular who considered the Army of the Potomac as their personal savior, saw the western army as a bunch of brash, unruly frontiersmen who might take over the whole country.

To overcome these differences, the "grand review" was planned whereby each army would march down Pennsylvania Avenue separately on two successive days, to receive the accolades of the citizenry and the reviewing officials.

Although Washington was still in mourning for the assassinated President Lincoln, with hotels, offices, and some homes draped in black, much effort was spent to make the "grand review" as spectacular as possible under the circumstances. Public buildings were decorated with blue and white bunting and arches of flowers were constructed along the parade route. There was concern that the Army of the Potomac, which was to go first, would receive more acclaim than the western army the next day, causing even more bad feelings. Meade's army started their march at 9:00 A.M. and the well-coordinated, spotlessly attired troops accompanied by elegant marching bands gave an impressive performance for seven hours, which was received with much applause, as expected in spite of exceptionally warm weather. It was also expected that the western army, unaccustomed to such parading, would give a less praiseworthy performance and that there would be less of a turnout for them.

The next day was not as hot, and there were more spectators than the day before. Ramón noted that their reception for the western army was more resounding and more emotional than for the more polished eastern army. Though less magnificent in attire and accompaniment, the westerners displayed more authenticity as to how the war was won. Behind each division were captured animals, some loaded with cooking utensils, captured chickens, and an occasional pig showing how the troops lived on the march. There was a corps of black workers carrying picks and axes. There was a group of horse-drawn ambulances with blood-stained stretchers strapped alongside, and the chief army nurse riding side-saddle. The soldiers themselves reflected the strength and resolve that brought these young pioneers from their farms, through the gruelling battles in the west and south, to the nation's capital. During seven and a half hours they won the hearts of the spectators and the newspaper reporters, and the east-west tension was at least temporarily diffused.[20]

The period of post-war reconstruction was almost as disruptive and harmful to the nation as the war itself, for which Ramón believed there was enough blame to spread around both major political parties and everyone else concerned. The ideal of freedom for slaves soon became corrupted by the personal greed of many northerners and southerners as well.

This post Civil War decadence reminded Ramón of the period following the secularization of the California mission system many years before, when the graft and corruption of the Mexican officials and citizens as well facilitated the takeover of California by the United States during the war with Mexico. Fortunately there was no foreign nation as ready to jump on the weakened United States after the Civil War.

After living through this period, Ramón wondered if there were any way this terrible war and its ugly aftermath could have been avoided. Thinking back over reports he had read of the 1858 debates between Lincoln and Stephen A. Douglas, preceding Lincoln's defeat by Douglas in the Illinois Senate contest,[1] Ramón wondered whether Douglas' principle of "popular sovereignty," which Buchanan shared, could have prevented the war.

The Kansas-Nebraska Act of 1854, sponsored by Douglas and opposed by the Republicans, repealed the "Missouri Compromise" and left the issue of slavery to vote of settlers in the affected states. If the Democrat Douglas had prevailed in the 1860 presidential election, there might have been no secession (as there was after the Republican Lincoln was elected) and no war, but a much longer and more gradual elimination of slavery, with its retention in some states perhaps indefinitely.

Ramón wondered if the continuation of such a moral blot on the United States could have been justified in terms of the saving of hundreds of thousands of lives lost in the war, not to mention the wounded and all the other costs to the country as a whole. To the slaves themselves, probably not; but to all the families which lost sons, husbands, and fathers, and to the hundreds of thousands of surviving casualties, he thought the answer might be less certain.

Anyway it could not now be redone and must be left to future philosophers and historians to decide. Ramón was certain that from this time forward there would be arguments between the two principal political parties, with much pointing of fingers, as to which was the party of war and which of peace—with the pendulum swinging back and forth over both parties depending on the current situation.

In analyzing the war's outcome, Ramón saw the importance of the new railroads linking the northeast and northwest, which helped keep the Union together. There had been differences between northern and southern politicians over selection of transcontinental routes. As Secretary of War, Jefferson Davis had favored earlier development of southern routes pursuant to surveys conducted under the 1853 Army Appropriations Act. This would have benefitted the south, but northern interests prevailed. In addition residents of the western Mississippi valley did not want its southern half in foreign hands, if the south seceded, which could block their river traffic outlet. Thus the railroads made it possible for most of the west to join the north against the south, and the Mississippi River held the northwest and much of the southwest together during most of the war.[19, 20] Of the eastern railroads, the B&O in particular, with lines located in slave states and near the battle front, held a strategic position that was of great value to the Union cause.[21]

Along with their mixed feelings about the divisive war just ended, and the many unfortunate deficiencies and excesses surrounding the sudden freeing of masses of southern slaves, Leann and Ramón were saddened by news of the death of composer Stephen Foster in New York on January 13, 1864. While they had not known him personally, they had followed his career and loved his music, as did most Americans. This was particularly true of Leann who recalled her father playing, and her singing, Foster's

"Open Thy Lattice, Love" in 1844, the year before she and Ramón were married. This was Stephen Foster's first published composition, wherein he wrote the music to a poem by George F. Morris that appeared in the *New York New Mirror*.[21] Soon thereafter came "Oh Susanna," introduced in 1847 at an ice cream saloon in Foster's hometown of Pittsburgh, and which later became the marching anthem of the "forty-niners" seeking gold in California.

Then there were the moving and soulful negro-dialect songs which Foster called "Ethiopian" songs, including "Camptown Races"; "Old Folks at Home" ("Swannee River"); "My Old Kentucky Home"; and "Massa's in de Cold Ground." Though these and other Foster songs dealt with the subject of southern slaves, the closest he came to the actual south was Cincinnati, Ohio, and Louisville, Kentucky, where he had travelled to visit relatives. Pittsburgh, at the head of the Ohio River, was visited by many river boats travelling to and from New Orleans and stopping every place in between, so their crews, deckhands, and passengers could bring the flavor of the south to anyone such as Stephen Foster who was receptive. Foster's family had two black servants, one of whom took Stephen to a negro church in which there was much music and singing that also had its effect on him.[22]

The Fosters were Democrats and hated abolitionists, but Stephen wrote many northern songs during the Civil War. He lived for a while with his brother William, whose brother-in-law James Buchanan had recommended him for a government job as principal engineer for canals and railroads in eastern Pennsylvania. Later, when Buchanan ran for president, Stephen Foster formed the "Buchanan Glee Club" in Allegheny City, Pennsylvania.[23]

Stephen's brother, Henry Foster, went to Washington in 1844 with his father, who had received an appointment with the Treasury Department. Henry got a job in Treasury's Land Office, which later became the Department of Interior. The senior Foster left after one year to become Mayor of Allegheny City, but Henry stayed on for eight more years. In describing Washington at that time, he wrote that "the principal amusement is promenading in the Capitol and President's grounds to the music of the Marine Band on every Thursday and Saturday evening at six o'clock." Henry Foster held his position at the Land Office until 1849 when Zachary Taylor became president and appointed Thomas Ewing secretary of the newly formed Interior Department. Foster, who had been appointed by the Tyler regime, was considered a

Democrat and dismissed.[24] In this respect, Henry Foster's brief career with the Treasury Department in Washington had something in common with Ramón Clemente's experience at the State Department nearly twenty years later.

Stephen Foster married Jane McDowell in 1850. Her family had an elderly black servant named Joe, whom Stephen promised to put into one of his songs. He did so some years later, and "Old Black Joe" was published in 1860.[25]

Early on Foster became associated with E.P. Christy, who formed the "Christy Minstrels" singing group which introduced most of Foster's "Ethiopian" songs. Foster allowed Christy to use his (Christy's) name on "Old Folks at Home." Apparently Foster did not want to become too closely associated with what some so-called refined whites considered "trashy" and offensive songs, as it might injure his reputation as a writer of other styles of music. Later, when the "Ethiopian" songs became more accepted, Foster asked Christy to reinstate his name as author, but this was not formally done until many years later when the first copyright term had expired.

Foster's more lively numbers, such as "Oh Susanna" and "Camptown Races," competed with songs of other composers, such as Septimus Winner's "Listen to the Mocking Bird" (1854) and Daniel Emmett's "Turkey in the Straw" and "Dixie's Land" (Dixie), which was adopted as the Confederate anthem even though Emmett was a northerner. Foster's many other songs, such as "Jeannie with the Light Brown Hair" (1854) and "Beautiful Dreamer," published posthumously in 1864, also became immensely popular.

Unfortunately Stephen Foster's life deteriorated in later years and he died at thirty-eight practically a pauper, after contributing so much to America's pleasure. His musical style was emulated by some later composers such as E.W. Nevin, who was known mostly for "The Rosary" published in 1898 and sung by Austrian-born contralto Madame Schuman-Heinck, but who also wrote the music to "Mighty Lak' a Rose," a poem in negro-dialect by Georgia's poet laureate Frank L. Stanton.[26]

Czech composer Anton Dvorak became interested in negro spirituals and Stephen Foster's songs on a trip to the United States. He disavowed use of American tunes in his famous 1893 work "From the New World Symphony" (Symphony No. 5, Opus 95) but did admit writing in the spirit of "national American melodies."[27]

But we are getting ahead of our story.

CHAPTER 11
POST-WAR PLATEAU

By the summer of 1865, Georgetown was no longer the pleasant village the Clementes had chosen for their home fifteen years previously.

Contrabands, the name given to blacks escaping from the south during the war, were arriving in increasing numbers now the war was over, causing problems for the residents of the District of Columbia, including Georgetown. This inundation of untrained black field hands unable to get jobs led to lawlessness. The overcrowding and lack of proper sanitation, creating health problems throughout the city, added to growing apprehension among the citizens.

The Washington & Georgetown Street Railway refused to let blacks ride inside cars until Congress threatened to revoke their charter. Resentment against blacks by white immigrants, principally Irish, grew with competition for low-paying jobs.

There was continued distrust of local citizens by Congress which considered Washington City, and Georgetown in particular, as hotbeds of southern sympathizers. Richard Coxe, who had sided with the south, had his Georgetown home confiscated and turned into a home for destitute black women and children. He was unable to reclaim his property until 1868.

One who fared better was Brittania Peter Kennon, who inherited Tudor Place on Stoddard Street between Congress and Valley Streets in Georgetown. Mrs. Kennon went to Richmond just before the war started and rented Tudor Place to a gentleman from Virginia who was a southern sympathizer. When Virginia seceded, he absconded and Brittania returned to protect her inheritance. Fearing

Tudor Place would be commandeered for a hospital, she set it up as a boarding house for Union officers, to the dismay of some of her southern friends. She was quoted as saying it was the best she could do "under the circumstances." Her belief was supported by the subsequent visit to Tudor Place in 1869, of defeated General Robert E. Lee, who was a relative of Mrs. Kennon's by marriage.[1]

There was, however, a more charitable side to this Civil War aftermath—more gallant, as in the case of certain Confederate spies held in the old brick Capitol building, used as such after the British burned the Capitol in 1814. It was later used to hold political prisoners, including several notorious female spies and a former mayor of Washington. When the war was over, the ladies were allowed to return south with safe passage guaranteed, but the men were detained—some were sent to other prisons and many died in prison, and some shot by guards for minor infractions.

Another chivalrous act was opening of the Louise Home at 15th Street and Massachusetts Avenue. It was built by William Corcoran in memory of his beloved wife and recently deceased daughter, as a refuge for southern ladies impoverished by the Civil War. Corcoran deeded the property for that purpose in 1869 and the home was completed in 1872.[2]

Of more lasting value was the founding of Howard University in 1867 by a group of Union Army generals and members of the First Congregational Church for the benefit of the recently freed slaves. Named after Major General Oliver Otis Howard, Commissioner of the Freedmen's Bureau, it began as a Theological Seminary with schools for teaching, medicine, agriculture, law, commerce, and military science added later. There was some initial friction as the first president, Charles B. Boynton, a prominent abolitionist who was pastor of the First Congregational Church and Chaplain of the House of Representatives, became concerned that the tremendous influx of illiterate blacks might cause racial problems in his church. He was soon replaced by Byron Sunderland, pastor of the First Presbyterian Church, who actually organized the University during its first two years. General Howard himself became the University's third president and shortly thereafter was involved in a conflict of interest scandal when it was learned that certain buildings on campus were constructed of materials manufactured by a firm he founded. He was finally exonerated but resigned anyway, and the University named for him went on to become an outstanding educational institution.[3]

Everyday living in Washington did not reflect these philanthropic accomplishments. Beggars besieged the residential areas; children of school age roamed the streets due to lack of truant officers; and cows, horses, sheep, and goats ran at large. Journalist Horace Greeley, speaking of the sheer discomfort of living in Washington, which had become close to intolerable, said: "The rents are high, the food is bad, the dust is disgusting, the mud is deep, and the morals are deplorable."[4] He recommended moving the capital to St. Louis.

Inflation of living costs, reaching more than 100 percent during the war, was especially hard on low-paid Federal employees.[5] It became apparent that the cost of correcting many of the post-war problems affecting the District of Columbia would rest largely on local citizens and homeowners with little assistance from the Federal government.

All of this, together with the proposed union of Georgetown with the city of Washington, caused the Clementes to decide to sell their Georgetown house and move elsewhere. Their decision, not reached lightly, was supported by the increase in demand and prices for housing. Real estate values, which had slumped after Lincoln's assassination, recovered and soared when it became apparent that the city was not in imminent danger from rebellious forces.

New row houses were being built on Capitol Hill for members of Congress and their staffs; stylish houses for the well-to-do arose along Massachusetts Avenue and K Street beyond 13th; speculators were purchasing land on Meridian Hill out 16th Street; and families of limited means were building houses in Mount Pleasant.

With only two of their little dogs left, it seemed an appropriate time for Ramón and Leann to make the change and realize a substantial profit from the sale of their home. The only question remaining—where to go from there?

Leann had the idea of forming a group to buy a larger house further out from the in-town area and turn it into several apartments which would provide the participants with desirable living accommodations at lower cost. With her extensive knowledge and experience in restoration, remodelling, and interior decorating, the Clementes believed they could develop an attractive project. The idea was discussed with, and met the approval of, several friends and neighbors, among whom was found the additional expertise in related fields of real estate, law, finance, and construction needed to mount a successful venture.

The next step was to locate and acquire a suitable property at a realistic, preferably below market price. Failing that an alternative would be to build from scratch what the group had in mind—a small apartment building in a good location, higher up and away from the stifling summer heat of the waterfront and the unsanitary over-crowded conditions of the downtown area.

After much searching and discussion, it was apparent they could not agree as a group, either on a suitable property or in what way such property would be divided up to meet individual needs. Reluctantly it was agreed to give up on the idea of a joint venture and continue on separate paths.

Leann and Ramón determined that their own best interests would be served by renting someplace where they could take their two dogs until the real estate market stabilized and its direction became clearer. Through Leann's contacts they were offered their choice of flats in a new building being constructed in the upper northwest section above Boundary Street, a block off Connecticut Avenue, and moved in shortly after the first of January 1866.

For the next year and a half they were very happy at being relieved of the cares of home ownership and enjoyed the relative freedom of their new surroundings. They soon were saddened by the loss of their next-to-last dog, who had mothered the brood. Leann was still working on two properties in Georgetown, but by mid-1867 had to slow down when stresses of work and earlier family problems began to take their toll. The stress led to a brief separation, during which time both Leann and Ramón were very unhappy and each was beset by concerns that the other might be involved with some-one else. Fortunately such was not the case, and they soon were reunited, with a few more scars for time to heal.

They were pleased when the Corcoran Gallery of Art reopened after its building at 17th and Pennsylvania Avenue was reclaimed from Quartermaster-General Meigs, whose offices occupied it since 1861. When the Clementes attended exhibits and dances in the Gallery's picture-lined halls, Ramón was reminded of its former occupant, General Meigs, who created the military machine that enabled President Lincoln and General Grant to produce victory in the Civil War.

Their interest in politics and international affairs was height-ened by the acquisition of Alaska from Russia through the efforts of Secretary of State Seward, which greatly increased United States' presence on the Pacific and gave new meaning to the term "manifest destiny." They followed the impeachment trial of President Andrew Johnson, widely thought to be a pretext for retaliation against the administration by Congress which had passed the Reconstruction Act over Johnson's veto. This act made possible some of the excesses of the reconstruction which Lincoln sought to prevent. Ironically Johnson, born in North Carolina, was said not to have supported Lincoln's original reconstruction plan. As a former member of Congress, Johnson had spoken out against black suffrage as early as 1844, and in 1864 as U.S. Senator and Lincoln's running mate, Johnson promised "a government for white men." There were rumors of alcoholism, given credence by an apparently drunken speech Johnson gave before Congress on Inauguration Day in 1865. There were also rumors of relationships with women other than his wife. The stated charges against Johnson were that he had removed Secretary of War Stanton from office without notifying the Senate, contrary to the Tenure of Office Act. The Senate finally acquitted Johnson by one vote, but Stanton resigned anyway.

In 1866 the new Harvey's Ladies and Gentlemen's Oyster Saloon was opened at 11th and Pennsylvania Avenue, where it moved from its original location in a renovated blacksmith shop at 11th and C Streets NW. After the Harvey brothers started out in 1858 they became known for their boiled oysters. During the Civil War they developed a faster steaming method and soon their food was so much in demand, especially with President Lincoln and his cabinet members, that larger quarters were required.[6]

The Clementes received a letter from the Graysons with the tragic news that their son Ned had been killed by Mexican robbers after a shipwreck during a birding expedition. They could share momentarily the Graysons' grief by recalling the happy little two-year-old boy they first met at his parents' boarding house in St. Louis. The letter also told of Assistant Secretary Baird of the Smithsonian asking for Andrew's help on a book about Mexican birds. Subsequently Andrew was commissioned by Mexican Emperor Maximilian to paint bird pictures for the Mexican Academy of Sciences, of the type James Audobon had done in the United States. Shortly after Andrew embarked on this assignment, Emperor Maximilian was abandoned by his French sponsor, Napoleon III, and the project was dropped. At the time the Graysons' letter was written in 1868, Andrew was finishing the bird portraits on his own with support from Baird at the Smithsonian.[7]

Ramón had previously contacted Professor Baird to see if he could help with the Grayson project and did so again on this occasion. Knowing of Ramón's interest in California and the west, Baird mentioned to him that U.S. Geologist Clarence King, head of the "Geological Exploration of the 40th Parallel" approved by Congress in 1876, had run short of funds and was in Washington to seek support for further Congressional action in his behalf.[13] Ramón regretted he had not cultivated contacts on the "hill" that could be of help but promised to bring up the subject with anyone he knew who did have such contacts.

In January 1869, Ramón's mother died and, although they had not been close for many years, it was a sad occasion as it had been when Leann's father died a few years earlier. The Clementes were dismayed at learning from friends in California that Doña Caterina's bitterness towards her son and daughter-in-law not only turned people away in her declining years but adversely affected Ramón's and Leann's reputations as well. Ramón became involved in a morass of legal matters concerning his mother's estate, which took further toll on both Clementes, emotionally as well as physically.

In May 1869, the Central Pacific Railroad from San Francisco and the Union Pacific from Chicago joined at Promontory Point above the Great Salt Lake in Utah to form the first transcontinental railroad. This was facilitated by Clarence King's survey but he unfortunately was unable to return to Salt Lake City in time for the "golden spike" ceremony.[14] Completion of the transcontinental railroad changed the face of the nation. It inaugurated a new era of greater westward expansion along with the growth of railroads in other parts of the country.

Collis P. Huntington, one of the Central Pacific's founders, invested money in the Chesapeake and Ohio Railroad, formerly the Virginia Central, which he planned to use to complete his vision of a coast-to-coast route over what Robert E. Lee, then President of Washington College, had called the best—via St. Louis to the Pacific, with easier grades and milder climate than any of the alternate routes.[8]

In July 1869, the Chesapeake & Ohio tracks were extended to White Sulphur Springs in the West Virginia foothills, which boasted mineral waters for drinking and bathing, also believed to be good for a variety of ailments. The Clementes took the occasion to visit the "Old White" resort in Greenbrier County, which had been popular with the southern aristocracy and had hosted Andrew Jackson and several other U.S. Presidents as well as many other American and foreign dignitaries.[9] The resort was used as a hospital by both Confederate and Union troops during the war, but had since been refurbished. Ramón and Leann felt no benefit from the spring waters, which smelled like rotten eggs, but they liked the surroundings so much they returned several times in later years.

While many Californians criticized Central Pacific's Huntington and his colleagues as having spawned a greedy heartless octopus in the west, some Virginians viewed him differently, as illustrated by an article in the *Richmond Whig* of January 12, 1870, describing Huntington as just, liberal, public-spirited, far-seeing with tact and energy, and "a better judge of practical advantages and ways to promote trade and prosperity than sly scrapping politicians."[10] This disparity between western and eastern opinions of the same man, who later became president of the C&O as well as the Southern Pacific, contributed to Ramón's awareness of differing viewpoints in American culture.

In 1870 the Senate approved a territorial form of government for the entire District of Columbia, including Georgetown. Political maneuvering began for control of the local government which would have a House of Delegates and a seat in Congress. The Republicans looked on this as an opportunity to entrench themselves in such a way as would affect the 1872 presidential election.

Henry D. Cooke, president of the First National Bank of Washington, who lived in Georgetown since 1863, was expected to be appointed territorial governor by President Grant. Cooke announced his intention to control the territorial government "in the interest of the Republican Party," and that "no one not a well-tried Republican should (with his consent) hold office." Later at his induction ceremonies, preceded by a torchlight parade with fire engines to Cooke's house in Georgetown, Norton Chipman, secretary of the new territorial government, reminded "all thoughtful citizens of their duty, first as members of the Republican Party, and second as citizens of the District."[11]

Although as an independent voter, Ramón had usually voted Republican and supported most Republican positions, he could not accept this philosophy espoused by the leaders-to-be of the new territorial government. It seemed to be undue political pressure and an infringement on the rights of citizens and government employees. Although it was directed specifically at employees of the District government, Ramón felt this same attitude could carry over to

Federal employees as well, and decided it was time to sever his connection with the United States government.

After tendering his resignation to be effective in February 1870, Ramón was pleasantly surprised when his colleagues at the War Department gave him a farewell party. It was held at the Washington Arsenal on Greenleaf Point, where the Eastern Branch flows into the Potomac.[2] The Arsenal complex had been augmented in 1869 by the transfer to the Quartermaster of the former Washington Penitentiary buildings designed by Charles Bullfinch in 1826. Parts of the buildings were redesigned to accommodate officers' quarters and the "model office," which contained models of American and European weapons. Included were many antique weapons, all of interest to visitors such as Ramón, a sometime collector of different weapons types.[12]

To return to the farewell party, it was well attended by Ramón's co-workers and superiors, military and civilian. He was deeply touched by the gift of a plaque commemorating his government service and by the warm sentiments expressed by most of his colleagues, while disappointed by the thinly disguised resentment of a few. Leann was invited to attend as an honored guest, but she was unable to do so, to Ramón's regret.

Being now unemployed, and with their twenty-fifth wedding anniversary nearly at hand, it seemed an appropriate time for Ramón and Leann to consider taking the European trip they had spoken of so often. They had one little dog left—Adonis, the only male. Although elderly and also blind, he was otherwise in good enough health to travel with them.

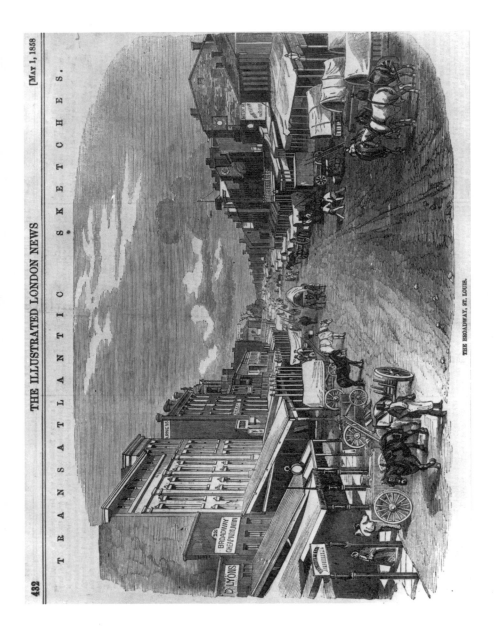

Illustration No. 14: The Broadway, St. Louis, 1858

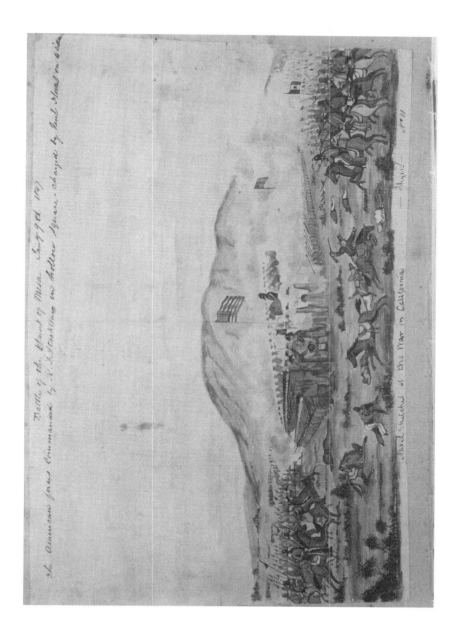

Illustration No. 15: Battle of the Plains of Mesa (near Los Angeles). Watercolor by William A. Meyers

Illustration No. 16: Col. John Charles Fremont
The Pathfinder of the Rocky Mountains

visitors such as Ramón, a sometime collector of different

Illustration No. 17: San Francisco, Lithograph S.F. Marryat, 1851

Illustration No. 18: Los Angeles, 1857. Lithograph by Kuchel and Dresel

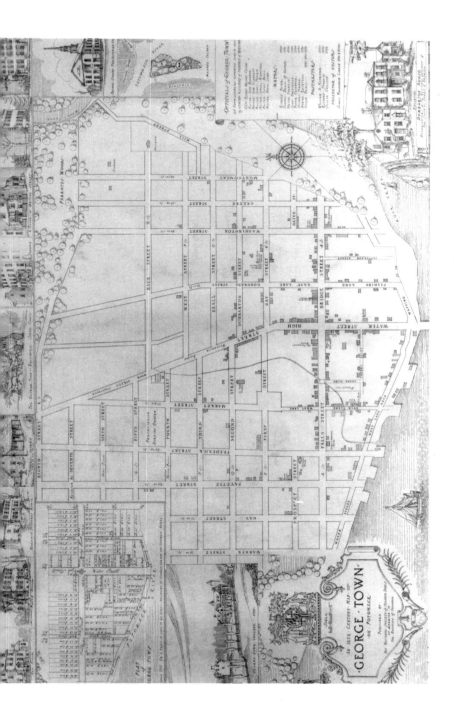

Illustration No. 19: Georgetown, 18th Century map, published in 1934 by National Society of Colonial Dames of America

Illustration No. 20: President's House. Aerial view about 1845

Illustration No. 21: Willard (City) Hotel and view of White House

Illustration No. 22: Georgetown, 1860, Lithgraph by E. Sachse

Illustration No. 23: U.S. Geological Survey field party of 1864
(Clarence King at far right)

Illustration No. 24: Edward F. Beale, 1862, founder of Tejon Ranch

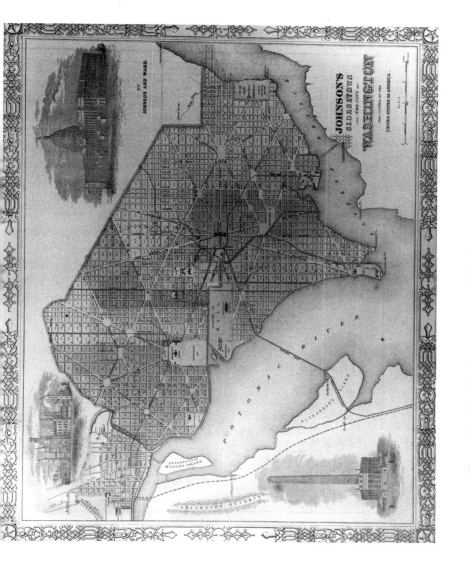

Illustration No. 25: Georgetown and Washington 1864 map by Johnson and Ward

Illustration No. 26: Map of the Defences of Washington, 1864-5.

PART VI
ROUNDING THE FAR TURN
(1870–1883)

CHAPTER 12
EUROPEAN ADVENTURE

Their plan was to select the first transatlantic crossing after the spring equinox to avoid the storms at sea and arrive in Europe in early spring. Then they would travel directly by rail to the major cities of the continent and decide where to spend their twenty-fifth wedding anniversary and the rest of the allotted time before returning in advance of the fall equinox.

They secured passage for the second week in April on the British steamship *Persia* which, though an older vessel, had made a record crossing in August 1856 of less than nine days at a speed of fourteen knots.

Their land route was planned in advance to obtain necessary visas for the countries they intended to visit. This was not a difficult task in Washington, in which all the foreign missions were close at hand. Most were not embassies but legations headed by ministers. Washington was not considered sufficiently "civilized" by European standards for assignment of top diplomats because of the hot summers and scarcity of what was considered adequate housing, restaurants and public entertainment. On the other hand, in democratic America ambassadors and embassies were associated negatively with old world courts and monarchies, so there was no pressure for change from either side.[1]

The mission staffs provided relevant information concerning conditions in their countries. The Clementes learned that Adonis also required a visa to enter certain countries, notably Italy and Spain, and could not enter England without a long wait. They decided to skip England for this trip but hoped to go there in the future.

They planned to disembark at the French port of Le Havre and take the boat train to Paris; from there by rail to Nice and Monaco on the Mediterranean; then to Rome and up through Florence to Venice; back through Switzerland to Basel and up the Rhine River to Strasbourg, through the Rhine Province of Prussia to the Netherlands, and return through Belgium to Le Havre.

After setting forth this route, they could see it covered too much for the time allotted, leaving no time to return to a favorite place for a longer visit. Furthermore, with roughly eighteen weeks to spend between mid-April and the end of August, and more than a dozen stops, there would be only a few days in each place, allowing travel time. This would hardly be enough to do more than rush through the major sights with no chance of absorbing the atmosphere of any location. In addition, there were indications of the possibility of war between France and Prussia, and that the Prussian leader Bismarck was planning actions towards unification of the German states, which could disrupt the Clementes' planned Rhineland excursion.

For all these reasons the plan needed revision, and there was also the matter of expense. Ramón had been able to save very little from his government salary, but with the profits from Leann's business, together with proceeds from the sale of their Georgetown house and property Ramón inherited in California, they were able to go abroad on more than a shoestring, but needed to retain sufficient funds to invest for the future.

They cut the itinerary to ten stops, allowing about twelve days for each including travel time, round trip to and from the port of Le Havre, as follows:

1. Paris
2. Nice
3. Monte Carlo
4. Rome
5. Florence
6. Venice
7. Lugano
8. Basel
9. Strasbourg
10. Paris

This seemed the best they could do within time and budget restrictions, and still get some flavor of these few famous places. They hoped to return another time to revisit those places they enjoyed most, and also to visit others they missed such as the British Isles; the German Confederation; and Spain, from where Ramón's ancestors had set forth for the new world.

As this visit would concentrate mostly on France and Italy, Ramón decided to broaden his language skills. He found these two "romance languages" had much in common with his native Spanish which enabled him to pick up basic knowledge without great difficulty. But as many of the words for the same thing were different, and some words which were almost the same had different meanings in the three languages, he had to be careful. He recalled the problem encountered when he learned English was that after carefully working out what to say to someone the reply came too fast for him to comprehend. Then he had to consult his pocket dictionary and attempt the painful process of translation while the other person waited for an answer. Fortunately by 1870 many persons in major European cities had enough knowledge of English or Spanish, so it turned out to be not as much of a problem as he expected.

Another preparatory problem was assembling appropriate clothing for the journey and packing large steamer trunks from which they would be living for about three months. From the foreign missions, they obtained information on climate, customs, and clothing advisable for the places they planned to visit. As many of the items they sought weren't available in Washington or Georgetown stores, they planned to shop in Europe where desirable items might be acquired at less cost than in the United States. Thus they packed less going over leaving more room for things to bring back.

The journey from Washington to the port of New York was only a blur that the Clementes hardly noticed in their excitement over the impending voyage across the Atlantic.

After boarding the *Persia*, Ramón kept a journal of the trip, much as he had after joining the Fremont expedition in April 1844. His journal of the European trip is reproduced herein in its entirety as follows:

> "April 13, 1870: We board the *Persia* at westside New York dock. After settling Adonis in cabin, we go on deck to observe departure from New York harbor and say farewell temporarily to our homeland, as shoreline fades in distance. We then explore ship from stem to stern before returning to attend to Adonis and dress for dinner.
>
> "Leann looks enchanting in her new evening gown. This is confirmed by the Captain's expression as he greets guests arriving in the dining salon. At our

request we are assigned a private table for two. The dining room steward is most attentive, and there is an excellent selection of comestibles to tempt our palates. While dining, we select a few items to take back to Adonis, which Leann secretes in her handbag.

"After feeding these morsels to Adonis and watching him enjoy the newfound gastronomic delights, we embark on a vigorous jaunt about the decks to help digest our meal and discourage any trend towards obesity. By 9:30 P.M., after this strenuous first day of our new adventure, we are ready to retire to our cabin. We are relieved to find Adonis sound asleep, his full stomach apparently quelling any anxiety he might have had at being left alone in unfamiliar surroundings.

"April 14, 1870: We arise early and enjoy huge breakfast, again requiring deck walk to digest. Take Adonis for walk on section of top deck reserved for passengers traveling with animals. Midmorning snack of bouillon and crackers is served in passenger lounge. Spend rest of morning in deck chairs watching sea and other passengers until lunch time. Afternoon seems good time for nap; then card game with new shipboard friends before dinner.

"April 15–20, 1870: Next six days at sea much alike. Fortunately my earlier tendency towards seasickness, displayed on the 1836 sea voyage around Cape Horn, did not recur on this voyage which was entirely pleasant throughout.

"April 21, 1870: Shortly after breakfast we sight land to our northwest. The Captain says it is the southeast coast of Ireland which we are passing on our way to Liverpool, where passengers going to England will disembark.

"We arrive at Liverpool in late afternoon. After those disembarking have done so, we are allowed to step ashore briefly while the ship prepares for departure. We see only a small glimpse of England, but enough to know we want to return another time for an extended visit. Reboarding the Persia, we are already sorry to be leaving, as we sail down the long estuary with green English landscape on either side. Enthusiasm returns on heading into the Irish Sea, then the Atlantic again for the remainder of the voyage to France.

"April 22, 1870: Our final day at sea is busy with packing and arrangements to disembark at Le Havre tomorrow. We say farewell to new friends, promising to look each other up when we return to the United States. Leann has put their names and addresses into her notebook.

"April 23. 1870: Our first view of the European continent is shortly after breakfast. Though not unexpected, we are struck by seeing signs in French language on buildings near our dock—perhaps I am more struck by this than Leann, who grew up in St. Louis with its French heritage. Anyway, we are both struck by the fast pace of the language as spoken by citizens ashore, particularly the customs officials as they peruse our passports and luggage.

"When the ordeal is finally over, in the early afternoon we board the boat train for Paris. We speed through the French countryside with new experiences arriving so fast one after the other, there is little time for it all to sink in. Before we know it we are in the outskirts of Paris as seemingly endless miles of suburbs rush by. They are teeming with activity—industry and small farms, plots of land growing every kind of fruit and vegetable, with chickens, hogs, sheep and goats, to feed the populace of one of the world's largest cities.

"Our initial view of the city is spectacular. A carriage takes us from the Gare du Nord through narrow streets to broad boulevards, finally arriving at the elegant Hotel de Crillon overlooking the Place de la Concorde, at the commencement of the Champs Elysees. We are greeted courteously and shown to our room where we order a light supper, being too tired to dress for dinner or explore further.

"April 24, 1870: Our first morning in Paris begins with breakfast of cafe-au-lait and croissants with jam, in our beautiful hotel room. We were told in

Washington before making reservations, that the Crillon is perhaps the best place to stay in Paris, not only because of excellent rooms, food and service, but also because of the beauty of the building itself—an outstanding example of 18th century architecture designed by Jacques-Ange Gabriel, who was commissioned by King Louis XV in 1758.[2]

"We spend a lazy morning enjoying the sights from our window. After a light lunch downstairs, we set forth to visit the Tuilleries gardens, a short walk from the hotel. We return for dinner and a good night's rest before starting serious sightseeing and shopping tomorrow.

"April 25–30, 1870: During the next five days before taking off for the south of France, we visit the Louvre museum and art galleries, taking two afternoons to see only the highlights; the Notre Dame Cathedral on the Isle de la Cite in the middle of the Seine River; the Bastille of French revolution fame; Napoleon's tomb at the Place des Invalides; and the new Opera building which is under construction. We go to the major shops and many smaller ones which Leann has discovered, to seek out all sorts of treasures for personal adornment, and household accoutrements.

"Whenever we feel hungry or thirsty there is always an excellent bistro or brasserie nearby. We enjoy returning to the Crillon, particularly for afternoon tea in the enclosed courtyard after a busy day on the town; then off to dress for dinner which we will have either in the hotel dining room or at one of the many 'haute cuisine' restaurants for which Paris is famous.

"Two restaurants we most enjoy are Ledoyen on the Champs Elysees, which has catered to prominent Parisiens since Robespierre and Napoleon I; and la Tour d'Argent, Paris' oldest restaurant and one of its most sumptuous.[3] I cannot begin to describe the huge variety of exotic dishes prepared and served in the most delightful and elegant manner at these two restaurants. Actually it is almost too much of a good thing. Although we wouldn't have missed going to either one, we prefer the simpler fare and less auspicious dining at the smaller bistros and brasseries of the city and surrounding countryside, which is better for us nutritionally as well as financially.

"May 1, 1870: We leave the Crillon early in the morning to board the Train Bleu of the PLM (Paris-Lyons-Mediteranee) for its fifteen hour run down the Rhone valley to the Cote d'Azur. This service began in 1863 as the Mediterranean coast became a fashionable resort area, surpassing the previously popular Deauville and Trouville resorts on the Atlantic coast of Normandy. Had we more time I would have visited that area (Normandy) from which my ancestors left for Spain nearly four centuries ago.

"Also, had we more time, we would have broken up the trip south into several stops along the way to visit, for example, the hospice at Beaune and some of the major sights of Provence such as the Roman arena at Arles; the ancient hilltop village of Les Baux; and Avignon's Chateauneuf-du-Pape (also the name of an excellent regional wine we both enjoy), all described by fellow train passengers on the Train Bleu.[4]

"Instead, we rush on through to Marseilles on the Mediterranean coast. After a late lunch of bouillabaisse (a highly touted local seafood dish including fish heads with staring eyes which neither of us fully appreciate) we continue by rail along the Mediterranean coast to Nice. It is dark when we check in at our hotel.

"May 2, 1870: We awaken to a bright sunny view of the Mediterranean from our hotel window, and order breakfast in our room. We haven't yet decided whether to spend the most of our allotted time here in Nice, or in Monte Carlo a few miles further along the coast. Both are in the same beautiful semi-tropical location, between mountain and seashore, reminiscent of my native California.

"The decision is made shortly after going outside the hotel, across the Promenade des Anglais, and down the steps to the beach. We are disappointed to find it quite narrow, with many pebbles, black sand, and water with a certain amount of floating garbage. This is not conducive to swimming or just relaxing on the sand, such as I have enjoyed on unspoiled Pacific coast beaches. The major activity here seems to be promenading along the walkways above the beach, and watching others do likewise which can't capture our interest for long. We decide to leave for Monte Carlo to concentrate on the indoor rather than outdoor pleasures.

"May 3, 1870: After consulting with the hotel concierge, we choose a scenic route by carriage, following the Grand Corniche, once the Roman Aurelian Way between Nice and Menton, which was reconstructed by Napoleon. This road, along the mid-mountainside, provides fabulous views of the coastal towns below. It also allows a close look at the ancient village of Éze, clinging to an almost vertical outcrop of rock, before our carriage turns off on a side road, dropping down into the Principality of Monaco.[5]

"We had heard of the Monte Carlo gambling casino which opened in 1862, said to be frequented by celebrities and potentates of all nations.[6, 9] What we did not know about were Monaco's other attractions as a tourist resort, including its magnificent scenery and historical interest. An independent principality since the 16th century, Monaco has belonged to the House of Grimaldi since 1297, except during the French revolution, and is now under the protectorate of France.

"We learned that Monaco's popularity as a place of residence has been growing rapidly since Prince Charles III abolished income taxes last year. This was done because of increased revenues from casino games accruing to the state through the Société des Bains de Mer, founded by Prince Charles, which owns the casino and the Hôtel de Paris, across the square, where we are staying.[17]

"Following our brief but exciting mountainside journey from Nice, we decide to stay in the hotel for the rest of the evening, and retire early to get a good start on seeing the sights tomorrow.

"May 4, 1870: After breakfast we set forth on our own personal tour of Monte Carlo, starting with the Prince's Palace. The oldest part of the palace was built in the 13th century, with additions in Italian Renaissance style and a Moorish entrance tower dating from the 15th and 16th centuries.

"Leaving the palace, we walk through 'La Condamine,' the commercial port district which occupies the low land between the promontories of Monaco to the west and Monte Carlo to the east. There are many interesting shops and restaurants which we plan to revisit when we have more time.

"At the east end of this area we approach the heights where the casino is located. The building was constructed in 1858 on authorization from the Prince of Monaco and is surprisingly simple in architectural style. We understand a new and grander structure is under consideration.

"We are introduced to the various games of chance and try a sample of each with negligible results. As it has been quite a full day, we decide to call a halt early and return for better luck tomorrow.

"May 5, 1870: After a leisurely breakfast we start out again. Time and financial limitations keep us from lingering at the casino, so after brief and occasional flings at the gaming tables, consisting mostly of flinging chips onto the table and seldom drawing any back, we venture out into the city and visit some of the shops and small restaurants we passed yesterday. One especially memorable restaurant serves the best crepes we have eaten anywhere, made even more delightful by the friendly welcoming demeanor of the owner/chef—a far cry from the haughty, disdainful attitudes of the staffs at some of the finer Parisian establishments. Much as we like it here, we decide to continue on with our journey tomorrow.

"May 6, 1870: Today we leave Monte Carlo early in the morning and travel eastward by rail along the Mediterranean, then south to the 'eternal city' of

Rome. It is located within the Papal States that extend from the Tyrrhenian Sea on the west to the Adriatic on the east coast of this long boot-shaped peninsula. We arrive late in the evening and go directly to the Hotel d'Inghilterra, which had been recommended as being 'central, healthy and cheerful.' Tired after the long days journey, we ring for tea and muffins in our room and retire early.

May 7–8, 1870: Before coming here, Leann and I had read the joint account of English clergyman Hall and his wife of their visit to Rome in 1853. We now recall Mrs. Hall's statement: 'I felt that I did not feel enough' in face of her husband's high enthusiasm at being finally among Rome's many cultural relics for which his classical studies had prepared him. Mrs. Hall wrote further: 'Sometimes I feel disgusted with myself for having been so indifferent.'[6]

"Thus prepared for experiencing mixed emotions, we set forth to encounter Rome's wealth of antiquities and art treasures, from the Forum to the Sistine Chapel. Our enthusiasm is further dampened by assertions of long-time English residents that the city has been 'completely spoiled' since their own earlier arrival. We are also deterred from full enjoyment of our surroundings by warnings that this is a bad time politically for tourists to be visiting because of anticipated movements by Italian troops to bring about a withdrawal of the French garrison in Rome, and annexation of the territory by the Kingdom of Italy.

"These warnings move us to arrange for departure from Rome earlier than planned, to avoid untoward delays or difficulties that could occur in such a situation. We enjoy an excellent dinner in the hotel dining room, from which we sequester a plate of fettucini and other delicacies for Adonis. We enjoy watching him enjoy his own Italian feast in the privacy of our hotel room on our final night in Rome.

"This unexpectedly early departure from Rome is a disappointment, particularly for me, having been raised a Catholic. Though I haven't been going to Church regularly or observing many Catholic rituals as often as I should, I wanted to spend more time visiting the Vatican and perhaps participate in an audience with the Pope, but it was not to happen.

"A further disappointment is not visiting Henry Van Owen, my friend from college days, whom we last saw in Washington on his way to Europe, and who now lives on the Isle of Ischia in the Bay of Naples. Henry's family was one of the first to settle in Greenwich Village where I visited them when in New York. He sought refuge on this Mediterranean isle after two unsuccessful marriages in the United States. When he wrote us suggesting a visit, he said that he had married an Italian widow and was pursuing his interests in writing and painting.

"We had intended travelling by rail from Rome to Naples and taking a ferry to Ischia. We now learn that dogs are not allowed to be brought on the island without a lengthy wait and there is nowhere in Naples we would feel safe in leaving Adonis while we make a quick trip across the bay and back. This, together with our decision not to linger in the area because of imminent politico/military disruption causes us to call off the plan. I know Henry will be disappointed as he indicated wanting very much to see us. I will write him the reason why we were unable to come, and hope he understands.

"May 9–15, 1870: We depart from Rome at noon today and travel by rail north to Florence. By leaving Rome sooner than planned, we can enjoy an extended stay in Florence. This is the principal city in the former Grand Duchy of Tuscany, which became part of the Kingdom of Italy by plebiscite in 1860. We have arranged to stay at the Villa San Michele, a beautiful spot high above the city. It was built in 1453, boasts a facade by Michelangelo, and statuary by Donatello which was added in the 17th century.[7]

"We could spend all our time at the Villa enjoying the view, fine cuisine and relaxing atmosphere. The day after our arrival we force ourselves to take a carriage down the hill and across the Arno river, to see the town itself and its renowned sights. After traversing the Ponte Vecchio with its interesting shops on both sides of the covered bridge, we visit the Duomo and Giotto's bell tower. On our way to the famed Piazza della Signoria, we see the house where Dante lived, and finally Michelangelo's statue of David in the great square. We browse in the wide variety of small shops on the surrounding cobblestone streets, and acquire some examples of fine Florentine leather-work—Leann selects very supple leather gloves and boots; my choices are a belt and billfold.

"There is no shortage of excellent restaurants in Florence but we prefer the open-air shops of the Mercato Centrale which offer every product imaginable, edible and otherwise, spread out under huge awnings covering several blocks of streets. We could spend days exploring these areas further, but decide to move on to more aesthetic diversions.

"We inspect the renaissance sculptures at the Borgello, the Boticellis at the Uffizi Palace, and the Boboli Gardens, then return to our Villa by way of the hillside town of Fiesole, where Boccacio set the 'Decameron.' A few more days at this pace makes us enjoy even more relaxing at the Villa on the hill before it is time to move on.

"May 16, 1870: Much as we enjoy Florence, only a week is allowed on our schedule, so today we set forth for Venice. From Florence the journey by train to Venice is a little over 150 miles, barely enough to get settled before arriving at the city of canals and gondolas. Our little dog Adonis enjoys the gondola ride to our hotel. Although he cannot see, the rocking motion of the vessel and the gondolier singing in Italian seem to please him. In fact everything Italian pleases him, including the food (he loves fettucini); and the Italians love him too. As we leave the gondola, the gondolier kisses the top of Adonis' head, pronouncing him *bellissimo.*'

"It is late afternoon as we check in at the hotel and we are a bit tired from the trip, with so many experiences to digest. We decide to remain in the hotel for the evening, have an early supper and leave further sightseeing until tomorrow.

"May 17–18, 1870: We get an early start to see the magnificent Piazza San Marco and the Doges Palace. After touring both, we watch the glass blowers at nearby shops creating their fantastic products. We linger over a delightful lunch at an outside table of one of the restaurants on the square. On our way back to our hotel on the Grand Canal, we pass under and marvel over the famous covered Rialto Bridge.

"After the initial excitement of seeing the unique sights of Venice, we conclude that this is not a place where we care to linger, as we begin to notice its somewhat fetid atmosphere from the nearly stagnant canal waters all around us. So after the second day, we decide to set forth again.

"May 19–21, 1870: I have arranged passage on a train which takes us from Venice first westward, then north through the Brenner Pass, by-passing Lugano which was on our original schedule. We stop first at Innsbruck, Austria; then through the Arlsburg Pass to Zurich, and on to Basel, Switzerland, where we arrive late at night. The fresh clean air of the Austrian Tyrol and the Swiss Alps is a welcome change from the swamp-like atmosphere of sea-level Venice. In Basel we enjoy feasting on their fondue specialties, and visiting the Fine Arts Museum with its Holbein portraits of the philosopher Erasmus, who lived and died in Basel.[8]

"Here we receive bad news concerning the increased danger of war between France and Prussia. Although still ahead of our original schedule because of reduced time at Rome and Venice, and the elimination of Lugano, we decide to cut short the rest of the trip and return to Paris as soon as possible to be ready for the voyage back to America—but not before visiting Strasbourg in Alsace, the former home of Leann's grandmother.

"May 22–23, 1870: A short trip by riverboat down the Rhine River brings us to this fantastic city of meandering canals, medieval architecture and tasty Alsatian cookery. From our hotel on Strasbourg's central square, we view the beautiful

rose-colored Gothic cathedral with its famous astro-
nomical clock. The next day we tour the narrow
winding streets, with carved timbered buildings, specialty shops, excellent restaurants and interesting
people.

"May 24, 1870: A side trip into the nearby wine
country takes us to the picturesque town of Colmar,
which exemplifies the blending of French and
Germanic cultures in this region. In the adjacent
countryside, we discover a small but elegant hillside
inn just outside the village of Trois-Epis, where we
decide to stop, at least for the night.

"May 25–June 8, 1870: On awakening we realize
that we have fallen in love with this place, and
Adonis seems to like it too. We decide to spend more
time just relaxing, getting the feel of what it is like to
be here, and meeting some of the local people. By the
third day we begin to feel we almost belong (perhaps
the spirit of Leann's grandmother is with us).

"Our room on the second floor faces the front of
the inn. It has a small balcony just above the terrace
where guests of the inn and local residents gather in
the late afternoon for a glass of Reisling, Pernod or
Framboise, and to discuss the day's events. On one
occasion Adonis, whom we let out on the balcony
above, lifted his hind leg against the balustrade and
sent a pale yellow stream down onto one of the tables
below. Sensing it was not Reisling or Pernod, the
affected customer called the manager who brought
this incident to our attention. We apologized and
assured him there would be no recurrence. The
understanding citizens and patrons are more amused
than annoyed. When we next bring Adonis to the
dining room, a practice not allowed in many places,
he is given his own chair and place setting, and welcomed as a special guest.

"Here in this lovely Alsatian countryside in early
June of 1870, we could linger indefinitely. But more
bad news of Prussian troop movements near the
French border, forces us to decide to return at once to
Paris, and hopefully have enough time there for one

more round of exploration and bargain hunting, while being in position to leave immediately for home if and when war actually breaks out.

"June 9, 1870: With mixed feelings of regret at leaving this happy spot, and enthusiasm for revisiting Paris, we return to Strasbourg to board the train for its westward run. We pause at the towns of Nancy and Chalons-sur-Marne before arriving in late evening at Paris' Gare de l'Est.

"June 10–11, 1870: Morning in Paris! It is exciting to reexperience the luxuries of the Crillon, where our former room is ready for our return visit, after I wired ahead for the reservation. The doorman warmly greets Adonis who seems to remember the sounds and smells of this now familiar place.

"We spend the day relaxing in our room and planning our next activities. We are fortunate to have returned in time to attend the Grand Prix de Paris at Longchamps, the day after tomorrow. This gives Leann time to plan her wardrobe and obtain any necessary missing items.

"June 12, 1870: We arrive at Longchamps amid milling throngs of enthusiastic race fans and people watchers. Much of the royalty and aristocracy of Europe are present in all their finery—quite a sight to behold, but not outdoing Leann in her finery, as she can more than hold her own in any gathering. Emperor Louis Napoleon and Empress Eugenie attend, but the Emperor remains seated during the entire proceedings, which we are told is unusual for him; and the Empress' dress and coiffeur are much simpler than usual, indicating for both their careworn condition over the increasingly tense situation with Prussia.[9] We do not bet heavily on the races, being unfamiliar with the participants and more interested in observing our surroundings. Thus we are not too disappointed when our selections do not win. We return to Paris feeling refreshed by the experience.

"June 13–July 9, 1870: This time in Paris we avoid the large expensive restaurants and patronize the smaller ones that are around every corner when we are shopping or sightseeing. We take a carriage to the Cathedral de Sacre Coeur on Montparnasse, overlooking the city. It reminds us of our first home in St. Louis near the school conducted by the Sisters of the Sacred Heart, who had come originally from this very place in Paris.

"The music of Offenbach, which we understand has captivated Paris for the last three years, draws us one evening to the Theatre des Varietes for a performance of "Orphee aux Enfers" (Orpheus in the Underworld). The maestro, born in Cologne, has become a favorite of Empress Eugenie and all of Paris is humming and dancing to his tunes.[10]

"One day we join a group tour to Versailles, just outside the city of Paris. We visit the Petit Trianon, built in 1762 by Louis XV and which became Marie Antoinette's favorite residence.

"As in Mexico City, where we compared that capital city with our own, we are intrigued by the similarities between Versailles, the former French monarch's 'country' capital, and Washington DC. We are shown by our guide, for comparative study, copies of the 1746 map of Versailles as planned by Le Notre for Louis XV, and a 1792 map of Washington DC as planned by Pierre L'Enfant and Andrew Ellicott. On the Versailles map, the palace and the Trianon are in the same relative positions as the Capitol and the White House on the DC map, joined by a broad avenue in each case. This similarity is said to symbolize the demise of the old monarchy and the ascendance of the new democratic institutions. Also notable on the Versailles map are the rondes or circles in the hunting forest which are analogous to L'Enfant's traffic circles at major intersections on the Washington DC map.[11]

"For Leann's birthday on June 30, we attend the new Folies Bergere and view the infamous 'Can-Can.'[12] It is risque even for Paris, but we find it merely amusing and thoroughly enjoyable. (Author's note: "risque" indeed, as indicated by Mark Twain's comments when he saw it a few years later and wrote that he had placed his hands before his face "for very shame" but admitted that he looked through his fingers and was astounded by what he saw.[7] To some, such as the author Emile Zola,[10] this sort of thing [the Can-Can] epitomized the increasing decadence of the Second Empire. Some foreign visitors regarded Paris as a kind of "gas-lit Venusburg" where those in pursuit of pleasure are offered temptations without limit.[13])

"One of our favorite spots to browse and eat is Les Halles, the gigantic glass and iron enclosed structure in the center of town, where hundreds of farmers from the surrounding countryside bring their produce early in the morning and remain until everything is sold—sometimes within a few hours and other times not until nightfall. We cannot be in this neighborhood without stopping in Les Halles for some of the fabulous onion soup served therein.

"On July 4 we meet with a group of Americans to celebrate Independence Day, and discuss how much longer it will be safe to stay in Paris. Within days our happy time is cut short by rumors of a pending declaration of war by France against Prussia. I secure passage on the U.S. steamship Baltic for the second week in July, so we will celebrate our twenty-fifth wedding anniversary at sea.

"July 10, 1870: Today we say a sad farewell to Paris and board the boat train for Le Havre, our port of embarkation for the United States. The train trip is marked by repeated recalls of all the things we had forgotten or neglected to do; assuring each other that nothing important of our belongings, old or new, was left behind; and that we had left the appropriate tips; and also in preparing for French Customs where our new possessions must be declared before boarding ship. We finally board the Baltic at dusk and watch the lights of the French coast disappear as our ship heads for home.

"July 11–18, 1870: The return sea voyage offers just as much as the trip over, with the splendid addition of our anniversary dinner which included a special cake, compliments of the chef and ship's Captain. Now the whole of our European adventure belongs to our twenty-fifth year of marriage. We are glad to have had enough time to get to know something of Paris, Monte-Carlo, Florence, and Strasbourg-Colmar-Trois Epis, which were the high points of our trip as well as the two transatlantic voyages. We can now commit these experiences to our store of happy memories to draw on in later years."

Here Ramón Clemente's journal of the European adventure ends. He learned later from the Fremonts that they too had been in Europe that fateful spring and summer and left just as abruptly, or at least their daughter did. The Fremonts were in Germany when the Clementes were in France. John Fremont was recalled to the United States on business and his wife Jessie accompanied him. Their daughter Elizabeth remained in Dresden (to "superintend the education" of her younger brother Charles, as she put it) and was there when a declaration of war seemed imminent. She got on the last passenger train out of Dresden for Hamburg, and returned on the last German passenger steamer available before the Franco-Prussian war began.[14]

The Clementes left France none to soon, for war was declared July 19, 1870, and thereafter France was not the same place they had so enjoyed. Having just been through America's Civil War they were happy to have missed the tragic events following Bismarck's defeat of Louis Napoleon's army at Sedan in September 1870, France's capitulation in January 1871 and Prussian troops marching down the Champs Elysées.[7, 12]

The outcome surprised many, as France appeared stronger before the war, with larger population, more experienced army, better weaponry, a superior navy, and aid promised from neighboring nations. But the aid didn't come; sea power was ineffective; and the Prussian army proved superior, with its more efficient mobilization and more effective leadership.[15] Furthermore, the unrealized industrial and technical superiority of the German States in support of Prussia, tipped the balance against France from the start, just as in the American Civil War the more industrialized north inevitably prevailed against the mostly agricultural south.

Leann and Ramón had witnessed the last days of France's second empire, which led to the beginning of a new era in Europe.

With France no longer able to manipulate the balance of power between the formerly fragmented states to her north and east, the wars of 1870–71 led to the unification of both Germany and Italy.

CHAPTER 13
BETWEEN EAST AND WEST

Arriving in New York harbor was a heart-warming experience for the Clementes. Even considering all the new sights and pleasurable adventures they had in Europe, there was nothing to compare with the satisfaction of returning to familiar surroundings of one's homeland, though in this case it first required contending with unsympathetic customs officials.

As the Baltic docked late in the day, they stayed overnight in New York and had one last fling of self-indulgence before returning to Washington. They checked in at the Fifth Avenue Hotel on Madison Square, where they were told the Prince of Wales had stayed in 1860.[1] It was also renowned as New York's first hotel with passenger elevators. After checking their luggage and freshening up, Ramón made dinner reservations at Delmonico's, and they took off for a window shopping excursion on Fifth Avenue. They made an unexpected stop at Tiffany's,[38] where Ramón bought Leann a gold pin with two birds in diamonds to commemorate their twenty-fifth wedding anniversary.

Dinner at Delmonico's was just as good as Ramón remembered from college days, but now in more elegant surroundings on Fifth Avenue at 14th Street. It was also known as the place where Samuel Morse, of telegraph fame, first made cable contact with Europe.[2] It had been a long day and night, and the Clementes were inclined to sleep late but arose early to complete the final leg of their journey.

Before taking the train to Washington they visited the Currier & Ives store on Nassau Street, where they purchased some last souvenirs of their trip—black and white prints of New York scenes at 15¢ to 20¢ each, and one colored print titled "The Lightning Express Trains" for $2.00.[3] They took a Currier & Ives catalog with them and bought the New York newspapers to read on the train.

Washington appeared much the same as when they left. They expected, on arriving at their apartment, to drop everything and just relax for a while. They did not expect to be greeted with a notice that the building was going to be sold, so they would have to begin immediately looking for other accommodations.

This development was so depressing that they considered moving to the new Arlington Hotel at Vermont and I Streets, already acclaimed as Washington's most opulent hostelry, catering to celebrities and foreign dignitaries.[4] Fortunately for the Clementes' budget, the Arlington did not accept dogs, even one in Adonis' aged condition.

They considered Miss English's Georgetown Female Seminary (Elizabeth Benton Fremont's "alma mater") on Gay and Washington Streets, which had been converted to a "flat" building.[1,6] However the rooms were quite small and pets were discouraged, so this did not solve their housing problem, although the prospect of returning to their former Georgetown neighborhood was enticing.

They kept looking and finally located other quarters to rent while deciding on something more permanent. They had considered moving out of Washington, perhaps to New York or the west coast. In fact the next several years seem to have been spent by the Clementes in drifting between the east and west while searching for their last real home before going to a final resting place.

Since Ramón left his government job and the properties Leann had restored/remodeled were sold, there was little to keep them in Washington. Ramón was still involved in legal matters concerning his mother's estate, requiring trips to California which now were facilitated by the new transcontinental railroad. On each trip there occurred a pull to and from the east and the west—a sadness at leaving one and an eagerness on arriving at the other and vice-versa.

The first such trip unfortunately was the last for their little dog Adonis. He had seemed to be doing very well on the way west and jumped around happily in the dry desert air when they took him out for a walk at a train stop in Nevada. But on the return trip the weather was unusually cold, too much for Adonis to withstand in his advanced years. Although the new railroad cars were quite elegant, with red plush upholstery and polished brass trim, the only heat

came from a single stove at one end of the long car, which was barely adequate in normal cold weather. Adonis' death marked the end
of the Clementes' small canine family. They spoke of getting another dog but decided to defer more serious consideration of the matter until they were permanently settled.

They were further saddened by a long-delayed letter from Frances
Grayson telling of Andrew's death in August 1869. He had begun to
receive payments from the Smithsonian for his bird paintings, but
became discouraged when his other business projects were unsuccessful, largely because of political unrest in Mexico. He succumbed
from a recurrence of the yellow fever contracted on an earlier bird
expedition. Frances tried to have his paintings published posthumously without success, and wrote later that she had donated them
to the University of California.[5]

On their next trip west, the Clementes decided to visit other
areas on their way to California—first Utah where the Mormons
had developed a flourishing community at Salt Lake City; then
Nevada where several towns such as Virginia City and Reno had
grown rapidly since the discovery of silver in 1858.

As before they took the Union Pacific west from Chicago,
enjoyng the relative luxury of a Pullman Palace car. Days were long
with stops for meals at stations sometimes as long as eight to twelve
hours apart. Excitement was brought about by male passengers
shooting at deer and buffalo along the way. At night porters lit
kerosene lamps and made up the berths. Women travelling alone
were said to keep hatpins in hand for protection during the night.[88]

Most noticeable on reaching Utah Territory, called by Mormons
the State of Deseret, were the extensive small family-run farms and
other thriving enterprises established by the thrifty and industrious
Mormons. One was the Zion Cooperative Mercantile Association
(Z.C.M.I.), a Mormon innovation for exchange and sale of community products.

They hadn't been in Utah (or Deseret) long before realizing that
the Mormons, in spite of what one might think of their religious and
social customs, had created a prosperous economy and made this
arid land bloom. Though raised a Catholic, Ramón tried to understand other religious concepts, as did Leann. While one might not
agree with all the Mormon beliefs, such as polygamy and the degree
of communalism they practiced, it was apparent the Mormons drew
a great deal of strength and wisdom from the totality of their beliefs,
enabling them to achieve outstanding accomplishments.

Among the most outstanding were the Mormon Temple, still under construction, and the Tabernacle which had just been completed. The 250-foot long building with its 80-foot high walls and huge sandstone buttresses, was topped by a 150-foot wide domed roof formed by a bridgework of timbers pinned together with wooden pegs and bound with rawhide to prevent splitting.[6]

To complement this vast auditorium, the Mormon leader, Brigham Young, wanted an organ befitting the grandeur of the building. A church member named Joseph Ridges from Australia, had brought with him an organ he made himself, which was used in the first Tabernacle, preceding the new structure. As the only organ-builder available, Ridges was assigned the task of designing and creating a larger organ for the new Tabernacle.[7]

Wood for the organ was hauled by ox-team from Pine Valley near St. George, 900 miles south, to Salt Lake City, where it was shaped into the finished product by skilled artisans under Ridges' direction. With completion of the building and the organ, a new Tabernacle choir was organized and the Clementes were privileged to hear one of its earliest performances.

While in Salt Lake City they visited the "Beehive House," built in 1854 as the residence of Brigham Young at the corner of State and South Temple Streets. They were impressed by the massive "Eagle Gate" marking the State Street entrance to Brigham Young's property.[8]

They found the physical grandeur of the city's geographical setting unique and compelling, with the Wasatch mountains to the north and east, and the Great Salt Lake stretching out to the west. The Mormons had found a beautiful place and were making the most of it.

Ramón recalled his experiences with Fremont's expedition in 1844, when they reached Utah Lake about fifty miles south, and Fremont's comments on what a rich agricultural area it could be. When Brigham Young was reported to have said: "This is the place," on first viewing the area, he may have meant "this is the place Fremont described" from his earlier expeditions.[87] Recalling some of the hardships of that journey, Ramón was glad they did not have to worry so much this time about Indian attacks and could enjoy the luxuries of hotels and train travel.

Their next stop was Reno, which enjoyed a building boom in 1870 and was overtaking Virginia City as the major town in Nevada. Originally known as Lake's Crossing,[29] the town of Reno was established in 1868 when the Central Pacific held a public land auction, selling 200 lots the first day starting at $600 for the first lot.

The forerunner of the currently popular Riverside Hotel received the Clementes on their arrival at Reno. Though not as elegant as the hotels of Europe, New York, or even Washington, it was quite adequate for the occasion. Looking around town the next day, they found the business district was mostly low-frame structures with false fronts and not very inviting. It was comforting to learn that Reno had become more of a family town that did not tolerate the usual frontier "rowdies."[9]

Reno had already replaced Virginia City as a center for expensive theatrical productions, thanks to the railroad company granting special stopover privileges to New York theater companies. The new Dyer's Theater had been built the previous year and the Clementes saw an excellent show the night after their arrival which was none too soon as the theater was destroyed by cave-ins shortly thereafter.[10]

Reno had a good newspaper, the *Nevada State Journal*, started in 1870, so Leann and Ramón did not feel as cut off from the rest of the country as they had feared. Within a short time they experienced most of what Reno had to offer, or at least all they cared to, and were anxious to move on. Ramón wanted to see the state capital at Carson City, named after his friend Kit Carson, and the boom town of Virginia City, of which it was said that life there was no more "wild and wooly" than in New York or San Francisco.[11]

Full rail service south of Reno was incomplete and uncertain at best. Stagecoaches of Wells Fargo and Pioneer Stage made the run to Virginia City in one and a half hours, turning the well travelled route into a sort of race-track. The route to Carson City was slightly less hectic, so the Clementes decided to visit there first, and then return by way of Virginia City to Reno to pick up the train to California.

It was a beautiful ride by stagecoach down the lush green valley, past Washoe Lake at the foot of the Sierra Nevada mountains. Leann and Ramón were tempted to consider Nevada as a possible nesting place but things were moving too fast. Reaching Carson City in a little over two hours, they found it not as fully developed as Reno, but were impressed by the new capitol building completed the previous year, the opera house built in 1861, and the Carson City Mint completed in 1867. This branch mint was established to mint coins from silver produced from the Comstock Lode in Virginia City, and began doing so in 1870. They made quarters, halves, and dollars that first year, and Leann obtained one of each for her collection. They also minted gold eagles ($10) and half-eagles ($5), and Ramón got one of each with the new CC mint mark.[12] For them as coin collectors, this was worth the trip to Carson City.

From there to Virginia City was a short stagecoach ride of less than twenty miles, hilly and rather barren, except for a few scrubby pine trees, lacking the lush forestation between Reno and Carson City. They passed through the busy mining towns of Silver City and Goldhill before arriving at their destination.

Virginia City, home of the famous Comstock Lode, is built on a treeless slope of Mount Davidson, directly above the mine. Some of the frame houses and brick stores had settled into cavities formed by tunnel cave-ins. The streets were crowded with coaches, wagons, and freight vans called "mountain schooners," which were drawn by twelve mules and loaded with every kind of merchandise from machinery and furniture to food and wine.[62]

The main street, C Street, runs through the center of town with parallel streets like stair steps high above and far below, intersected by steep cross streets. The best residential section is high above on A and B streets with commercial and industrial activities on the lower levels. At the north end of town is the "Sierra Nevada Glory Hole," the northern part of the Comstock Lode, where steam shovels chewed away at the hillside. Downhill below C Street the Union Shaft drops 3,000 feet inside the earth and meets the north lateral of the Sutro Tunnel.[13] Leann and Ramón did not venture inside but were interested in having this mine described to them, the production from which helped finance the Civil War, the transatlantic cable, and turned San Francisco into one of America's most fashionable cities.[14]

They stayed at the International Hotel, called the "boast and glory of the Comstock" at the corner of C and Union Streets, which provided excellent accommodations for a frontier town. It was in easy walking distance of Piper's Opera House at Union and B, a block uphill; and the Crystal Bar a block south on C Street, with its tremendous crystal chandeliers.[2] Also nearby were St. Mary's Catholic Church and an Episcopal church within a block of each other on Taylor Street between E and G.[13]

The following year in Washington, the Clementes read Mark Twain's *Roughing It*, about his experiences in Nevada, particularly

Virginia City. He worked as a cub reporter on the *Enterprise* which moved from Carson City in 1860. The rival *Virginia Evening Bulletin* in 1863 referred to Twain as "that beef-eating, blear-eyed, hollow-headed, slab-sided ignoramus, that pilfering reporter Mark Twain," giving some idea of the tenor of newspaper reportage of that time and place.[15] When Ramón learned the author's real name was Samuel Clemens, he wondered if they might be distantly related.

Before leaving Virginia City, they inquired about visiting Las Vegas, some four hundred miles south, where Ramón had camped with Fremont in 1844. The area had been settled in 1855 by Mormons who saw it as a good stopping point on the route between Salt Lake City and Los Angeles, and built an adobe fort to house a small garrison and protect passing travellers.[16] Ramón was advised the trip from Virginia City to Las Vegas would be long and difficult with not very much worth seeing after they arrived there so they gave up the idea.

The Pioneer Stage back to Reno was filled to its nine-person capacity inside, with six more riding on top, including a "shotgun messenger" to guard a valuable shipment. The well-built Concord stage, once described by Mark Twain as "a cradle on wheels," seemed something less than that for Leann and Ramón, each crowded into fifteen inches of seat space allowed per person, their knees nearly pressed against those of passengers seated opposite them. They listened uneasily to stories of stagecoach robberies and shootouts between armed robbers and Wells Fargo agents. Fortunately they reached Reno in near record time without incident, and boarded the Central Pacific for the run over the Sierra Nevada into California.

In San Francisco they stayed overnight at the Russ House, still the city's finest hostelry, built by 1847 pioneer Christian Russ on Montgomery Street between Bush and Pine.[17] Before settling in, they took a horse-drawn streetcar out Pine Street past Van Ness to visit the site of the newly created Golden Gate Park, then returned downtown for a Chinese dinner. The next morning Ramón went to the Wells Fargo Bank at Montgomery and California Streets to collect the funds he had sent by telegraph before leaving Washington, and to establish an account for use on future trips west. Then he and Leann boarded a stagecoach for the trip south. They had considered a sea voyage down the coast, but selected the land route so they could make a side trip to Yosemite, fulfilling a vow Ramón made to himself in 1844 after hearing Joseph Walker's description of the place.

In 1864 Congress had passed legislation making the Yosemite valley and the Mariposa Grove of giant sequoia trees on the western slope of the Sierra Nevada, a national preserve.[18] Because of his interest in geology and the geography of his native land, Ramón particularly wanted to see Yosemite, ever since reading Clarence King's treatise on the valley's formation. King's theory was that the gigantic domes along the preglacial valley were formed by upsurges of molten rock; then later glacial flows carved U-shaped troughs leaving hanging valleys, giant waterfalls, and house-sized boulders in their wake. The Merced River and Tuolomne Glacier remain as evidence of these geologic events, together with their results—such as: Half Dome, Sentinel Dome, El Capitan, Vernal and Bridal Veil Falls, and Cathedral Rock, most of which Leann and Ramón could view from Glacier Point high above the valley floor.[19] They could agree with author Ralph Waldo Emerson who later observed: "This valley is the only place that comes up to the brag about it and exceeds it."[70] After a day of sightseeing, they returned to the Hutchings Hotel in the valley, where the amenities did not "come up to" the views, but they enjoyed an excellent dinner of broiled fresh trout, venison, and strawberries from the hotel garden.

Yosemite was becoming one of America's foremost tourist attractions, popularized in paintings by Albert Bierstadt, who first visited the valley in 1863. Some believed that Yosemite surpassed Niagara Falls as the nation's best display of natural wonder, particularly, as novelist Henry James noted, the natural attraction of Niagara Falls was being stifled by commercialism.[20]

Leaving Yosemite the Clementes took the same stage route down the central valley as they had twenty years earlier. They noticed that small farms were beginning to replace the large cattle ranches. At the lower end of the San Joaquin valley were two new stage stations, one at Los Alamitos where the Tejon creek disappears into the sand, and the other about four miles from the foot of Grapevine Canyon, called Rose's Station, known to have been a stopping place for local bandits such as Joaquin Murieta and "Three-fingered Jack."[21]

Continuing on the southwesterly route to Los Angeles, they found on arrival that the city had changed considerably since their last visit. The great drought of 1862 had practically wiped out the old cattle ranches, but the wealth and power of the former Mexican land owners—Pico, Figueroa, Sepulveda, and others, was recalled by the names of streets and locales in southern California. Los Angeles was beginning to look more like an American city and less like a

Mexican pueblo. This was due largely to the efforts of transplanted Americans like Abel Stearns and Phineas Banning, who had settled into the California scene and lifestyle but also contributed their own Yankee ingenuity to further the area's growth. In addition to El Palacio, built by Abel Stearns for his fourteen-year-old bride Arcadia Bandini in 1829, there was the Arcadia business block, completed in 1858 at a cost of $85,000—two-story brick with iron doors, balconies, and shutters.

There was a railroad south to the port of San Pedro and vaqueros from the adjacent ranchos Los Cerritos and Los Alamitos would race their horses against the locomotives.[75] Phineas Banning, from Delaware, had founded the nearby settlement of Wilmington (named after his home town) where he built a pier and a carriage factory and was becoming a factor in both land and sea aspects of the growing transportation industry in California.[86]

While in Los Angeles, the Clementes stayed at the Pico House at 430 North Main Street, a hotel built in 1869 by Pio Pico, the last Mexican governor of California.[24] The three-story romanesque style hotel, with its multiple arches facing the sidewalk, had become popular because of its fine cuisine and guest rooms with hot baths and gas lights. The lobby, with its central fountain surrounded by fresh flowers and cages of singing birds, was a welcome respite to travellers after crossing the Mojave desert or coming down the central valley. The Pico House was a definite improvement over the Bella Union, in which the Clementes stayed on their last visit.

Los Angeles had a reputation for lawlessness and was trying to soften its image as "the toughest town in the state" with help from the *Evening Express*, the *Southern Californian* (the two major newspapers) and *La Estrella de Los Angeles*, a four-page weekly half in Spanish and half in English.[23]

Adding to the problem was the accidental killing of an American by a Chinaman, which led to looting and pillaging of the Los Angeles Chinatown, and the lynching of nineteen Chinese.[22] There were also many lesser levels of unseemly behavior. On Sunday morning Ramón noticed citizens on their way to mass carrying game cocks, and there was a cock-fight ring behind the church presided over by the priest himself.[61]

On Monday morning, Ramón opened an account at the new Farmers and Merchants Bank which would provide them greater financial flexibility on their now frequent visits to California and would be a necessity if they decided to move out here permanently.

They considered several locations in southern California for permanent residence, but could not convince themselves to make the commitment. Perhaps it was due to the nature of Ramón's business there—trying to settle his mother's estate matters and becoming unpleasantly involved with other family members and their representatives. This situation was not conducive to a lengthy visit, much less a permanent stay, so they decided to leave as soon as business could be brought to a logical interim conclusion. With mixed feelings, they returned to San Francisco, this time by ship up the coast, and boarded the eastbound train to further deliberate their future.

They returned to find Washington in the midst of a gigantic public works program designed to remove the stigma described earlier by Horace Greeley and make it worthy of being the nation's capital. President Grant had appointed his friend and business associate Alexander Shepherd to the Board of Public Works, and Shepherd was personally responsible for much of the city's physical improvement but at great cost to the taxpayers. He was a dynamic and controversial figure, opposed by civic leaders such as Riggs and Corcoran and by most property owners, but supported by the Freedmen's Bureau, General Howard (founder of Howard University), and of course President Grant. Shepherd's association with land speculators and paving companies, directorships in streetcar companies, and ownership of a large plumbing firm were considered by some to present a conflict of interest. He had a country estate on 300 acres in the upper northwest corner of the territory and an elegant mansion on Farragut Square, in which he gave large parties that Congressional leaders refused to attend.[82]

While reluctant to provide Federal funds to the Territory of Columbia, Congress had authorized a multi-million dollar edifice to contain the State, War, and Navy Departments, to be located just west of the White House. The architect, Alfred Mullet, designed a highly ornate building based on the "Nouveau Louvre" in Paris, which had been designed in the 1850s under direction of Louis Napoleon.

The new State, War, and Navy building took seventeen years to complete and became highly controversial for its alleged fiscal and aesthetic extravagance. Mr. Mullett, who had designed other public buildings in New York, Boston, Cincinnati, St. Louis, and Philadelphia, quit his job before the building was completed. Washington was shocked to learn later that he had committed suicide—a sad commentary on the exigencies of contemporary life in the public eye.[25]

The fact that funds were approved for the building helped allay fears that the nation's capital would be moved to another city, such as St. Louis, which had been proposed as an alternative. This plus Shepherd's public works program fueled a real estate boom that brought even California and Nevada mine operators to Washington for real estate investment.

In 1872 the Clementes welcomed repeal of the income tax which began ten years earlier to finance the Civil War. When signed into law by Lincoln in 1862, it was the first income tax to be collected by the United States government. A tax of 3 percent was levied on incomes over $600 and 5 percent on incomes of $10,000 or more. The newly established Bureau of Internal Revenue placed notices in newspapers and public places, and most people paid their share willingly as long as the Civil War lasted. The few who didn't received visits from Bureau representatives. After the 1872 repeal, other income tax bills were introduced but none were successful for the rest of the century.[26]

The DC territorial government under Governor Cooke was now in full swing and making pronouncements that confirmed, in Ramón's mind, the wisdom of his earlier decision to leave government service. The territorial government was growing rapidly at taxpayers' expense, without Federal funds. Congress had developed a distaste for the local government and for the citizenry as well, identifying all, however unjustly, with "carpetbaggers," the newly rich and the ostentatious.

The term "carpetbagger" was commonly used to describe northerners who went south after the Civil War and joined with poor white southerners known as "scalawags" for political and financial advantage contrary to Lincoln's intended fair treatment of the defeated Confederacy.[36] The term had a different meaning when it originated in the period between the expiration of the charter of the Second Bank of the United States in 1836 and the introduction of government-issued paper currency in 1861. During the intervening years, a large number of small banks were organized primarily to issue their own paper currency. Such banks were frequently located in out-of-the-way, hard to reach places. Keeping their currency in circulation required hiring men to carry large quantities of banknotes to sometimes distant locales to purchase farm commodities which were resold for cash. These men, who used carpet bags to carry huge amounts of sometimes nearly worthless paper, became known as "carpetbaggers." The term was later used by political satirist

Thomas Nast in a caricature of a Union General, who went south after the war, giving the term its new meaning.[27]

The term "carpetbagger" was also associated with the infamous Ku Klux Klan (KKK), long a symbol of bigotry and hate. Not always such, it began as an heroic band fighting to free the south from the oppressive rule of Republican "carpetbaggers" and "scalawags," who maintained their power by controlling negro votes. As an example, when elections were held in the south, where there was a separate ballot for each candidate, and most negroes could not read the labels on the separate boxes, they were trained in advance to recognize the boxes of Republican candidates by their position in the line of boxes. Though considered heros in the south, like the vigilantes in lawless western towns, the KKK was outlawed by the Federal Government, went underground, and operated in secrecy.[28]

Ramón read Clarence King's book *Mountaineering*, published in 1872, on completion of his work on the 40th Parallel Survey. The book was praised as surpassing anything done so far in later-day western exploration, but also was criticized as containing exaggerations and too much local color. Ramón enjoyed it as a treatise on geology as well as having much to do with his native California, which the author obviously loved.[68]

The following year King achieved acclaim for his detective work in exposing the "Great Diamond Hoax," which began when two men "salted" an unidentified western mesa with loose diamonds and convinced a group of investors the land was worth $600,000. After the men disappeared with the money, King was called upon to utilize his geographical and geological expertise to locate the mesa in which the diamonds were located. By determining its fraudulent nature, he was credited with saving other investors from further losses.[81] Ramón was dogged by the thought that a man of lesser reputation might have been suspected of complicity in the hoax.

The panic of 1873 and the depression that followed had far-reaching consequences. Partly responsible was Philadelphia banker Jay Cooke's failed attempt to extend the Northern Pacific Railroad across the Dakotas and Minnesota for a second route to the Pacific, which caused his bank to close and others to do likewise. Many railroads defaulted on their bonds and one, the Erie, was forced into receivership.[29]

At the beginning of the 1873 depression, the First National Bank of Washington closed, and Governor Henry Cooke resigned as head of the DC government. To make matters worse, he was replaced as governor by Alexander Shepherd, derisively called "asphalt Shepherd" because of suspected personal gain from vast sums spent on improvements to the capital city during his tenure.[30]

The anger of property owners and taxpayers of the District led to a Congressional investigation of the territorial government, culminating in abolition of the territorial system and its replacement with a Board of District Commissioners answerable to Congress. President Grant nominated Alexander Shepherd to the Board but the Senate rejected the nomination.[82] The U.S. Government once again was responsible for District finances, which brought a measure of stability back to Washington and was a positive factor in the Clementes's consideration of where to live permanently.

About this time they received news of having been disinherited from the will of Ramón's deceased aunt, Lolita Calderon, who had always been loving and seemingly understanding but apparently also manipulable by others. It was not for financial reasons the Clementes were concerned, but because they had done their best to maintain good relations in face of damaging remarks by Doña Caterina and felt that aunt Lolita might not have been affected by such remarks unless someone had influenced her with false information so others could divide what would have been Ramón's share of her estate.

Ramón decided to contest his aunt's will, if only to clear what appeared to be a blot on his and Leann's names. This meant retaining a lawyer in California, where the case would be heard—not an easy matter from such a distance. Ramón had little appetite for further involvement with family members, even on an adversarial basis, but proceeded anyway albeit very slowly given the distance and normally sluggish pace of the legal system, which apparently was gauged so as to increase the lawyers' fees.

It was largely because of this development in their lives that the Clementes became aware of the notoriety surrounding the legal difficulties of multi-millionaire heiress Hetty Green. She had contested her aunt's will in 1865 in Massachusetts, only to have the case finally dismissed in 1870 after a series of bitter court battles and acrimonious exchanges between Mrs. Green and her relatives, which benefitted only the lawyers, trustees, and the newspaper circulation.[31]

After a while, Leann and Ramón found themselves sharing Mrs. Green's distaste for lawyers, judges, executors, trustees, and anyone connected with them. Ironically Ramón had to undertake the role of trustee for a brief period and tried to do the best job he could under the circumstances, for all concerned. The will contest was finally dismissed for lack of conclusive evidence, resulting in added expense and stress for the Clementes, which may have contributed to a partial blindness in Ramón's right eye that occurred at this time.

After a series of unsuccessful treatments and recurring infections, the Clementes decided, on advice from Ramón's physician, to move at least temporarily to a drier climate for his speedier recovery. Their plans were facilitated by news of the completion in 1876 of the Southern Pacific Railroad connection between San Francisco and Los Angeles, which would eliminate the need for a bumpy stagecoach trip or damp sea voyage.

Another reason for going west was to search further for a permanent home and perhaps stay there until they found it. They reasoned that if they travelled west every time a drier, more temperate climate was needed, they may as well be there all the time. This required maintaining the flat in Washington as a place to come back to if they were unsuccessful, and to hold their furniture and personal belongings until a new place could be found. It created added expense and worry but seemed necessary under the circumstances.

Once again they headed west through Chicago, Omaha, and Salt Lake City, viewing what had now become familiar scenes. Most of it was still exciting to them but crossing the plains of Nebraska was least exciting of all. It held a certain fascination, however, perhaps best described in Robert Louis Stevenson's later account of his own cross-country train trip. He wrote: "We were at sea—there is no other adequate expression—on the plains of Nebraska...a world almost without a feature, an empty sky, an empty earth; front and back the line of railway stretched from horizon to horizon, like a cue across a billiard board; on either hand a green plain ran till it touched the skirts of heaven. Now and again we might perceive a few dots beside the railroad which grew more and more distinct as we drew nearer, till they turned into wooden cabins, then they dwindled and dwindled in our wake until they melted into their surroundings, and we were once more alone on the billiard board. The train toiled over this infinity like a snail; and being the one thing moving, it was wonderful what huge proportions it began to assume. It seemed miles in length and either end of it within but a step of the horizon."[32]

On reading these lines from Stevenson's *Across the Plains*, Ramón at first felt resentment at the implied criticism by a foreigner of this section of his adopted country as boring and featureless. He thought its thirty-seventh state deserved better treatment as being one of the sources of America's strong pioneer spirit that turned the western plains into a supplier of food for the United States and foreigners alike. He thought that Stevenson, having crossed the Atlantic in cramped steerage accommodations, could have been more appreciative of the "wide open spaces," and that had he not been travelling west to improve his ill health and also chasing after a California divorcee he met in France[71] he might have viewed Nebraska in a better light.

During this cross-country trip, the Clementes could see that farmers were replacing cattlemen on the western plains, and space available for cowboys as well as for Indians was considerably diminished. Ramón recalled his less peaceful trip with Fremont's 1844 expedition when they crossed the Kansas plains about two hundred miles further south. This time they hadn't the Indians to contend with and there were fewer buffalos to be seen.

Leaving Nebraska the train ascended from the Laramie plains through mineral lands, to the Devil's Gate bridge near Medicine Bow, and shortly thereafter passengers viewed the majestic buttes along the way to Green River. Then they crossed the Wasatch range to Salt Lake City, passed through the deserts of Utah and Nevada, and crossed the Sierra Nevada range to arrive in San Francisco.

They checked into the elegant new Palace Hotel, said to be the world's largest, and enjoyed an excellent evening meal in its magnificent dining room. The next morning Ramón headed for the Wells Fargo Bank to obtain funds as before and found them in the process of moving to a new location at Sansome and Halleck Streets. He was interested to see that they still had the huge scales for weighing gold dust brought in by miners for conversion into bullion and coins. Afterwards he and Leann shopped at Gump's for unusual Asian art objects to take home as gifts then had lunch at the same Chinese restaurant at which they ate on their last visit.

Their meanderings were facilitated by the newly installed mechanical cable cars, designed by Andrew Halliday to negotiate the city's steep hills, and replacing the horse drawn cars.[69] In the afternoon they visited the Mission San Francisco de Assis, also called Mission Dolores, which was celebrating the centennial of its founding by Fra. Junipero Serra as the sixth of the California missions. Then they went to Washington Square and enjoyed a delightful dinner at a small Italian restaurant before returning to the Palace.

The following day they boarded the Southern Pacific to Los Angeles. The route traversed the central San Joaquin valley, where Ramón and Leann could see its transformation from a land of cattle ranches, as it was on their first visit, to becoming one of the world's richest agricultural areas.

They found Los Angeles bursting with added population since their previous trip, partly due to New York journalist Charles Nordhoff's articles and later his book titled *California: For Health, Pleasure and Residence.* Nordhoff had been sent west by the *New York Herald*, with transportation provided by the Southern Pacific Railroad, to write articles on California. He was particularly impressed by the Ojai valley a few miles inland from Ventura, and by the Tejon Ranch, then owned by Edward Beale. His enthusiasm over the healthy climate and other aspects of California life, as expressed in his book and news articles, encouraged many easterners to head west.[33]

Also attracting immigrants was the prospect of profits from cultivation of citrus trees which Ramón recalled were grown on mission lands near his childhood home. Commercial orange growing, which began in the 1840s, expanded in the 1870s from Los Angeles to Riverside, and from Santa Barbara to San Juan Capistrano, giving indications of becoming a significant cash crop for California. In 1873 the navel variety from Brazil via Washington DC was introduced, which ripened in winter and was grown inland. Later there came from a Long Island, New York, nursery the Valencia-type that ripened in summer and prospered in coastal regions.[77]

New residential and commercial subdivisions were being laid out from the coastal community of Santa Monica to San Bernardino seventy-five miles inland, with real estate agents active everywhere in between. Most of the land was now owned by large corporations and a few private individuals, with small farms mostly tenant operated. "Lucky Jim" Baldwin, who made a fortune speculating in silver mining stocks, had acquired Rancho Santa Anita which bore extensive orange groves.[83] Baldwin expanded it to 54,000 acres by subsequent acquisitions and raised sheep, dairy cows and a variety of agricultural crops, but in the old California tradition he also bred race horses.[79] To his credit, Baldwin maintained Hugo Reid's original tile-roofed adobe casa near his own more ornate residence, which was built in Queen Anne style with marble floors and stained-glass windows.[84]

Los Angeles itself was now much like other American cities, with brick replacing adobe, paved streets, horse drawn streetcars, gas lights, a lending library, and a 400-seat theater. The Los Angeles High School, founded in 1873, would have been helpful to Ramón about forty years earlier in preparing him for Yale, instead of his relying on tutors from Mission San Gabriel.

Although they were excited by all these new developments, the Clementes' first priority was Ramón's recuperation before getting down to serious home-hunting. It was during this time that Mark Twain's *Tom Sawyer* came out, which Leann read aloud, transporting her back to her childhood by the Mississippi River. Leann also read the newspaper account of the loss of the clipper ship Flying Cloud, which was wrecked off the coast of Newfoundland in 1874.[34] They recalled that the Flying Cloud had set a record for the 14,000 mile voyage from New York to San Francisco around Cape Horn in 1854, which was followed by a series of rapid developments in coast-to-coast transportation and communications.

Another clipper ship, the Comet, soon beat the Flying Cloud's record by thirteen days, but it still wasn't fast enough to meet the demand for speedier mail service. Congress provided subsidies for the Pacific Mail Steamship Company to transport mail and passengers to and from the west coast and the Isthmus of Panama; and for the United States Mail Steamship Company between the east coast and the Gulf of Mexico. Crossing the Isthmus was a nine-day trip by mule train. With completion of the trans-isthmian Panama Railroad in 1855, the overland portion was reduced to a few hours and the total time from New York to California was cut to thirty days. This was still not considered fast enough, leading the Post Office to contract with the Butterfield Overland Mail Company in 1857 for semi-weekly mail and passenger service by stagecoach from St. Louis to San Francisco, cutting the total cross-country time to twenty-five days. Further pressure for speedier delivery in 1860 brought into being the Pony Express with over one hundred relay stations, which carried the mail from the railhead in St. Joseph, Missouri, across 1,500 miles of the largely uninhabited west to San Francisco in ten days. This made a total of less than two weeks from New York, nearly six times as fast as the clipper ships.

The Pony Express continued for nearly two years until its record time was eclipsed by completion of the transcontinental telegraph in 1861. The need for fast delivery of documentation was met by completion of the first transcontinental railroad in 1869.[35]

While on the west coast, the Clementes read about the "Statue of Liberty" planned for New York Harbor[39] and the 1876 Centennial

Exposition in Philadelphia, with the new Bell telephone on display for the wonderment of visitors. Developments had come so fast during their lifetimes that it was difficult for Leann and Ramón to comprehend how much progress had taken place in America's first century, which the Philadelphia exposition was designed to show. Unfortunately it soon was overshadowed by news of the massacre of General George Custer and his troops at the Little Big Horn on June 25, 1876.

Between keeping up with the news, searching for a suitable home at a reasonable price, and Ramón's recuperation, the Clementes were fully occupied. They didn't need what happened next—a robbery and assault by intruders in their hotel room. On previous occasions they had stayed at the Pico House but this time they had decided to try the newer Lafayette Hotel. They learned later that one of the robbers was a hotel employee who may have obtained a room key through hotel sources. After hitting Ramón on the head with a pistol, they tied up both Leann and Ramón and threatened their lives for an hour while searching for significant valuables without much success. After their assailants left and the Clementes freed themselves, they learned from otherwise uncooperative police that the robbers were part of a group that committed other more violent crimes in the same neighborhood and time period, so they considered themselves fortunate not to have suffered more serious consequences.

A side effect of this occurrence for the Clementes was finding themselves referred to as "elderly" in the police report. Both had identified for so long with younger images of themselves that it was hard to realize their time as "old folks" had arrived.

As a result of the robbery/assault, they were drawn once again into a prolonged legal battle—first in identifying and testifying against the robbers, who threatened to have killed anyone who did so; and then in bringing action against the hotel as being responsible for allowing the crime which took place on their premises and involved at least one of their employees. Three years were spent in pursuing these matters, finding and changing unsatisfactory lawyers, and moving from one place to another, sometimes under assumed names, to avoid detection and attack by the robbers' associates. Finally the Clementes dismissed the case when it appeared there would be no satisfactory outcome but only more time and money spent on lawyers with added stress for themselves.

Getting back to 1878, Ramón and Leann again crossed paths with the Fremonts, who arrived in Los Angeles on the Southern Pacific from San Francisco, after seven days on trains from New York. John Fremont had been appointed Governor of Arizona Territory by President Hayes and on his way there was being honored at parties given by his many California friends. The Clementes attended one such gathering hosted by Robert Baker and his wife Arcadia, widow of Don Abel Stearns and daughter of Juan Bandini, former secretary to Governor Pio Pico. Baker, who owned Rancho San Vicente, was a partner of Edward Beale who now owned the Tejon Ranch.

Ramón felt shy about greeting Fremont, his friend and expedition leader of many years back, who had since become a national celebrity. At age sixty-five with grey hair, Fremont was still lean, erect, and just as open and direct as ever, with an added gregariousness perhaps born of political maneuvering to overcome career obstacles. His wife Jessie, also turning grey, was still attractive and gracious. They greeted the Clementes warmly and invited them to visit as soon as the Fremonts were settled in Prescott, the territorial capital.

One of the prominent citizens attending the gathering was Don Juan Temple, owner of Rancho Los Cerritos south of Los Angeles. A native of Massachusetts, Temple acquired the 200,000 acre property by marriage to Rafaela Cota, who was descended from Manuel Nieto, the original Spanish grantee.[85] Juan Temple had other California property interests and had joined with Ignacio del Valle in selling the Tejon Ranch to Edward Beale for $21,000 in gold coin, which amounted to about $216 an acre. Ramón learned that Baker and Beale planned the railroad to San Pedro making Los Angeles a shipping port. He also learned that Baker built the "Baker block" on Main Street near the Plaza at a cost of $250,000 during the depths of the depression. This block, where the Bakers maintained a luxurious suite, was now a center of business and social activity, replacing worn out adobe and frame shacks on the site.[36]

Edward Beale and his wife Mary were at the party, and when they met the Clementes told them they lived in Washington about half of each year and invited them to visit at their home on Lafayette Square when they returned. Ramón was impressed with General Beale, a bicoastal resident of considerable accomplishment. He appeared to be in his mid-fifties with a strong face and solemn yet attentive expression. His eyes were piercing but with a trace of weariness. His graying hair was thick and well-groomed. He had a flowing moustache and a small Van Dyke beard.

Ramón was already favorably disposed towards Beale based on reading of his encouragement of Indians to develop cooperative farms and ranches on Tejon lands for which he employed former Fremont Scout Alex Godey as Superintendent. The resulting "Sebastian Indian Reserve" was a successful social experiment for which Beale was acclaimed personally as embodying the best of American enterprise merged with old Spanish culture—a welcome exception from the more common exploitation of the native inhabitants.[78]

From Beale's conversation and from what others had said and written about him, Ramón knew him to be a man of great imagination, daring and courage, and he welcomed the Beales' invitation.

For the first time since they had known the Fremonts, Leann and Ramón talked more with their daughter Elizabeth, now in her mid-thirties, who resembled neither parent but had inherited her father's directness and her mother's friendly manner. After the Fremonts left for their new assignment, Elizabeth maintained correspondence with their many friends in California and elsewhere. Her letters described their experiences, such as the trip from Yuma to Prescott by horse-drawn Army ambulances, as there was no rail service beyond the Colorado River. She described the congenial surroundings of their new home in the small frontier town of Prescott which supported a local opera company among other amenities.

There was the related story of the "Battle of Yuma" when the Southern Pacific bested the Texas Pacific which intended to build its railroad through to the west coast and compete with the planned Southern Pacific route. To counter this, Southern Pacific's owner, C.P. Huntington, extended his line from Los Angeles to Yuma where the Texas Pacific planned to cross into California. The Army garrison at Yuma was supposed to provide protection from Apache Indians and also to keep out railroad companies that hadn't received a government land grant. The Southern Pacific crew proposed sharing a supply of whiskey with the cavalry troopers, which led to several days of revelry, allowing time for the Southern Pacific work force to complete a wooden bridge across the Colorado River and establish a beachhead in Arizona. Their presence was supported by the Arizona legislature, which wanted railroad service in the area sooner than the Texas Pacific would provide. With persuasion from Huntington, President Hayes authorized the Southern Pacific access to Arizona October 9, 1877.[37]

Elizabeth Fremont wrote about how she enjoyed horseback riding in Arizona as she had when the Fremonts lived in northern California. She suggested their guests might enjoy riding around Prescott, where the Fremonts had access to Army stables, and repeated her parents' invitation for the Clementes to visit. This appealed particularly to Ramón, who hadn't been riding much since selling Cristobal after the Fremont expedition arrived in St. Louis in 1844.

The Clementes accepted the invitation, deciding to visit Prescott before returning to Washington. Ramón's recuperation was complete, and they had been unsuccessful in finding a suitable home. Further, they received notice that the building where they had been renting in Washington was going to be sold, so they had to return to relocate.

The Clementes' trip to Prescott took less time than in 1878 when the Fremonts made the 200-mile trek from Yuma by horse drawn ambulance, which took nearly a week. The Clementes took the Southern Pacific which was now completed past Yuma to Tucson.[17] They got off at Gila Bend, about 120 miles east of Yuma from where the stagecoach ride to Prescott was less than 150 miles, and took three days, with overnight stops at places not much more civilized than those where the Fremonts had camped two years before.

Tension mounted as they neared Wickenburg, where the 1873 stagecoach massacre by Apache Indians took place. Although that was seven years ago, there had been enough similar incidents in the general area since then to keep the memory alive. Realizing that worry would not help, they determined to enjoy the scenery. The sight of yucca trees, cactus, black rock, and desert flowers was fascinating to Leann and reminded Ramón of April 1844, when he set forth on the Mojave desert with the Fremont expedition. By comparison the Clementes' arrival in Prescott was like returning to civilization.

The Fremont home was simple but comfortable by frontier standards. Its walls were solid planks cut from nearby pine and juniper trees, covered with cotton sheets.[38] All necessities were provided, including excellent food prepared by their Chinese cook. Particularly enjoyable was the crisp mountain air, the sight and scent of pine and juniper trees on surrounding hills, the masses of wild flowers dotting the hillsides after the rainy season, and the gorgeous sunsets.

Since the Fremonts' arrival two years before, there had been established two churches, Catholic and Methodist, and a hospital run by the Sisters of St. Joseph, who had come from St. Louis at the urging of Jessie Fremont.[21] The Fremonts gave a party at which the Clementes met many Fremont friends and associates, including E.P. Clark; M.H. Sherman; and his sister, Lucy. Clark had travelled by covered wagon from Missouri to Prescott in 1867, where he met and went into business with Sherman, who came west from Vermont. Both men were now on Governor Fremont's staff and Clark was engaged to Lucy Sherman, who had arrived recently via the same Cape Horn route travelled by Ramón many years before. The Clementes were invited to the Clark-Sherman wedding in April 1880, which they attended before returning to Washington.[89]

They had planned to return on the new Santa Fe Railroad which projected its westward route to pass about one hundred miles north of Prescott but was not yet complete west of Albuquerque. The Santa Fe was delayed by a dispute with the Denver and Rio Grande Railroad regarding the route through southeast Colorado. The Santa Fe hired Dodge City Marshall Bat Masterson to protect its property at Pueblo, Colorado, but the Denver and Rio Grande paid him more and took over the Santa Fe roundhouse. The dispute was settled peaceably in February 1880, with the Santa Fe allowed to continue its route to the west coast while the DRG expanded locally in Colorado.[39]

Because of this delay, the Clementes had to return the way they had come, by stagecoach to Gila Bend where they took the Southern Pacific back to Los Angeles, then north to San Francisco from where they would head east.

As the train approached San Francisco, they learned from fellow passengers about the Del Monte Hotel, being built by the Southern Pacific as a luxury resort near the ocean at Monterey, to attract business for trains that were only partly full.[40] Ramón thought what a change this was from the early Spanish/Mexican days of his youth, when Monterey was the principal settlement in Alta California and the presidio its main attraction. They were tempted to visit the site of the new hotel and delay their departure from California a while longer, but reason prevailed and they continued reluctantly on their journey east.

By this time the passenger accommodations on railroads, particularly transcontinental, had become not only safer and more comfortable, but in some cases quite luxurious. Technical improvements such as the Westinghouse air brake brought added safety and comfort, and passengers enjoyed such amenities as steam heat, reclining chairs, and dining saloons which made the trip more pleasant and eliminated the need to stop for meals, which usually were bad and, perhaps appropriately, there was little time to eat them.

Back in Washington, the Clementes concentrated first on finding a place to move. The summer of 1880 was unusually hot, and Leann suffered badly from heat exhaustion which limited her activity considerably. Their spirits rose when they looked at Washington's first "luxury" apartment building—the Portland Flats built in 1879. The six-story structure at 14th and Vermont was described as "an ocean liner sailing into Thomas Circle" because of its long triangular shape with the apex pointing at the circle. All units had twelve foot ceilings, parlor, and private bath. Sizes ranged from one to three bedrooms or "chambers." The largest units also had a dining room, kitchen, pantry, and maid's room. The building had an elevator, a central steam heating plant, and a telephone in every unit connecting to the public dining room, the janitor's room, and also to the elevator for some purpose the Clementes did not fully comprehend. In addition to the public dining room on the ground floor there was a drug store off the lobby and two iron staircases lit by skylights for the residents, with a separate staircase for servants. The building was designed by Washington architect Adolph Cluss for developer Edward Weston of New York, where apartment buildings like this had been prevalent for the past decade.

The unit Leann and Ramón liked most had two bedrooms, one of which they planned to use as a work area. It was at the apex of the building with an octagonal-shaped bay and windows overlooking Thomas Circle. The drawbacks were that it cost an unheard of $150 a month, and had no kitchen, so they would have to use the public dining room.

As an alternative, they looked at the Fernando Wood Flats, a four-story structure built the same year by another New York developer at 1418 I Street NW. This building bore the name of the controversial former mayor of New York City who favored secession of the southern states in 1860 and even advocated secession of New York to facilitate trade with the south. But when war came, Fernando Wood patriotically urged people to unite in the Union cause and became active in working for the New York Democratic organization in Congress. The price of units at the Fernando Woods Flats was more reasonable at $50 a month—about what it cost to rent a house in Mount Pleasant.[42] But it didn't compare with the unit the Clementes liked at the Portland Flats which spoiled them for anything else, so they decided to splurge and take it.

Now that they had found such a nice place to live, their urge to move west subsided. Their last trip, while not diminishing their love for the west, had made them appreciate the east even more, particularly Washington DC. They realized the need to establish a home base and felt Washington might be the best place for it. Telephone service had expanded greatly since the first one page listing for the city in 1876. The new Boston Dry Goods Store opened February 25, 1880, providing another source of merchandise for the city. The Washington Monument was finally to be completed after a long delayed Congressional authorization in 1876. There was the newly opened Yale Club of Washington, at which President Hayes attended a dinner in his honor. The capital now had over 140,000 residents, plus 9,000 in Georgetown which was still counted separately.

In 1870 the Washington Canal was filled in just north of Pennsylvania Avenue to form B Street between 7th and 9th Streets NW. The area was designated Market Space and the new Central Market was built there. It was an excellent facility providing good light, space, ventilation, and drainage. Four years later the Northern Liberty Market, with its enormous arched roof, was completed on 5th Street between K and L Streets NW.[43] Both compared favorably with the Georgetown Market at Falls and Potomac Streets built in 1860. Thus the area had several alternatives to the small neighborhood grocery stores with limited inventories, where clerks plucked individual items off shelves for waiting customers or made deliveries by wagon.[44]

The new *Washington Post* newspaper, established in 1877 by Stillson Hutchins of St. Louis, already rivaled the *Evening Star* which was founded in 1854. In 1880 the Post established a Sunday edition, becoming the first to publish seven days a week.[45]

On the negative side, increased population and the aftermath of the 1873 depression brought swarms of beggars and tramps into the District. There were inflated prices, with bread "rising" to 7¢ a loaf. But all things considered, the Clementes were glad to be back in Washington and leaned towards staying.

Pressure from silver mining interests and representatives of western states resulted in the Bland Allison Act of 1878, which restored legal tender status to the silver dollar, missing from U.S. coinage for five years (except for the Trade Dollar that circulated mainly in the orient). The new dollars were designed by George Morgan, formerly of the Royal Mint in London, and the Clementes obtained samples for their collection. The "free silver" movement that brought about the act and these coins resulted from an 1873 law that had eliminated the silver dollar and made the gold dollar the unit of value. This law was called a crime by western silver interests.[20] The free silver advocates contended that foreign interests had manipulated Congress into passing the law without its full impact being known. They claimed the Rothschild syndicate in Europe conspired with certain eastern U.S. bankers to eliminate bi-metalism so as to weaken U.S. economic power and reduce the country to poverty and a state of servitude to England. They believed that unlimited coinage of silver dollars would be beneficial to farmers in particular, and to the economy of the country as a whole.

The opposing gold supporters feared that a return to bi-metalism by the United States unilaterally would drain the country's gold reserve, flood it with silver, and undermine the dollar's purchasing power worldwide. The controversy was evidenced by running arguments in the press. An editorial in the *St. Louis Globe Democrat*, which supported gold coinage, charged that the new silver coins contained less than a dollar's worth of silver and were privately minted with silver bought at lower prices than for U.S. minted coins. A reply from the *Rocky Mountain News*, which supported silver coinage, stated there was no evidence of any such counterfeiting on a large scale, and if there were, it would indicate a strong public demand which should be satisfied by the U.S. Mint.[46]

One of the results of the Clementes' 1877 robbery and assault, wherein Ramón received a concussion from being "pistol-whipped," was a resurgence of his earlier tendency towards nightmares which became more frequent and often featured threatening intruders. Leann and Ramón had become interested in the subject of psychology and welcomed a physician's suggestion to read certain books on the subject of dreams. He recommended three German works: Schubert's *Die Symbolik des Traumes* (1814); Scherner's *Des Lebens des Traumes* (1861); and Volkelt's *Die Traum Phantasie* (1875).[47]

Not being fluent in German, Ramón obtained translations of these works, hoping to get some insight into his problem. It was also a matter of concern to Leann, whose sleep was adversely affected by Ramón's unfortunate affliction. Schubert declared dreams to be "a liberation of the spirit from the power of external nature and a freeing of the soul from the bonds of the senses." Scherner and Volkelt believed more conservatively, that dreams arise essentially from mental forces that have been prevented from expanding freely during the daytime.

With these and other considerations in mind, Ramón began writing down all he could remember of his dreams immediately on awakening, with particular attention to nightmares, of which he kept a more detailed record. Analysis of the information collected in this manner indicated the robbery/assault experience as possibly a major cause of the resurgence of nightmares. It also indicated that some of them could result from earlier fears originating in childhood, that may have been rekindled by the robbery/assault. While such record keeping and analysis did not cure or even significantly diminish the frequency of Ramón's nightmares, it did provide a basis for better understanding of some of the factors that may have caused them. Unfortunately it did not provide much relief for Leann. There were times when Ramón thought he should check in at the National Mental Institution in southeast Washington, and there were times when Leann agreed with him.

The Clementes read of European actress Sarah Bernhardt's American tour and how during the stormy crossing from Le Havre to New York she saved from serious injury an American woman who turned out to be President Lincoln's widow. Interviewed by reporters on her arrival, Bernhardt denied rumors that she slept in a coffin, smoked cigars, and wore men's clothes. Her first performances at New York's Booth Theater were sold out at unheard of prices of $10, $15, and $25 per seat. She was reported to have demanded and received payment of $1,000 in $20 gold pieces, plus 50 percent of the gross over $4,000. She reportedly earned nearly $50,000 in New York, and netted almost $200,000 for the six month tour.[48]

The Smithsonian Institution was now headed by Spencer Baird, replacing Joseph Henry who died in 1878, and Clarence King was appointed to head the newly created U.S. Geological Survey the following year.[63] When Ramón called on Professor Baird to congratulate him on the promotion, Baird suggested the Clementes join the Bairds for dinner some evening when Clarence King would also be their guest. King had planned to resign his position in July of 1880 to go into private practice as a mining consultant, but agreed to stay on a few more months at the request of President Hayes. He had returned from California to Washington in February 1881 to support his agency's upcoming funding request, and was staying with his friends Mr. & Mrs. Henry Adams at their home on 1607 H Street NW.[64]

The Bairds had just returned from a vacation at Woods Hole on Cape Cod in Massachusetts, and their home was not yet ready to receive guests, so they invited the Adams with their houseguest Clarence King and the Clementes to dinner at Harvey's Restaurant on Pennsylvania Avenue. Ramón and Leann enjoyed the urbane and witty Henry Adams and his wife Marian and were impressed by King who was smaller than they expected. He seemed the type of person who enjoyed everything in life as well as sharing his enjoyment with others. Ramón learned he had several things in common with this man, some twenty-three years younger than himself. King's father had died when King was only six years old; and an ancestor on his mother's side was an associate of William the Conqueror. In 1862 King had graduated from Yale—not the college but the Sheffield Scientific School, and had experienced the contempt of academic students who looked down upon "scientifics" as if they did not "belong," much as Ramón had been looked down upon as an Hispanic Catholic by Anglo-Saxon Protestants when he was at Yale College.

King's family were abolitionists and supported Fremont against Buchanan for president in 1856. There was some conflict in his feelings as he also supported Stephen Douglas' concept of "popular sovereignty," allowing states to decide on slavery, but he expected most western emigrants would be northerners and vote against it. He did not fight in the Civil War or even register for the draft, believing literally in the Commandment "Thou shalt not kill," and he suffered some criticism as being a "draft dodger."[65]

On the lighter side, both had enjoyed Offenbach's "Orfée aux Enfers"—King having seen it in New York and the Clementes when they were in Paris. King was particularly fond of California and enjoyed visiting the Spanish missions, all of which endeared him to Ramón. In King's latest publication, *Systematic Geology*, he advanced the theory of evolution based on catastrophic change, drawing from his western explorations, which was of great interest to Ramón as a former student of geology.[66]

One thing on which Ramón did not agree with King was the latter's derogatory description of certain California rural farmers who had migrated from Pike County, Missouri, and were known as "pikers."[73] While they were less successful than some other Americans who came west, King's description of them as "degenerate" and "chronic immigrants" seemed to Ramón unnecessarily harsh, indicating an elitist side to King's nature.

All in all it was a most enjoyable and enlightening evening for the Clementes who were pleased when Mrs. Adams said she would be inviting them one evening to their home, which the Clementes had heard was considered one of the most distinguished literary salons in the country.[67]

With renewed feelings of connection to the Washington scene, the Clementes became more attentive to national politics, which had been a subject of lesser interest on the west coast of California.

The 1880 Presidential election was one of the most bitterly contested in U.S. history. In the Republican primaries, Grant was running for a third term against Blaine, a liberal, making way for the nomination of Garfield, who was a dark horse. Chester Arthur was selected as his running mate to please conservatives. There were no real issues, and Garfield defeated the Democrat Hancock by a small margin in a contest marked by bitter personal attacks on both candidates. An unlikely by-product was the most elaborate inaugural parade Washington had ever seen. It included the Marine Band led by John Philip Sousa and thirty-nine massive inaugural arches erected just for the occasion along the Pennsylvania Avenue parade route.[49]

In July of 1881, the nation was shocked by news of the shooting of President Garfield in Washington by a mentally deranged office-seeker. People all over the country prayed for the president's recovery, but he died in September of that year, succeeded by Vice President Arthur.

The Clementes attended the auction sale of the extensive Randall coin collection in 1882. Ramón got a 1794 half dime for $7 but was outbid on a 1797 half dollar and a 1796 half cent that went for $23.50 and $31 respectively. He learned the price differences were due to rarity—the two highest priced coins having less than 2,000 pieces minted of each, while there were nearly 90,000 dimes minted in the two years 1794–95.[50]

During this period the Clementes expanded their investments in stocks which they began in the 1860s. They had met with some success by avoiding the most speculative offerings and limiting their investments to companies with good financial condition that paid some dividends. They believed in as much diversification as possible within funds available, preferring to have a few shares of more companies than more shares in fewer companies.

These guidelines were established as protection against "robber barons" such as Jim Fisk and Jay Gould, noted for manipulating securities and their effort to corner the gold market, culminating in the disastrous "Black Friday" September 24, 1869. Fisk, known as

Wall Street's "Great Bear," had previously gained and lost two fortunes during the Civil War years—first when Jordan Marsh, the Boston dry goods firm, employed him to represent them in Washington. Fisk was so successful in selling blankets to the Union Army that he convinced Jordan Marsh to acquire mills to manufacture their own cloth at greater profit, using cotton he bought from sections of the south under Union occupation. His cotton fortune was lost before the war was over. Fisk formed a group in 1865 to sell confederate bonds abroad at a discount before news of the confederate defeat was received, giving him a second fortune which was lost again on Wall Street.

By this time Fisk had become associated with New York financier Jay Gould, who was forming a group, including President Grant's brother-in-law Abel Corbin, to control the gold market. Hesitant at first, Fisk joined the group thinking there would be no Federal intervention. When Gould discovered Corbin had no governmental influence, he began selling his recently acquired gold contracts but neglected to notify Fisk of the change in plans, so Fisk continued buying. Fisk eventually saved most of his third fortune by repudiating his gold contracts under protection of friendly judges who benefitted from his largesse.[51]

Fisk's notoriety was based not only on what he did but how he did it—largely through self-publicity, which he learned after joining the circus at age fifteen, and later adapted to a wide range of management and marketing activities. He acquired the title of Colonel by paying the debts of the New York State National Guard, buying their uniforms and recruiting for them an award-winning marching band. He became an "admiral" by purchasing a steamship company. In 1869 Fisk and Gould bought Pike's Opera House at 23rd Street and 8th Avenue in New York City, and renamed it "Grand Opera House." They used the top floors as offices for the Erie Railroad in which they owned controlling interest, while continuing to offer public entertainment on the floors below. In the basement was a printing press convenient for issuing more stock, or "stock-watering" as it became known.[52]

Fisk's flamboyance made him a natural target for newspaper columnists and illustrators such as Thomas Nast. The conservative appearing Jay Gould who was Fisk's partner in several ventures of dubious legality received less attention, although the newspapers referred to him as "the Mephistopheles of Wall Street." Gould was a slight, quiet man with a happy home life, apparently unconcerned about his poor public image. Though widely depicted as a greedy pirate, he performed many charitable acts for which he seldom received recognition.[53]

The exploits of Fisk and Gould typified the American drive for wealth Ramón had observed during his college days. Since then he had noted the increasingly large fortunes left by men of wealth. John Jacob Astor, "czar" of the fur trade, set the pace for fortune accumulation when he died in 1848 leaving an estate worth $20 million—a record at the time.[54] When N.Y. financier Cornelius "Commodore" Vanderbilt died in 1877 he left $105 million, reflecting a substantial rate of increase over the thirty year period.[55]

Returning to the Clementes' investment programs, they agreed initially on a division of effort whereby Ramón would concentrate on a conservative income-producing portfolio, and Leann would take chances on speculative issues having more appreciation potential than current income. Accordingly Ramón accumulated shares in bank, insurance, and utility companies such as Chemical and City Banks in New York, Cincinnati Gas, and Travellers Insurance. Leann acquired shares of industrial companies such as Singer Sewing Machine and Stanley Works, along with Washington Gas Light and Boatmen's Bank in St. Louis for some income. In 1881 they diversified further, with Ramón acquiring shares of American Express, Chase Bank of New York, and Security Bank of Los Angeles; while Leann bought shares of American Telephone, Corning Glass, and Standard Oil. They avoided most railroad stocks as being excessively volatile and subject to manipulation by the likes of the aforementioned "robber barons."

Ramón could not resist taking a chance on a gold-mining issue that actually turned out to be a good long-time performer. After General George Custer's 1874 Indian hunting expedition into the Black Hills of South Dakota, gold miners followed the soldiers into that area. Two miners named Fred and Joseph Manuel hit pay-dirt and named their find "Homestake." Later some San Francisco investors led by George Hearst, purchased claims in the area including the Homestake, for $70,000. To offset their costs, this group started selling shares on the New York stock market in 1879.[56] Ramón bought a few shares whenever the market dipped and, except for temporary downs, it was never a disappointment.

Although they used a broker to buy and sell stocks of their own choosing, Leann and Ramón relied on their own judgement in selecting issues to be bought and sold rather than stockbrokers or other "experts" who usually were more interested in making money for themselves.

The Clementes continuously devised new systems for managing their current investments and "stalking" new ones. Leann was most active in this regard, and planned a guide for amateur investors such as themselves, including guidelines for buying and selling stock and forms for recording stock data which she had developed and found practical for her own use. As conditions constantly changed, with repeated cycles of panic/depression followed by upswings, whatever guidelines were set down needed constant revision. Realizing the need for more lasting guidelines, Leann's goal became development of a master cycle chart for investment decisions.

When travelling Leann packed into a small "office bag" all the books, papers, and office supplies needed to keep up with investment matters, so their hotel room took on the aspect of a business office. Whenever concern was expressed by housekeeping personnel, who preferred to have "everyone out" when they were ready to clean the room, Leann dealt with it by conversing on other subjects, thereby learning more about local goings-on while diverting the housekeeping complaint.

One such travelling time occurred when periodic infections in Ramón's right eye reached a point where an operation was advised, which he underwent reluctantly. During his recuperation, Leann began to have pains in one of her wisdom teeth. Dr. Hoffer, their Georgetown neighbor, was no longer there and the only other dentist in whom Leann had confidence was in California. So once again they headed west—Ramón to convalesce in the dryer climate and Leann for dental needs.

This time they took the Santa Fe railroad which now connected with the Southern Pacific at Deming, New Mexico, completing the new transcontinental link. The route passed through areas Leann hadn't seen and some which Ramón recalled from the 1844 trip with Fremont's expedition.

The trip across Kansas and southeast Colorado closely paralleled the Old Spanish Trail but was comfortable and less hazardous. The discovery of gold in 1858, and of silver in 1864, had contributed much to the growth of Colorado and Denver City which became its capital when statehood was achieved in 1876. Ramón thought how close they had been to these gold and silver mines when the Fremont party passed through the Middle and South Parks along the branches of the upper Arkansas River nearly forty years before.

At La Junta, Colorado, the Santa Fe tracks passed near Bent's Fort, at the junction of the old Navajo and Santa Fe trails, where Kit Carson had made his headquarters as a hunter and scout. Ramón recalled the warm welcome accorded the Fremont party's arrival at Bent's Fort when they descended from the mountains on July 1, 1844, and how the group seemed considerably diminished after Kit Carson remained at Bent's Fort, and the others went on without him. A few miles further south the Santa Fe route passed through Trinidad, Colorado, a supply center frequently visited by Carson in preparing for the many expeditions in which he served.

Newspapers at La Junta carried the story of a man being tried for cannibalism in the community of Lake City. The accused, Alfred Packer, was born in Pennsylvania in 1842, discharged from the Army in 1862 because of epilepsy then migrated west to become a prospector. In December 1873 he left Bingham Canyon in Utah Territory with a group of twenty men and emerged alone from the San Juan mountains of southwest Colorado in April 1874. Subsequent investigation found evidence of consumed human bodies along the route, corroborating his initially unbelievable confession. Packer escaped from custody but was recaptured later in Wyoming and returned to Colorado where he was sentenced to hang, then granted a stay by the Colorado Supreme Court. The Clementes learned later that the court reversed Packer's murder conviction and sentenced him to forty years for manslaughter.[57]

The trip beyond La Junta was new to Ramón. As they crossed the continental divide, further south than where he had crossed with Fremont, he found the event still awe-inspiring even by rail. After entering the Territory of New Mexico, the train stopped at Albuquerque, then at Tucson in Arizona Territory, where Ramón recalled his mother's family lived near the Presidio at Tubac before moving to California. The route continued a few miles north of the town of Tombstone, where U.S. Marshall Wyatt Earp and his brother Morgan were said to be keeping lawless elements under control since winning the 1881 gun battle at the O.K. Corral. The vast southwest desert stretching the rest of the way to California had now become familiar to the Clementes who enjoyed immensely its dry clean air and majestic scenery.

They also enjoyed eating at the Harvey restaurants along the Santa Fe route. Englishman Fred Harvey first opened a restaurant in St. Louis in 1860 which failed when his partner absconded and joined the south during the Civil War. After working on several railroads,

Harvey became disgusted with the notoriously bad food at stops where passengers were allowed only ten minutes to eat, and unfinished items were saved for the next arrivals. Harvey convinced Santa Fe management they needed better passenger food service and that he could provide it.

The first Harvey restaurant was established at Topeka, Kansas, in 1875, and the system expanded to other locations in 1877. The food, service, and surroundings were such an improvement that passengers were lured from other carriers to the Santa Fe, which became famous for its Harvey House chain and service provided by waitresses called "Harvey Girls." Passengers were allowed twenty-five minutes to eat, which was adequate as the first course was on the table when passengers arrived, and they were asked immediately for their choice of main course which followed shortly thereafter. A typical 75¢ menu included such delicacies as: blue point oysters on shells, filet of whitefish in madeira sauce, young capon with hollandaise sauce, roast sirloin of beef au jus, pork with applesauce, stuffed turkey with cranberry sauce, prairie chicken with currant jelly, sugar cured ham, pickled lamb's tongue, and lobster salad. Customers were welcome to partake of all items but usually limited their choices to only a few. Men were required to wear coats, which was challenged in Oklahoma but upheld by court decision. Once in New Mexico, Fred Harvey personally requested boisterous cowhands to leave, thus assuring proper decorum in his restaurants.[58]

Arriving in Los Angeles, the Clementes decided to stay at the Pico House, which had served them well on previous trips, and they were glad to see its familiar arched arcade and central courtyard with splashing fountain, surrounded by banks of fresh flowers and cages of singing birds.[43] The city now had about sixty thousand population. The *Los Angeles Times*, first published in 1881 when there were only 17,000 inhabitants, was under new management headed by Col. Harrison Gray Otis. The paper was beginning to have labor problems, as unions which were powerful in San Francisco attempted to enter Los Angeles. Otis outspokenly favored the "open shop," incurring the wrath of union leaders who promoted unrest among the workers.

There was news of oil deposits in southern California and drilling had begun near Ventura, north of Los Angeles. Ramón recalled Yale Professor Silliman's articles in the 1850s about the possibility of oil in California and was saddened to learn that three exploration companies backed by Silliman experienced difficulties causing him to lose his position on Yale's faculty.[80]

Los Angeles looked less like a "cowtown," as San Franciscans liked to describe their growing rival to the south. Old adobe and false front frame buildings were being replaced by larger ones of granite and brick, as in the older "Baker block." There was now the "Temple block" with its impressive clock tower, and the Merced Theater was changing its name to "Wood's Opera House."[74]

To attract conservative easterners and midwesterners, promotional literature changed its "semi-tropical" description to the less exotic "Mediterranean," a term used by Fremont in his 1848 *Geographical Memoir Upon Upper California* in which he compared California with Italy.[72]

A throwback to the Spanish/Mexican days was the hanging of bandit Tiburcio Vasquez, who was treated as a celebrity. His words in justification of his actions: *"Yo soy un caballero con el corazon de un caballero"*[76] caught the imagination of those who wanted to preserve the romantic image of early California.

Soon after they arrived, the Clementes read of the murder of a Cahuila Indian near San Bernardino by a white settler named Sam Temple for the allegedly unauthorized use of his horse. The Indian's wife, who was part Spanish/Mexican, was barred as a "squaw" from testifying at the trial in San Jacinto, after which Temple was freed. There was much controversy about the administration of justice in this matter. The following year in Washington, Ramón read with interest the semi-fictitious novel *Ramona*, which dealt with this case, written by Helen Hunt Jackson, a crusader for Indian rights.[59] While Jackson attempted to do for the Indians in *Ramona* what Harriet Beecher Stowe did for negroes in *Uncle Tom's Cabin*, her book was more successful in promoting southern California as a sunny enchanted Spanish/Mediterranean kind of place, especially attractive to easterners and middle-westerners tired of winter snows and industrialized cities.

Los Angeles was booming in the mid 1880s largely because both the Southern Pacific and Santa Fe railroads were competing in rate wars. The Southern Pacific charged $125 fare from the midwest to Los Angeles before the Santa Fe came on the scene. Now rates of both railroads were reduced to $5 and once were as low as $1, to attract passengers from the rival railroad. This brought hordes of people to southern California and much scrounging for places to live.

The price of a building lot in Los Angeles rose from $500 to $5,000, with outlying truck gardens and vineyards rising from $350 to $10,000 an acre. People were paying $20,000 to $50,000 for waterfront lots on a lonely stretch of shore named "Redondo-by-the-Sea." Leann and Ramón visited their favorite beach location at Santa Monica, hoping to find something more reasonable. They pictured a home overlooking the Pacific from atop the palisades, where wooden steps were being constructed to the beachlands below. Disappointed at finding prices just as exorbitant in Santa Monica as elsewhere in southern California, they stopped at Rapp's Saloon to drown their sorrows before returning to Los Angeles.[60]

When the real estate bubble finally burst a few years later, there were networks of roads running into sagebrush, unoccupied hotels on the desert, and many former millionaires who went broke. Perhaps if they had stayed those few more years, the Clementes might have found their dream home at a reduced price compatible with their pocketbook. Having failed thus far, when their dental and recuperative needs were met, they again headed back to Washington, this time they thought for good—for sure!

Illustration No. 27: Nice's Promenade des Anglais (at the turn of the century)

Illustration No. 28: Interior of palace car, Ohio Railway, circa 1875.

Illustration No. 29: Zion's Cooperative Mercantile Institution,
Salt Lake City, 1869

Illustration No. 30: The Great Palace Reclining Chair Route,
Chicago and Alton Railroad

Illustration No. 31: Across the continent on the Pacific Railroad—
Dining Saloon of the Hotel Express Train

Illustration No. 32: The Portland Flats, Washington's first apartment house.

Illustration No. 33: Harvey's Restaurant, Washington, D.C.

Illustration No. 34: Garfield Inaugural Arch at 15th Street and Pennsylvania Avenue NW, 1881

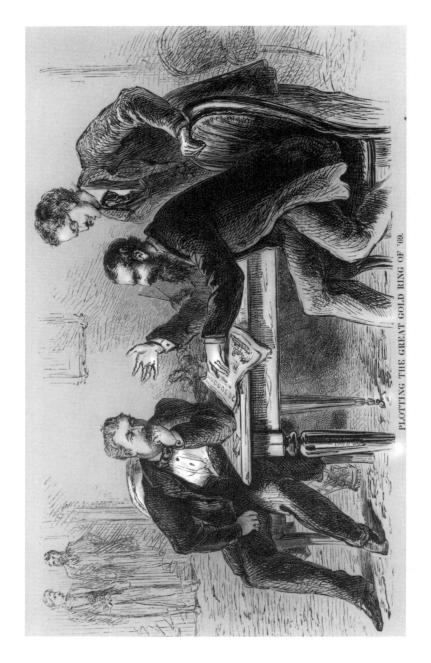

PLOTTING THE GREAT GOLD RING OF '69.

Illustration No. 35: Plotting the Great Gold Ring of 1869, James Fiske (left) and Jay Gould (right).

Illustration No. 36: John C. Fremont in General's uniform.

Illustration No. 37: Jessie B. Fremont (in long dark dress).

Illustration No. 38: Santa Fe Railroad bridge over Canyon Diablo, Arizona.

Illustration No. 39: Harvey House at Syracuse, Kansas
with "Harvey girls" in front.

Illustration No. 40: Pico House, Los Angeles, (right center) opened in 1870.

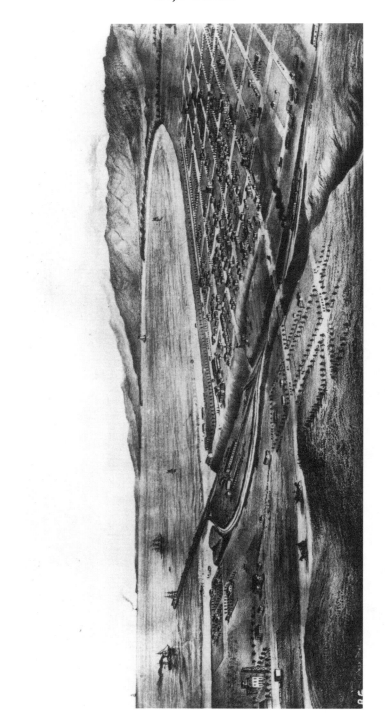

Illustration No. 41: Santa Monica, California and bay, circa 1877.

PART VII
INTO THE HOME STRETCH
(1883–1900)

CHAPTER 14
HOME IN WASHINGTON

After returning to Washington, as if by unspoken agreement, neither Leann nor Ramón mentioned moving to California. They noticed more things they liked about the District of Columbia and began to speak of it more often as their home.

Although they had lived longer in the District than anyplace else, they still felt ties to other parts of the country and lacked a permanent home in spite of all their searching and debating. They liked the Portland Flats, but it was expensive and they missed having their own kitchen. They had not yet unpacked most of their belongings because of uncertainties over their future.

They were curious about the new Richmond Flats recently completed at the corner of 17th and H Streets NW. Patterned after Chateau Chambord in France's Loire Valley, it was more advanced in design and services than the Portland Flats and provided a kitchen for each apartment. On inspection they found the kitchens were not actually in the apartments but were located in communal areas in the attic and basement with dumbwaiters to service each apartment dining room. Further the Richmond Flats contained only ten apartments which were all five bedroom units, really too large and too expensive for the Clementes.

They looked at other rental possibilities. One was the Montrose mansion in upper Georgetown, which had been renovated after falling into disrepair, but it turned out to be more space than the Clementes could use or afford and not big enough to divide economically for use by more than one family.[2] They reconsidered

Leann's earlier idea of forming a syndicate to buy or build a small apartment building, retaining a unit for themselves, or to buy an older home and divide it into apartments. They even considered older homes in outlying areas such as Sandy Spring in Montgomery County, founded by Quakers in 1727. Beautiful and tranquil as was this Maryland countryside, it was too far out for year around living to suit the Clementes, who had become accustomed to city life.

When Robert Baker; his wife, Arcadia; and her mother, Señora Bandini came to Washington for a visit, the Beales gave a party for them at their home, Decatur House on Lafayette Square, to which the Clementes were invited. The stately Federal-style townhouse was built by English architect Benjamin Latrobe for Commodore Stephen Decatur in 1819. It was the first private residence on the square across from the White House. After Decatur's death, it was home to a succession of secretaries of state and foreign ministers until acquired by the Beales.

During the party, Ramón and Leann learned more about Edward Beale's experiences. He had met General Grant during the "gold ride" across Mexico in 1848 and much later was minister to Austria-Hungary for a brief period under then-President Grant. After the Mexican War, Beale had been the first commissioner of Indian Affairs for California and Nevada, the first surveyor general for the same area, brigadier general for the State of California, and commanded the Army's first and only Camel Corps. Beale told how he missed on the California oil boom, having prematurely sold oil properties to a group of San Francisco investors. Apparently he and Baker had some harsh words over the matter, and this visit was a move towards reconciliation.[3]

Of his many activities, Beale recalled with particular pride his recommendation as surveyor general that President Lincoln not issue a Civil War draft proclamation in California, which might have upset a delicate balance and pushed the state into the Confederacy. He was particularly sad that another of his recommendations, the acquisition of Baja California by the U.S., went unheeded.[4]

In the mid-1880s, Washington (like Los Angeles) was experiencing a real estate boom. The Federal Government commitment to share District expenses kept property taxes low, which already were below those of most major cities. Wealthy out-of-towners, lobbyists, members of Congress, and Federal appointees now could afford more easily a part-time residence in the nation's capital.

With the opening of new stores adjacent to the Market Space, Washington was becoming a better place to shop. Saks' and Kann's stores came to Washington from Baltimore. The Saks brothers who started in 1867 in a small building on Market Space, purchased the Avenue House Hotel in 1884 and razed it for their new store building.[5] Woodward and Lothrop, successors to the Boston Dry Goods Store, opened their new building at 11th and F Streets NW on April 4, 1887.[6] It was expected that such new stores would help Washington compete with New York and Philadelphia.

America's rising importance abroad also contributed to Washington's growth. Pressures grew to upgrade foreign missions to Embassy status headed by Ambassadors who would deal directly with the president rather than Ministers who went through the secretary of state.[4] Although Congress had not yet passed the necessary legislation, just the potential of mushrooming foreign embassies added to the real estate boom. The British Legation on Connecticut Avenue, ten blocks from the White House, was considered far out when it first opened in 1874, but in ten years was surrounded by private residences. Further development of embassies and residences was anticipated up 16th Street and along Massachusetts Avenue.

The replacement of gas lamps with electric arc lights in 1882 helped reduce crime and furthered real estate development. Some of the gas lamps were so elegant in design that people hated to see them go, but some electric replacements were just as attractive if not so elaborate.[2] Visitors now compared Washington favorably with New York or Chicago as "a city of rest and peace, although full of commotion and energy," a reversal of earlier criticisms.[7]

Local residents built houses as investments to sell or rent. Rents ranged from $75 to $3,700 a month, averaging about $200. There were over one hundred real estate offices in Washington in 1885 and close to twenty-five hundred building permits were issued in 1887. Ground sold for 48¢ a square foot, which had been 8¢ five years before.[8] Some said Washington was becoming "a city for the rich." Syndicates acquired large chunks of land in Cleveland Heights, Meridian Hill, Kalorama Heights, Washington Heights, and Chevy Chase on the District border.

Cleveland Heights was so named because of the President's fifteen-room "summer cottage" on Woodley Road near Tenleytown Road. A month after his marriage ceremony at the White House, President Cleveland had purchased the former Forrest Hill residence for $21,000 and remodelled it as a country home. It became known as "Red Top" because of its barn-red roof.[9]

Meridian Hill was mostly woods and farmland when Joaquin Miller, the "Poet of the Sierras," built his log cabin there in 1883. Miller, whose real name was Cincinnatus Heine, came from California to seek a job in the Arthur administration and became quite a sight around town in his frock coat, corduroy trousers tucked into high-heeled boots, and large tasselled sombrero over his long blond hair.[10] The area around Miller's cabin became more desirable in 1886 when Missouri Senator Henderson started his home known as "Boundary Castle" at 2200 16th Street. Its cost was estimated at $50,000, and it was the first important residence to be erected on this new subdivision just outside the city limits.[11]

Leann and Ramón looked at all these new areas but were drawn back to Georgetown. Leann read in *Godey's Lady's Book* about "Cooke's Row" of double villas built in 1868 by Henry Cooke a block north of their former home. Cooke had come to Washington as manager of the local office of Jay Cooke and Company, later headed the Georgetown Street Railway and the First National Bank of Washington, then became the first territorial governor of the District of Columbia.[47] The villas he built differed from the flat front federal houses, like the Clementes' first home, in having rich detailing with mansard roofs, prominent bay windows, and many outside surface moldings. Inside they were compact and square with flat walls and high ceilings.[12]

The Clementes looked at these and also at a newer house the Albert Jacksons built in 1880 on Congress Street, described as a late Victorian "cottage." It was too large for the Clementes and had, for their taste, excessive ornamentation exemplified by something resembling lacework around the roof line. They were not disappointed when the owners decided not to sell.[13]

They considered the double houses built in 1880 by Dr. Grafton Tyler on Washington Street between Gay and Dunbarton. The northern half of the Tyler double house was occupied by the present owner, Samuel Wheatley, but the southern half was available. A good example of the new Victorian architecture, it provided more space and versatility than the earlier federal style houses. In Dr. Tyler's words, they were designed to meet "the comfortable living standards of the upper middle class," somewhere between the large detached mansions and the small tenant houses. Leann liked the sliding panel "pocket" doors between the first floor rooms, providing convenient alternatives of more space or more privacy.[14]

Before making a decision the Clementes inspected a row of new Romanesque style houses in the 1700 block of Q Street NW[8] but disliked their lack of individuality, the same reason they passed up the more ostentatious Cooke's Row in Georgetown. They also considered a frame "salt box" house on the northwest edge of Georgetown. Its front entrance was on the side, with side porches off both first and second floors, like Charleston houses Ramón so admired in the 1830s. They decided against it, preferring to have a masonry house. Then they returned to make an offer on the Grafton Tyler house, but someone else had already bought it. This stopped their house search and sent the Clementes back to their apartment at the Portland Flats.

Though still filled with wrapped furniture and packed boxes awaiting shipment to an unknown destination, the apartment was well located, with agreeable neighbors, and the Clementes were used to it. Then the building management announced plans to make certain improvements which could require vacating the apartment temporarily, so they were unable to unpack and use all the beautiful things Leann had collected to make their Georgetown home a showplace. To uplift their spirits, they turned their attention to contemporary art. The work of Frederick Remington, who had begun painting and sculpting images of life in the American west, first caught their attention. They noted that Remington, like many other artists and authors portraying western subjects, were easterners often working in eastern surroundings. An exception was Charles Russell, the "cowboy artist" born in St. Louis, who worked and lived in the west, mostly in Montana.

They noted increasing demand for the work of George Caleb Bingham, whom they had met in St. Louis in 1845. Born near Staunton, Virginia, Bingham grew up in central Missouri and painted portraits of local people. In 1840 he moved to Washington and had a studio in the Capitol basement, where he painted portraits of members of Congress, including one of former President John Quincy Adams. After four years he returned to Missouri, became a member of the state legislature, and also served as State Treasurer and Attorney General. Eventually Bingham devoted full time to painting, portraying the life he was familiar with in scenes such as "The County Election," "Fur Traders Descending the Missouri," and "The Jolly Flatboatmen," which seemed to capture the real spirit of Americans who migrated west.[48]

They also liked the French impressionists who dominated the art scene when the Clementes were in Paris in 1870. Impressionists' works were less sought after in the 1880s, which offered the possibility of obtaining attractive specimens at reduced prices. They were impressed by the new work of Paul Gaugin, a young Paris stockbroker who left work and family in 1885 to paint, and became an accomplished impressionist. Later, dissatisfied with impressionism as being too exact and mechanical, he again broke with his past and moved to Tahiti where he developed a new style, describing it as "a synthesis of what you see and feel." The Clementes particularly liked his "Still Life with Three Puppies," which reminded them of their own family of five in earlier years.

A welcome visitor to Washington was Leann's cousin, Edna, whom she had not seen in many years. Through her the Clementes met John Philip Sousa, a native Washingtonian born of European immigrants, who was commissioned in the Marine Corps in 1880. Leann's cousin first met Sousa when his Chicago theater company came to St. Louis with a touring light opera company before he left to lead the Marine Band. The Clementes went with cousin Edna to a Marine Band concert on the grounds of the Smithsonian Institution, where she introduced them to the maestro who told them he was writing several new marches, and working on a light opera.[15] Leann had begun to feel closer to Edna on this visit and was sorry when it ended.

In the spring and summer of 1883, both the *Washington Post* and *Evening Star* carried articles about the proposed Washington Casino which was expected to become the social and cultural hub of the capital. It was to be located on Connecticut Avenue between K and L Streets and would include an opera house, restaurants, ballroom, and covered tennis courts. Its business form would be a public company which was backed by several prominent citizens, with shares selling at $1,000 each. The Clementes were considering participating but the venture was terminated when funds ran out in 1884.[16]

In October 1884, they attended the wedding of Emily Beale and Cincinnati newspaperman John McLean at Decatur House.[17] At the reception afterwards, Ramón talked with the bride's father about California and Edward Beale's experiences during the six years it took, from 1860 to 1866, for him to acquire the four Mexican land grants which made up the 300,000 acre Tejon Ranch. The Clementes were invited to visit the ranch on their next trip to California.

They learned that the bridegroom, John McLean, came to Washington from Cincinnati, where his father had become wealthy as a steamboat manufacturer and purchased the *Cincinnati Enquirer*. In 1880 John's family moved to Washington, to a home on Jackson Place, where he became acquainted with his neighbor, Emily Beale.[52] Subsequently John leased the house at 1500 I Street, which he later purchased for $127,500 from the estate of Senator Morgan of New York. The house, previously leased to Secretary of State Hamilton Fish, was only a five minute walk across Lafayette Square from the White House. President Grant, who apparently visited often, called the house "one of the finest in Washington," in spite of its rather plain exterior. For ten years after the Beale-McLean wedding there were extensive alterations and additions for the now famous mansion, but as McLean also owned a country estate called "Friendship" on Tenleytown Road, the newly married couple was not wanting for a quiet place to live during the remodelling.[18]

A neighbor of Beale's on Lafayette Square was President John Quincy Adams' grandson Henry Adams and his wife, Marian, whom the Clementes met at dinner with the Bairds and Clarence King in 1880. Adams had written a novel, *Democracy*, dealing with financial and political scandals of the Grant administration, which led to establishment of a literary salon where the Adams entertained at breakfasts and at teas that sometimes lasted until after midnight.[19] Mrs. Adams, also known as "Clover," was an amateur photographer who delighted her guests with pictures as well as conversation. Originally the group consisted of the Adams, the John Hays, Clarence King when he was in town, and whatever guests each of them invited. On one occasion that the Clementes attended, Henry Adams described meeting King in 1871 on a western surveying trip in Estes Park, Colorado where, after a hard and dirty workday, King would appear at the evening campfire immaculately attired in city clothes that his personal valet kept cleaned and pressed daily.

In 1885 Henry Adams and his friend Secretary of State John Hay had H.H. Richardson design and build for them two adjoining Romanesque style houses at 16th and H Streets, directly across the square from the White House. Before it was finished, Clover Adams committed suicide following a period of depression after the death of her father.[49] Henry Adams moved into the new house alone, and after a period of grieving, resumed the literary salons he and his wife had made famous.[20]

Another literary social center the Clementes visited was at 1219 I Street NW, the home of Washington hostess Frances Hodgson Burnett, author of *Little Lord Fauntleroy*, who entertained British author Oscar Wilde during his 1882 tour of the United States.[21]

An unexpected visitor in 1886 was John Barnard, a distant relative from the English branch of Ramón's family. Royal and Helen Clement, the Worcester relatives with whom Ramón spent Thanksgiving in 1836, wrote that their cousin John was coming to Washington from St. Joseph, Missouri, where he was president of that city's new Electric Light and Power Company and had just become president of the Ohio & Mississippi Railroad, so he would be in town on company business.[54]

Leann and Ramón could not ask him to their apartment due to their unsettled circumstances, but they got together for dinner at the Willard Hotel. Ramón and John enjoyed exchanging information concerning their respective branches of the family, and Ramón was fascinated in learning more about this distant relative, only ten years his junior. After graduating from technical school in New York, Barnard worked for the Grand Trunk Railroad in Canada for the next twenty years so was not involved in matters in the U.S. such as politics or the Civil War. Barnard described himself as a "man of peace who tried to make his life work constructive rather than destructive." He also admitted to being a man of strong prejudices with sometimes a hot temper that may have precluded him from certain career advancements.

Barnard returned to the United States to become superintendent of a railway serving northeast Missouri, which later became part of the Chicago, Burlington, and Quincy system.[54] He remained as general manager for the area until assuming his present position. For one trained in engineering, he was all too frequently immersed in legal and financial problems ranging from costly litigation to a $30 reimbursement for the "appraised value of a cow" caught on one of his engine's "cowcatchers."[55]

Ramón and John found they shared many of the same feelings and reactions on a variety of subjects and might have become close friends had their paths run closer together. They did, however, maintain a correspondence after this initial meeting.

Buffalo Bill Cody's Wild West Show was an entertainment the Clementes greatly enjoyed when it came to town. Ramón considered it somewhat exaggerated from what he knew of the American west, but with good entertainment value. Cody was a former Pony Express rider, cavalry scout, and hunter for the Kansas Pacific Railroad crews, until lured by author/promoter Ned Buntline into the entertainment field. Buntline made Cody a national folk hero, first in the 1872 dime novel *Buffalo Bill—King of the Border Men*, previously serialized in a New York weekly; then in a live show "Scouts of the Prairie" featuring Cody and Texas Jack, a lariat expert. Later Cody and Texas Jack left Buntline to form their own show, featuring a display of the scalp of Cheyenne Indian Chief Yellow Hand, whom Cody took time off to kill in revenge for the Chief's part in the 1876 massacre of Custer's forces at the Little Big Horn River.[22]

By 1883 Cody was a skilled showman who brought real Indians and renowned gunfighters like Wild Bill Hickock on stage. It was now called "Buffalo Bill's Wild West Show" and included the "Old Glory Blowout" which became immensely popular. The show capitalized on the romantic image of the "cowboy," a term used by President Chester A. Arthur in his 1881 report to Congress and more widely seen in *Leslie's Illustrated Weekly*. A more utilitarian cowboy image was featured earlier on the Texas $2 bill in 1841, but Ramón felt the concept really evolved from the Spanish vaqueros, who had herded cattle in the southwest since the 16th century.[23] He liked to watch the show's trick riders, ropers, and shooters, and all the Indians who seemed to have forsaken their earlier animosity towards whites in order to partake of the benefits of civilization. The Wild West show drew increased interest and revenues years later when evening performances were made possible by introduction of outdoor electric lighting.

Dining out at restaurants was still a major divertissement for Leann and Ramón, although now more for lunch than dinner. They still frequented the dining room at the Willard Hotel; the Ebbitt House Grill with its elaborate paneled bar; Harvey's Fish House; and Hall's Restaurant on the river front, with its huge painting of a nude Venus over the bar. Harvey's had become a favorite eating place not only with presidents and other Washington notables, but also with such national figures as Ralph Waldo Emerson, Walt Whitman, and New York cartoonist Thomas Nast. Nast was noted for inventing the donkey and the elephant as symbols of the Democrat and Republican parties and the tiger as the symbol for Tammany Hall, the New York Democratic organization. He was a member of the Canvas Back Duck Club, which met monthly at Harvey's, and he drew a caricature of founder George Harvey which hangs in the restaurant.[24]

The Washington Light Infantry built an Armory at 15th and E Streets NW in 1884, which also housed Albaugh's Opera House, the third largest theater in town after Ford's and the National.[25] In addition to theatrical performances, Albaugh's was the scene of many conventions, including the International Council of Women presided over by Susan B. Anthony which Leann attended.

The Washington monument was finally completed, after an interval of eighteen years when funds were not forthcoming from Congress to finish the project.[26] Leann and Ramón went to its formal dedication by President Cleveland on February 21, 1885, but did not take the twelve minute ride to the top of the monument in the new steam elevator that was installed three years later.

In 1886 the Cosmos Club, already located on Lafayette Square, acquired the former home of Dolly Madison at the corner of H Street and Madison Place, giving the Club a larger presence on the east side of the square. The Clementes had followed the activities of this organization since its founding in 1878 by a group of men who went to Colorado to see the eclipse in August of that year. Clarence King was a founding member and met with associates there in 1879 to plan his campaign strategy for nomination as head of the U.S. Geological Survey.[50]

The club was patterned after the London Atheneum, "where learned gentlemen would meet like-minded philosophers." Ramón was surprised to learn in 1882 that the club had to take "stern measures against the use of club sofas for undignified lounging or sleeping," presumably by some of its less gentlemanly members who were unmindful of the social graces.[27]

The Clementes read Stevenson's *The Strange Case of Dr. Jekyll and Mr. Hyde*, in 1886, and noted its difference from some of the Scottish author's other works. In addition to *Across the Plains*, created after travelling across the American continent looking for a healthier climate, he wrote *Treasure Island*, a book for children, inspired by his walks along the California beaches near Monterey.[28]

News of the disastrous earthquake in Charleston, South Carolina, in 1886 evoked memories of Ramón's visit in the 1830s. The earthquake surprised everyone, including Ramón, who was used to such things but usually occurring in California. He wrote to his college friend Hosea Stewart to ask whether his home or any of the beautiful houses along the Battery had sustained damage. Hosea replied his home had been damaged, but not destroyed, and that many of the buildings along Meeting Street, where serious damage had occurred, were being restored with cast iron support rods called "earthquake bolts" as a precaution against any recurrence.[51]

He said further havoc was caused by slates falling from roofs with resulting rain damage to plastered walls and ceilings. Holes were drilled in floors to release water, but replacement of roof slates, mostly imported from England, was delaying the rebuilding process.

In 1887 Ramón was surprised to see the discredited former territorial Governor Shepherd honored with a parade down Pennsylvania Avenue, after having regained his lost fortune through Mexican business ventures.[53] He was still controversial, but many citizens credited him and his costly public works programs of the late 1860s and 1870s with securing Washington's position as the nation's capital and its subsequent growth.

A letter from Elizabeth Fremont in December 1887 told of the family's move to Los Angeles for health reasons after living in Tucson and New York. They had left Prescott for Tucson in March 1881, because her father suffered from mountain fever, needed a change of climate, and wanted to see more of the Arizona countryside. Later her parents went to New York while she stayed in Tucson. John Fremont was in New York to promote the Jerome, Arizona, copper mine and to purchase arms for defense of the territory against Indian attacks such as occurred at Fort Apache near Tucson.

Elizabeth described the extremes of summer heat and sudden cloudbursts, one of which temporarily wiped out the Southern Pacific track from Yuma to Tucson. With outside supplies cut off and ice at 20¢ a pound, there was a scarcity of fresh food. She mentioned watching a great comet brighten the sky just as a nearby powder magazine exploded, causing concern as to whether the end of the world was at hand. A further shock came with news of a fire at Morrell's warehouse in New York, which destroyed all their household goods stored there when the Fremonts left for Arizona Territory.[29]

After a year in Tucson, Elizabeth joined her parents in New York, where her father was writing his memoirs after resigning from the Army. When he came down with pneumonia, his physician ordered him to Los Angeles for the climate. The Fremonts arrived on Christmas Eve 1887, and were staying at the Marlborough Hotel while looking for a furnished house.[30] They were reunited with many old friends in Los Angeles, including the E.P. Clarks, whose wedding Leann and Ramón attended in 1880. Elizabeth wrote that the Clarks now had three daughters and a son.

It seemed that Clark was instrumental in building a railroad from Prescott to Seligman, where it connected with the Atlantic and Pacific Railroad, giving Prescott its first rail link. The family then moved to Los Angeles, where Clark and his brother-in-law M.H. Sherman participated in the real estate boom and established a street railway.[56] Elizabeth closed with the wish that Ramón and Leann would be coming soon to the west coast, unaware of their current plans to remain in Washington.

When Fremont's memoirs were published, Ramón obtained a copy and studied carefully those parts concerning the second expedition in 1844 and Fremont's later role in the acquisition of California for the United States. He was interested in Fremont's version of what took place, including such lesser known aspects as: Father McNamara's ill-fated plan to colonize California with Irish Catholics; Buchanan's ill-timed effort at peaceful acquisition of California, temporarily delaying naval support to Fremont and the uprising American settlers; and the heroic actions of Edward Beale and Kit Carson after the defeat of General Kearney's forces by insurgent Californians.[31]

The memoirs stop short of describing Fremont's court-martial but reflect his bitterness and disappointment over the circumstances that helped bring about the challenge to his otherwise spectacular career.

Ramón could see how Fremont had earned the friendship and respect of Californians by being more understanding and compassionate than General Kearney or Commodore Stockton before, during, and after the war with Mexico. When President Polk allowed him to resign from the Army, Fremont returned to California to live, where he was welcomed warmly. While criticized by some, he was praised by most who had known him personally and had first hand knowledge of his accomplishments. Reviewing Fremont's memoirs confirmed in Ramón's mind the rightness of his decision in 1856 to vote for Fremont for President over Buchanan, even though Fremont lost the election and Ramón lost his State Department job as a result.

The Clementes interest in the stock market and in railroads, at least for cross-country travelling, led them to follow further the adventures of Hetty Green as reported in the newspapers. She piqued their interest not only because of her legal problems that related to some of their own but also because of her widely recognized astuteness in investments, particularly regarding railroads.

The *New York World* of December 27, 1887, reported that Mrs. Green as a stockholder of the Houston and Texas Central Railroad became involved in a dispute with C.P. Huntington, one of the founders of the Central Pacific and now owner of the Southern Pacific of which the H&TC was a part. Huntington was apparently trying to squeeze out Mrs. Green, who had bested him in some previous deals. One could not help but admire this fearlessly outspoken woman who stood up to and prevailed against one of the most prominent business tycoons of the time.[32]

Anther quality that endeared Hetty Green to the Clementes was her affection for her little dog "Dewey." His name appeared on the doorplates of various apartments she inhabited in New York and New Jersey, as reported in the press. Her son Ned was quoted as saying she used the dog's name in place of her own "to avoid annoyance and publicity, as frequent discussion of her wealth in public prints had subjected her constantly to pursuits by reporters, photographers, cranks, beggars, and people with something to sell."[33]

Mrs. Green's rival, C.P. Huntington, who had taken over the Chesapeake and Ohio Railroad in addition to his western holdings, was extending it from Huntington, West Virginia, to Cincinnati on the Ohio River. This would replace the "White Collar Line" of C&O packets carrying freight and passengers between the two river ports. He established a C&O steamship line from Newport News, Virginia, to ports in England so that, together with the Occidental and Orient Steamship Line in the Pacific, that he and his associates founded in 1873, their transportation empire would extend eventually from Europe to the Orient.[34]

Huntington started building a bridge across the Ohio from Covington, Kentucky, to Cincinnati to carry the C&O but his funds ran out and the "Huntington Bridge" was not finished until 1888, after his ownership of the C&O was transferred to receivers.[35]

The tremendous growth of railroads, which reached its peak in the 1880s, brought immense personal wealth to a select few who financed and constructed them. One such was William H. Vanderbilt, president of the New York Central, who left a fortune of nearly $200 million when he died in 1885. Wealthy people such as Vanderbilt, Huntington, and Mrs. Green received much unflattering press attention, often because inept, unseemly comments such as Vanderbilt's "the public be damned," about which there is still controversy concerning the context in which it was made. Public resentment at the arrogant behavior of some railroad managements, largely due to near monopolistic conditions in certain areas, resulted in establishment in 1887 of the first governmental regulatory agency—the Interstate Commerce Commission, to look into claims of excessive freight charges, customer kickbacks, and inadequate passenger service.[36]

In May of 1888 the Clementes attended the 18th running of the Preakness stakes at Baltimore's Pimlico Race Course, named after the winner of Pimlico's first stakes race in 1870. The winning horse in 1888 was the seventh Preakness winner trained by Robert Wyndham Walden since 1875.[37] (Author's note: The name of the winning horse is not found in Ramón Clemente's papers, indicating that neither he nor Leann bet on the winner.)

In June 1888, George Eastman introduced his "Kodak" camera, which allowed ordinary people to take quick "snapshots" of desired subjects, without all the technical equipment and supplies required by expert photographers. For example, the American Optical Company's four-by-five inch camera required a tripod, chemicals, and other expensive supplies and devices, whereas Eastman's Kodak, with its self-contained film and adjustable lens, could be hand held. The Clementes were sorry this had not been available for their 1870 trip to Europe or earlier to record the growth of their puppies. The Kodak's introductory price of $25 put off many amateur photographers, including the Clementes. Later, when the price was reduced to $5 for the 1895 "Pocket Camera," they couldn't resist getting one. Introduction of the "Brownie" camera in 1900 for only $1 was the turning point which assured the popularity of "snapshooting" as a national pastime.[38]

For some time Washington's Corcoran Gallery of Art had allowed local art students to work in public areas; but in 1888, bowing to widespread criticism of the practice, the gallery board voted to remove the students. The following year they voted for a separate School of Art building to be erected adjacent to the Gallery on 17th Street. The building was scheduled to be completed and opened to students at 1890.[39] Leann and Ramón planned on attending art classes there, but during the interim turned their attention to writing, which was more practical in times such as the "great blizzard" of 1888 that kept people indoors for extended periods.[5, 21]

The blizzard of '88 occurred in two parts. On January 12, preceded by unusually warm weather, it hit in the west, killing hundreds of people in South Dakota, Iowa, Nebraska, and Minnesota. The temperature dropped fifty degrees in twelve hours, and winds reached seventy miles an hour. Two months later, on March 12, the same thing occurred in the east. The U.S. Signal Service had predicted fair weather throughout the Atlantic states. Then a hard rain began Sunday afternoon, knocking out telephone and telegraph circuits. By 10:00 P.M. there were hurricane winds at Cape Henlopen, Delaware.[40]

More than one hundred vessels sank along the Maryland and Delaware coast. By Monday morning there were ten inches of snow. Rail lines were shut down and all public transportation stopped. People were stranded all over town. Hotels set up cots in their lobbies, and restaurants were overrun. Fortunately the Clementes had a supply of edibles to augment what was available in the public dining room, so they did not venture out and could concentrate on writing.

Leann, who had written short stories in her youth, began writing poetry. Ramón followed with some poems of his own and later was encouraged to do more by the appearance of the poem "Casey at the Bat" in the *New York Times*. This poem by Ernest Thayer of Worcester, Massachusetts, was first published in June 1888 in the *San Francisco Examiner*, at which the author was employed by his college classmate William R. Hearst. It did not become well known until recited by entertainer William deWolf Hopper at a special performance for the New York Giants at Wallach's Theater later in the summer. While Ramón's work never reached the level of quality of that now famous poem, his efforts were stimulated by the appearance of "Casey" in print.[41]

Along with their writing, Ramón and Leann were aware of significant new developments as the last decade of the nineteenth century approached. For example, Dr. Herman Hollerith of New York developed a data processing computer using punch cards for the U.S. Census Bureau in 1889.[37] That same year the *Washington Post's* founder, Stillson Hutchins, sold the newspaper to a pair of Ohio journalists so he could devote full time to the new type-setting machinery system called "linotype," which he had been supporting financially since its 1883 invention by Ottmar Merganthaler of Baltimore.[42]

The introduction in 1889 of a daily newspaper dealing exclusively with the stock market and related financial and business news, called *The Wall Street Journal*, was of special interest to the Clementes as investors. The Journal was founded by Charles Dow, who also invented an index to measure the rise and fall of the stock market. In 1882 Dow and two partners formed Dow Jones & Co., that distributed business news to customers in New York's financial district. The following year, Dow Jones began publishing a two-page news bulletin called the Customers' Afternoon Letter, which grew into the four-page *Wall Street Journal*.[43]

The year 1889 presented a possible solution to the Clementes' housing problem with the opening of the Shoreham Hotel at 15th and H Streets NW. From the start it was popular with members of Congress as an apartment hotel for use as their Washington residence, and it could serve the same purpose for the Clementes. Leann and Ramón had reached that stage in their lives when they didn't need so much space after disposing of some excess items accumulated over the years. Hotel amenities such as regular cleaning and room service were most desirable and becoming more of a necessity.

The hotel was a business investment for New York Congressman and later Vice President Levi P. Morton, who owned the site and lived in the former Alexander Graham Bell mansion at Scott Circle. The new hotel was named for Morton's birthplace—Shoreham, Vermont.[44] After further consideration, the Clementes determined the cost would prohibit any other activities such as travel, so they decided to stay where they were for the time being.

The United States Congress was 100 years old in 1889, and the 51st Congress that year had to deal with a Treasury surplus for the second time in its history. The first federal surplus from the sale of public lands in 1829–37 was resolved by distributing the excess to the states. This time the surplus of $265 million arose principally from high protective tariffs, which were strongly supported by American laborers and farmers but contributed to rising living costs in the 1880s. President Cleveland tried to lower the tariff and lost the 1888 election to Harrison. The 51st Congress reduced the surplus to less than $25 million with pensions to Union Army veterans, civil and military capital improvements, and silver purchases. In answer to critics who named it the first "Billion Dollar Congress," the Republican House Speaker said "we are now a billion dollar country."[45]

On June 2, 1889, the Clementes were amazed at the aftermath of the Potomac overflowing its banks and flooding of downtown Washington. The Long Bridge across the river to Virginia was washed out, and Pennsylvania Avenue was under water from Second to Eleventh Street NW. Railroad cars were submerged at the Baltimore and Potomac Depot on Sixth and Constitution. A schooner was washed from the Georgetown channel to the foot of the Washington Monument, and in town, people were fishing from second story windows. This disastrous occurrence finally led to steps being taken to prevent future flooding of city streets and monuments.[46]

When the year 1889 drew to a close, Ramón realized the last decade of the nineteenth century and perhaps of his own life was about to begin. He wondered if his life had any meaning or was he just an observer of the passing parade. As a young man growing up he had set no specific goals other than to witness the turn of the century and always had done what seemed best as he went along. Now he began to wonder if that was good enough.

CHAPTER 15
DIFFERENCES

The following passages, in Ramón's own words, are taken from a paper he wrote apparently for further study, or for discussion with Leann, concerning a subject he believed needed serious attention:

> "One of the things that brought Leann and me together was that we were different in many ways—each having qualities the other admired but did not have ourselves to the same degree; yet also having many similar qualities we valued in ourselves and welcomed in the other.
>
> "After forty-five years of marriage, the differences have begun to loom larger than the similarities. Perhaps we have taken the similarities for granted, and in later years allowed the differences to become obstacles, as if they had never been there before.
>
> "In physical size, of course, we differ immensely—by nearly a foot in height and almost 100 pounds in weight. This is of no consequence to me, being the larger, but it matters considerably to Leann who often says that I sometimes 'tower' over her in what seems a threatening manner. It is a relief for her sometimes to stand on a step above me so that our eyes are at the same level, instead of always having to look up at me. I can understand this feeling, such as a child has among adults. I sometimes think of myself still as a

small boy, taking up little space, seeking approval of others and looking for answers to things I don't understand. At other times I see myself more realistically as an old man becoming increasingly irrelevant to things going on in the world around him.

"While growing up, what I wanted most was to fit in, get along and be accepted. I cared less about excelling, competing, or defeating an opponent unless attacked or tormented excessively. As I grew older, I wanted one more thing—someone to love and share my life with, which I have found in Leann.

"Leann, on the other hand, has always wanted to succeed, excel and to be outstanding in whatever she did. As a child she prayed for talent in whatever field she would pursue. She imagined us achieving great success together as 'two against the world.' In a sense we were on a collision course unless we reconciled our two different attitudes towards life.

"In later years we have had increasing arguments, often related to our uncertain living conditions and past problems incompletely resolved. I began to keep track of what seemed to have been my part in causing these arguments, as I understood it, in an effort to discover and correct my own mistakes and inadequacies. While this approach might seem too methodical, it is typical of my approach to many problems, and illustrates one of our differences.

"We both agree that arguments are a normal part of married life and that marriages without any arguments would be most unusual if not impossible. I think we would also agree that there are good and bad ways of arguing, but might not agree as to exactly what that entails, and when either of us is being fair or unfair in a specific instance.

"Sometimes upon hearing the first part of a statement which strikes a particular note, one's mind disengages and forms a mental picture that may vary what actually occurred or was said, so that when the instance is recalled one person's recall may be different from the other's. There is also the problem of commingling facts of two or more separate occurrences with resulting inaccuracies of later recall. Both of these types of mental aberrations occur increasingly with age and can lead to arguments.

"Other factors leading to arguments may be personal characteristics that one can attempt to discover and modify. Referring to my recordations of what has been my part in causing arguments, I established a list of guidelines for myself in trying to reduce arguments and improve relations. From May 1886 to April 1888 I recorded my violations of these guidelines which resulted in arguments. A review of my records indicates I have such faults as: frequent loss of temper; being petulant, pedantic, impatient, insensitive, unappreciative, selfish, rude, boastful, indecisive, and more.

"This self-assessment reminds me of Dana's words in *Two Years Before the Mast* which Leann and I read together in the early 1850s. Therein he describes 'the average lazy Californian as a man blighted by a curse which had deprived him of all good qualities but pride, a fine manner and cultivated voice.'[1] At the time I felt I had perhaps escaped such curse, but now am not sure.

"I am now aware of a fault that my mother often referred to as 'our kind of humor.' It consists of saying the opposite of what you mean, or something so outrageous that anyone should know you couldn't possibly mean it and would therefore take it as a joke—only some don't and may be angered or hurt by it.

"I can recall one time when I was about 11 or 12, I purposely used the term *'avoirdupois'* in place of the French expression *'savoir faire'* in describing a characteristic of a mutual acquaintance to a friend of my mother. The lady assumed I didn't know the difference between the two expressions and told my mother, who replied:

'My son was just making a joke!'

My mother's friend didn't believe her and continued to regard me as a person of limited knowledge, at least insofar as the French language was concerned.

"Another time, as a youth of about 15, I went to call on the beautiful daughter of a neighboring Don, and felt very nervous and self-conscious. While awaiting the appearance of the señorita whom I greatly admired, I said to her father:

'I am here only because you are a friend of my family, otherwise I wouldn't be calling on your daughter.'

My remark was obviously inappropriate, extremely rude, and intended as a joke—the opposite of what I really felt. The Don looked at me first in surprise, then with a half smile, he replied:

'But of course.'

It was as if he understood my intended humor, but I wasn't really sure. I have often thought how stupid it was to have said that and wished many times I could have retracted it.

"Extravagant flattery was also used as a form of humor on my mother's side of the family. Expressing sincere feelings was considered banal except under conditions of extreme stress. I came by this naturally, but have tried to change, particularly after meeting Leann, who is not that way at all. When I say to her what I really feel it comes out flat and, to her, unbelievable. So, in a way, I may have the 'curse' as Dana described it.

"As to my temper, I can recall my father's which would flare suddenly and with more frequency as his debilitating illness kept him more and more confined to his room and bed. When I am aware of having expressed anger inappropriately, I recall my father lying in bed being 'testy.' I may be trying to emulate him in some way, selecting perhaps his least desirable trait if only to feel closer to one whom I never felt close enough to when he was alive.

"I remember lying in bed one night at the age of about 12, and hearing a particularly bad argument between my father and mother. Usually I didn't hear my mother's voice, only my father's, loud and angry. This time I heard my mother cry out:

'Oh Guillermo, how can you say such things to me!'

Her audible sobs tore at my heart. Then I heard their door slam as she left for another room to be alone with her hurt.

"I marched from my room down the hall to my parents' room to confront my father, something I had never done before. I looked him squarely in the eye and said:

'You are sick and are making her sick too. If it continues I will take her away so you can't hurt her more!'

As I looked at my father, sitting up in bed with his arms on his raised knees and his head bent, he seemed very tired and dejected. He said in a low, soft voice:

'Maybe you'd better do that, my son.'

"Feeling confused and regretting my impetuous act, I marched back down the hall to my room. After a while my mother came to my door and said, in a firm but kindly tone:

'You must never do anything like that again. Your father and I may argue, but we love each other very much, and some arguing is part of a good marriage. You must understand that and never interfere between us.'

"I often remember the entire episode and my parents' words to me, particularly after arguments Leann and I have now.

"Regarding Leann's and my differences, I am given to understatement, whereas Leann sometimes exaggerates to make a point. If I could accept over-statement for what it is, many arguments might be avoided. I recall arguing with my mother over some of her (mother's) remarks I thought were overstated or ill-founded, and perhaps some of my present attitude carries over from that.

"When discussing political developments and current events, Leann and I agree that a watchful eye on the party in power by the 'loyal opposition,' the press, and an informed citizenry is essential to the proper functioning of democratic government. While retaining a degree of skepticism, I often err on the side of accepting statements at face value, whereas Leann looks carefully between the lines for other meanings and motivations.

"I have warned Leann that sometimes she is overly trusting of certain people or expecting too much of them at first. Then when the inevitable disappointments and disillusionments occur, she becomes, in my opinion, overly suspicious of them. To be fair, she too has warned me of being overly trusting, as when I rejected her suggestion of difficulties in my sister's marriage which subsequently proved to be correct.

"I still believe it is better to trust most people's good intentions than to regard all with suspicion because of a few bad experiences. Most interpersonal and business relationships Leann views in terms of a 'power struggle,' whereas I believe in sharing control relative to the rights and responsibilities of all concerned. This often leads to divisive arguments about the merits of our conflicting premises, thus detracting from our ability to work together in dealing with the matter at hand.

"Some of our differences relate to the hypothetical question of whether a glass is half-full or half-empty, with my leaning more towards the full side. For example, when it comes to eating, I usually think of what is available, easily obtainable, or on the menu. Leann thinks of what she would like most which may not be available, but also leads to something more creative. Enthusiasm is one of Leann's qualities that first attracted me to her, yet I frequently dampen it by questioning new ideas which comes across as negativism. I understand it is not necessary to react every time a view is expressed with which I disagree, but failure to speak up may be interpreted as agreement, passivity or not holding strong convictions, thus presenting me with a dilemma.

"While I believe that extremists on opposite sides of an issue are necessary to define the middle and move forward, I seldom favor either extreme and see a wide area of alternatives in between as a basis for compromise. Leann sees each extreme as being either right or wrong and regards the middle only as a 'gray area' incompatible with black and white decision making.

"I received criticism from my superiors at the War Department (but not the State Department) for indecisiveness in certain situations, because of my tendency to consider all sides of a situation as well as the view of others, and I strive for better discrimination in this area. Hopefully we can learn to understand and accept our individual differences.

"When Abraham Lincoln became President, and for many years since, there has been talk of differences between him and his wife, Mary Todd Lincoln. Apparently the Lord gave them the strength and wisdom to overcome or deal with their differences, which is what we pray for now.[2]

"In addition to our differences, there are those similarities that we sometimes find fault with in the other, but fail to see in ourselves. But what person who has ever been married, or been close to another person, does not already know of this feature of the human condition?

"In spite of our differences, I believe we still have the same hopes, basic beliefs, and sense of belonging to each other that brought us together many years ago, and has broadened into a deep and everlasting love. It can be difficult to hold this thought during an argument, but afterwards the belief returns stronger than ever and will remain long after these words are written.

"One of my warmest memories of the feelings we share is of one day when we were going shopping during the holiday season. As I helped Leann down from the carriage, she turned to me with the sweetest most loving smile and said: 'We'll always be a close little couple, won't we?' I smiled back, agreed and gave her a quick hug as we approached the store entrance.

"Whenever I recall that moment, and a myriad of others like it, our differences seem much less important and even trivial within the context of the deep love we share."

(Author's note: There is nothing in the records available to indicate what, if any, discussion or resolution there was of this matter. It is deemed sufficiently significant for inclusion in the story to provide a fuller picture of the persons herein described.)

CHAPTER 16
LOOKING BACK AND FORWARD

As Ramón and Leann approached the start of the twentieth century, their own mortality became increasingly apparent. They also became more aware of new things happening—fruition of the "industrial revolution" bringing widespread application of recent discoveries and inventions with accompanying social changes. It was an exciting time to be living yet sad knowing they hadn't much time left to enjoy it. Ramón believed this is what life is about—ambivalence and ambiguities and how to deal with them—like the differences between those who love each other. In this latest and potentially most satisfying period of their lives, he felt their greatest achievement could be fuller knowledge and understanding of themselves and of each other.

In the three decades before the Civil War, not only had the United States spread itself across the continent but living conditions had greatly improved with the introduction of interior lighting, cook stoves, ice-boxes, the telegraph, and mass circulation newspapers. Central heating became possible in the 1840s when railroads lowered the cost of coal. In the 1850s inside water closets and running water in bathrooms and kitchens were not only welcome conveniences but also reduced disease, thus increasing life expectancy. The many technological advances in the latter half of the century such as electric lights, telephones, and automobiles were further improvements on the significant developments that occurred before the Civil War.[1]

After the Civil War, the United States could freely exploit its natural advantages with few of the disadvantages of its European rivals. Postwar growth in agricultural production, raw materials extraction, and technological development transformed the country from an exporter of raw materials, principally cotton with gold to make up the deficit, into a net exporter of manufactured goods and a wider variety of farm products.[44] The introduction of refrigerated rail cars in 1886 enabled broader distribution of local farm products and expanded grocery shopping for the entire nation.[2] The remaining years of the nineteenth century saw greater industrial expansion, with improvements in transportation and communications and the many adaptations of electricity, such as Thomas Edison's motion pictures.

In 1894 Edison used his new Kinescope to film Buffalo Bill Cody's Wild West Show and the International Congress of Rough Riders at the Columbian Exposition in Chicago. Motion picture theaters showed Cody, dressed in characteristic fringed buckskin, with his complete show, including Pony Express riders; rescues of covered wagons and stagecoaches from marauding Indians; and the Battle of the Little Big Horn as the climax.[3] Through electricity and motion pictures, Cody became more widely known and successful. In 1890 he founded the town bearing his name—Cody, Wyoming, located on the Shoshone River about sixty miles east of Yellowstone, America's first national park, which was established by Congress in 1872 after seeing Albert Bierstadt's paintings of the area.

Urban growth was accelerating nationwide because of developments enabling almost unlimited vertical construction. Steel structural systems with "I" beams, independent of building walls, made possible the creation of "skyscrapers" exceeding the previous six-floor limit, and Elisha Otis' elevator with a new safety latch made the taller structures usable.[4]

When motor cars arrived on the scene, there began a continuing debate as to whether they would replace the horse, which had provided basic transportation for so many years. Judging by the rapid growth of railroads and other mechanical developments of the period, one could conjecture that the automobile would prevail, but that was by no means the consensus.[2] The Clementes only regret was that the auto came so late in their lives as to preclude their fuller enjoyment of it.

The Duryea Motor Wagon Company launched the U.S. automobile industry in 1893. Two more companies—Olds and Detroit Automobile Company, began making "horseless carriages" in 1896.[5] By 1900 there were several other manufacturers and many new models. The Packard single seat roadster was said to be "superior to any on the market."[6] There was a new Duryea, which was the first car with a muffler and with a fuel additive available to mask the smelly fumes. All the makes and models were at the first New York Auto Show, which opened November 3, 1900, and which the Clementes hoped to attend. They read later that the attendance of about eight thousand people was approximately the same as the total number of automobiles in the U.S. at that time. There was much competition between gasoline, steam, and electric powered engines, with the latter preferred as being quieter, safer, and without offensive odors. In spite of strong initial interest, the popular consensus, as stated in *Automobile Topics* November 10, 1900, edition, was that "the horse would continue to be indispensable for a long time to come."

A less glamorous but equally important example of American industrial accomplishment was development of new and improved farm machinery. This helped turn the United States into the world's foremost granary and also a worldwide supplier of farming and other industrial equipment.

The 1890s saw the disappearance of the western frontier which had influenced national life, thought, and character for most of the nineteenth century. Now the work of consolidation would have to replace expansion, with emphasis on resolving conflicts between divergent interests such as eastern industry and western agriculture, and, within industry, between capital and labor. These and other socio-economic problems brought on by the industrial revolution became of concern later in America than in Europe because of America's earlier preoccupation with its western frontier.

Throughout the period of westward expansion, the front line of white settlers had been in constant contact with the retreating Indians. The racial pride of the Anglo-Saxon settlers prevented any amalgamation such as took place in Latin America. While the black slaves in the south were cared for as property like domesticated animals, the Indians were considered as wild beasts to be exploited or exterminated.

One of many broken U.S. promises to the Indians received unusual attention in 1889 at what was called "Harrison's Hoss Race," named for the incumbent president. Indian tribes from the east had been moved to what became known as Oklahoma Territory, by an 1830 Congressional Act, with then-President Jackson's promise that it would remain their land forever. Growing pressure from white settlers known as "boomers" forced President Harrison to revise this promise. The government bought back from the Indians two million acres which was opened to homesteaders in 160-acre plots effective at noon on April 22, 1889. As there were many more would-be homesteaders than plots, and some individuals known as "sooners" had already jumped the opening gun to claim the choicest sites, the resulting rush into the territory became completely undisciplined, and much valuable prairie grassland was destroyed as rival "boomers" raced their wagons against each other to establish claims.[8]

In January 1890, the Clementes read of the return of reporter Nelly Bly from her record-breaking trip around the world. Born Elizabeth Cochrane, she began reporting as a teenager for the *Pittsburgh Dispatch* in 1885. She took the name "Nelly Bly" from a Stephen Foster song[7] and soon became known for going into disguises to uncover unsavory situations for news stories. Joseph Pulitzer, editor of the *New York World*, hired her in 1887 and published her sensational stories on subjects such as conditions of the New York Lunatic Asylum, certain factories labeled as "sweatshops," and bribery of state legislators. In 1889 he sent her on a round-the-world trip, using commercial transportation, to beat the record set in Jules Verne's *Around the World in 80 Days*, apparently as a ploy to boost newspaper circulation. She did it in just over seventy-two days and six hours. On her return she herself became the story and a celebrity in her own right.[9] The Santa Fe Railroad shared in the accolade by claiming the fastest time for an American train, taking the famous reporter from La Junta, Colorado, to Chicago, Illinois, at an average speed of 78.1 miles per hour.[10]

Leann and Ramón saw Nelly Bly arrive at the Washington train station during one of her personal appearance tours. They were struck by her youthful appearance and distinctive apparel—a long black and white check fitted top coat with matching cap and bag, looking as if she were ready to start off around the world again. Not long thereafter a new game was introduced bearing her name and likeness, which the Clementes acquired. Though not as intellectually stimulating as chess or even checkers, it provided a pleasant pastime in addition to the jigsaw puzzles they had come to enjoy.

The news of John Fremont's death in 1890 was especially saddening. He was a distinguished and noble citizen who had performed great services for his country that Ramón felt were not sufficiently recognized. At the time of his death, Fremont's wife and daughter were in Los Angeles, where he had expected to join them after Senate restoration of his Army rank of Major General. Jessie and Elizabeth Fremont were fortunate in being surrounded by friends who provided support during this tragic time and also a home in Los Angeles for the rest of their lives.[11]

Later that year came better news for the Clementes—the availability of a highly desirable apartment on an upper floor of their same building, the Portland Flats, which seemed to resolve their long-standing housing problem. After a nerve-wracking move in February 1891, they finally started to unpack, albeit only a little at a time. They were pleased at the prospect of seeing again all of their valued household furnishings and belongings, some of which had been packed away since they sold their Georgetown house.

On the fortieth anniversary of their arrival in the nation's capital, Leann and Ramón decided to revisit their first home there—the former Georgetown Hotel, originally the City Tavern in 1796, and now the Morgan House. They had followed the changes in its name and ownership over the years. In 1864 Boyd's Directory listed the property at 129 Bridge Street as Lang's Hotel under the direction of John Lang, the son of Eleanor Lang, who in 1863 had purchased the Town House next door. In 1866 Lang's Hotel was advertised as being at the western "terminus of the Washington and Georgetown railroad," the area's first street car line completed in 1862. In 1875 the property was listed as the Morgan House, Richard W. Morgan proprietor, and in 1883 Eleanor Lang's grandson John R. Lang was listed as co-proprietor using the Washington Street numbering system for its 3206 M Street address. The 1890 directory showed John R. Lang and his brother William H. Lang in charge. The Clementes enjoyed dinner with the Lang brothers and told them of their good treatment with their little dogs at the hands of Eleanor and John Lang forty years earlier.[78]

Ramón was glad to receive a letter from Richard Woodward, his shipmate aboard the *Valiant* in 1836, whom he had been trying to contact. Woodward wrote that his wife of forty-five years had succumbed after a long illness, and he had recently remarried. He was living in southern California and had been active in real estate which piqued Ramón's interest. Another voice from the past was Ramón's Yale classmate Walter Peterson, who wrote that he had been assigned the task of raising funds for the college from 1840 alumni. Walter wrote that he (too) had remarried and was spending much of his time travelling about the country and abroad. Ramón was grateful to God that he still had Leann, his bride of forty-six years, and that they could now relax and live more comfortably in what probably would become their last permanent home on earth, above the ground.

The Clementes continued to follow the financial adventures of Hetty Green, which were widely covered in the newspapers. Her personal fortune was rumored to be about $100 million, making her probably the wealthiest woman in the United States and reputedly one of the most eccentric. Her holdings included real estate in most major cities, paper and cotton mills, gold mines, and stocks and bonds of most American railroads and many foreign ones.

In 1891 John Barnard wrote that Hetty's son Ned had approached him regarding acquiring an interest in the Ohio and Mississippi Railroad, and that Ned, then twenty-one years old, was made a director.[75] Knowing of the Clementes' interest in Mrs. Green, John sent them a letter of introduction, warning that she might be difficult to contact. As the fabulous Sarah Bernhardt was again in New York for one of her "final" U.S. tours, Ramón and Leann went to see both of these famous people. They bought tickets to see Sarah play Cleopatra, wearing a live garter snake.[12] They also visited the Metropolitan Museum of Art, which Leann had long wanted to see.

This time in New York, they stayed at the Brevoort Hotel on Lower Fifth Avenue at 8th Street,[13] in which presidents of the New York Central, Pennsylvania, and B&O Railroads had met in the 1870s to resolve rate wars.[14] The Clementes chose this hotel to be nearer to where they thought Mrs. Green might be living. Actually finding her was not so simple because of her frequent moving and using the name of her dog Dewey on the nameplate. When they finally located her current lodging, a flat in Hoboken, New Jersey, she was just returning from the Chemical Bank in Manhattan, in which she maintained office space, and could not avoid the visitors at her door. When she read the note Ramón had brought from John Barnard, with whom she had been doing business, Mrs. Green invited them in, although somewhat grudgingly, as if suspecting a trick. At fifty-six years of age, Hetty Green was a vigorous and active woman but hid natural good looks under heavy, dowdy dark-colored clothes that actually looked soiled. Her lodgings were simple and plainly furnished, with no indication of her great personal wealth. With much pride she introduced to her visitors her beloved Dewey, a small Skye terrier who seemed as reluctant as his mistress to greet the guests.

They spoke of their mutual acquaintance John Barnard, who Mrs. Green said was hoping for her support in preventing a merger of his railroad with the B&O.[75] She was concerned about newspaper reports, which she vehemently denied, that her son Ned was considering buying the *Chicago Times*, a development which would appear to align her with the world of reporters and publishers whom she strongly disliked.[16] As the conversation became more open, she expressed her concern about reports of her son's expanded social life and activities with presumably predatory women since his business trip to Chicago on her behalf.[16] She did not volunteer much else about her personal affairs, and the Clementes respected her privacy by not probing. They did exchange views on various stocks and the stock market in general. They had differing views on the new Sherman Anti-Trust Act, passed in 1890, which declared illegal "every contract, combination in the form of trust or otherwise, or conspiracy in restraint of trade...."[10] Mrs. Green feared this might open the door to excessive government interference with free enterprise. Ramón and Leann felt it was an action needed to control the excesses of some of the "robber barons." When they left promptly after the appropriate half-hour visit, they felt they had almost come to know the famous Hetty Green and liked and admired her very much.

While in New York, Ramón called his college classmate Homer Bradford, who met the Clementes for lunch at Fraunce's Tavern. Afterwards Homer took them to the Stock Market a block away, then to his brokerage firm of A.A. Houseman & Co. at 52 Exchange Place. Here he introduced them to Bernard Baruch, who was a friend of his grandson and had just joined the firm. Homer's grandson had decided against Yale as being too "stuffy" and enrolled instead at the City College of New York, from which he and Baruch graduated in the class of 1889. When Baruch heard the Clementes were originally from the west, he told them of his temporary diversion from the financial world of New York in hopes of making a fortune in the Colorado gold and silver mines, which didn't "pan out" for him. In Colorado Baruch said he became familiar with the mining activities of Tom Walsh, later to become a U.S. Senator whose daughter Evelyn would marry the son of Emily Beale and John McLean.[15]

The following year, the Clementes were delighted to receive a note from Hetty Green, then living at a boarding house in Morristown, New Jersey, inviting them to her daughter Sylvia's debut on December 7, 1892. This seemed out of character for Mrs. Green, who was known to abhor and avoid most social activities as being wasteful and ostentatious. They made a special effort to attend and were pleased to meet some of the Green friends and relatives, including Annie Leary, a longtime friend and now a papal "countess," and who, it was said, had convinced Hetty Green to have the party for Sylvia and helped with the arrangements; also the Green cousins Nina Howland and her sister, Mrs. M. Ford; and others from New York and Massachusetts as well as some of the local citizenry.[16]

At twenty-one, Sylvia Ann Howland Robinson Green was not particularly pretty but was tall and slender with clear pale ivory skin. She seemed quite shy and actually blushed on being introduced. She seldom danced that evening and seemed uncomfortable with others, except for her brother, Ned, who came from his current home in Texas to be her escort. Ned Green, at twenty-five, was more outgoing than his sister. He was a large man, well over six feet tall and weighing about 200 pounds, with a round friendly face and gregarious manner, not consistent with his reputedly austere upbringing. He did not dance at the party, presumably because of his artificial leg, the result of an amputation four years earlier. Ramón thought that he seemed to be trying hard to please his mother and sister while also striving to break away and make his own life.

On the business front, Mrs. Green had out-maneuvered Collis P. Huntington for a piece of the Houston and Texas Central (H&TC RR), known as the Waco and Northwestern, which included nearly two hundred thousand acres of land and a franchise to extend the line north to Red River on the Texas border. This later became the Texas Midland Railroad with Hetty's son Ned Green as President.[17]

In the 1890s Charles Dow expanded his stock market index, begun in 1884 as an average of nine railroad and two industrial stocks, into two separate indices—one for twenty railroads, and one for twelve industrials, which the Clementes found useful in managing their investments more effectively.[18]

The decade of the 1890s saw the beginning of organized labor's challenge to industry moguls and the "robber barons" who had been abusing the industrial system during its growth in the 19th Century. As reported in the *Wall Street Journal* July 6, 1892, striking workers at the Carnegie Steel Plant in Homestead, Pennsylvania, opened fire on Pinkerton Detective Agency guards who were brought in by management to break the strike. By July 10th, strikers controlled the plant, and by November 14th they voted to return to work with a pay cut. Charges brought against the strikers were dropped except for those against two men who were convicted of assault and battery. Generally this was seen as a turning point in favor of labor against complete management dominance of the industrial scene.[19]

A by-product of the Homestead steel strike was the assassination of industrialist Henry Clay Frick, who was blamed by many for causing the disastrous Johnstown flood of 1889. Frick and other wealthy Pittsburgh businessmen, including Andrew Carnegie and Andrew Mellon, had developed an exclusive hunting and fishing club, using an inadequate dam above Johnstown, Pennsylvania, to form a lake. When the dam collapsed through allegedly careless or inept contractors and maintenance techniques, Frick and his colleagues were held responsible by many for the thousands of deaths from the resulting flood.[20]

The 1890s were the end of one era in the financial and economic development of America and the beginning of a new one. Conditions of unrestrained individualism that created the "robber barons" of the earlier period were changing. Dominant financial figures such as Morgan, Harriman, and Rockefeller were at the peak of their power and prestige. After the Spanish-American War in 1898, America was recognized as a world power, and by the turn of the century the financial arena would be too large to be dominated by any one man or group of men. The newer generation of younger financiers, such as Bernard Baruch, presented themselves as less satisfied with mere money-making and reflected a growing sense of social responsibility.

Financial markets became unstable after the near collapse in 1890 of a London banking house which had bad investments in Argentina and was heavily invested in the United States. This aggravated more fundamental U.S. instability caused by outflow of gold from foreign redemption of U.S. Treasury Notes following the Silver Purchase Act of 1890. Confidence in the U.S. dollar was restored temporarily when New York financier J.P. Morgan, the "Lion of Wall Street," led a group of U.S. and European bankers, at the request of President Cleveland, in exchanging gold for government bonds. Financial panic followed a market sell-off in 1893. Ramón and Leann owned their stocks outright so were not subject to margin call and their losses were only on paper. In fact they considered it a buying opportunity but proceeded cautiously as the Dow-Jones index dropped 25 percent. By year end scores of railroads and thousands of other businesses were bankrupt, and 5 percent of the nation's banks had failed. Two years later the whole country was on the verge of bankruptcy.[21]

Economic depression followed the 1893 panic. The labor movement received a temporary setback when a strike against the Pullman Company in Chicago erupted into violence. After a mail train was wrecked, President Cleveland ordered the Army in to restore order. The strike leader, Socialist Eugene Debs, was arrested and sentenced for contempt of court. The Supreme Court rejected his appeal, upholding the government's right to remove barriers to interstate commerce.[22]

An unusual form of labor protest occurred in April 1894 when "Coxey's Army" of 500 unemployed workers marched from the midwest into Washington DC. Their leader, Jacob L. Coxey, was arrested for trespassing on Capitol grounds, and the group disbanded when there was insufficient popular support.[23]

While financial panics in 1893 and 1896 slowed economic growth in the rest of the country, more business came to Washington DC, where services to the Federal Government and tourism in the nation's capital provided a sound basis for the local economy. This situation almost brought to Washington the Columbian Exposition—the 400th anniversary of Columbus' discovery of America. There was great disappointment in Washington when the exposition was held in Chicago instead.

On the positive side, the occasion of the Columbian Exposition led to the "City Beautiful" movement, which encouraged formation of a Public Arts League in Washington by members of the Cosmos Club and the American Institute of Architects. Its objective of establishing a mechanism for government acquisition or commission of works of art and architecture, was presented to Congress in 1897, but would not become law until much later.[24]

In the spring of 1893 Leann was invited to tea and a book review at the Washington Club by a friend of Mrs. Fremont, recently elected as an honorary member. The club was organized in 1891 by a group of Washington women "for literary purposes, mutual improvement, and the promotion of social intercourse." It was located in the Richmond Hotel at 17th and H Streets, NW,[71] which Leann recognized as having been converted from the Richmond Flats, once considered by the Clementes as a possible home.

The following year Leann was asked to join the Club and witnessed its move first to the Everett, a block west on H Street, and then to its new home at 1710 Eye Street, NW.[72]

On one occasion Leann and other members who invited husbands or gentlemen friends to an evening lecture and ordered tea afterwards were reprimanded for conduct likely to create an unseemly appearance. In later years a more relaxed atmosphere apparently prevailed as the Club's seventh anniversary was celebrated with a breakfast including wine for $12.50 per person, and on another occasion when light refreshments were served, members were allowed to bring an escort.[73] After that Ramón felt more at ease accompanying Leann to her club.

Not much of a club man himself, Ramón did become associated with the older Army and Navy Club, located nearby at Connecticut Avenue and Eye Street, NW,[74] on the basis of his earlier activities at the War and State Departments.

The Clementes attended the opening of the National Zoo at its new location near Rock Creek. Formerly the Smithsonian's "Department of Living Animals," the zoo was moved from its cramped location on the Mall by 1899 action of Congress.[25] The first head zookeeper was William Blackburne, who previously worked for a circus. He negotiated for the first kangaroo, costing $75, which the zoo couldn't afford. Blackburne arranged to trade guinea pigs at 15¢ each, taking three years to pay for the kangaroo. For the elephants, he developed a stomach-ache remedy of mustard plasters followed by a gin and ginger drink they enjoyed so much it seemed they sometimes feigned illness to receive the cure.[26]

The following year, Congress passed a bill creating Rock Creek Park, due to the efforts of Charles C. Glover, president of Riggs & Co., and other local leaders. This saved Rock Creek and its beautiful surrounding valley from having its upper portion become a battleground for real estate developers. It also saved the lower portion of the creek from O Street to Pennsylvania Avenue, from being covered over as an arched tunnel to form an open sewer for Georgetown's industrial waste.[59]

Leann and Ramón enjoyed cultural developments such as the center at Glen Echo just above the District line in Maryland, built for the National Chataqua Assembly in 1891;[27] the "Hall of Ancients" with its reproductions of Egyptian and Roman architecture; and the new Lafayette Square Opera House which opened September 30, 1895, with Lillian Russell in "Tzigane."[28]

The "Redwood Tree House," a popular exhibit at the Chicago Fair, was moved to Washington for permanent display on the Mall near the Agriculture Department. The house was made from a section of a 2,000-year-old redwood tree cut in California in 1892. So many of the trees were being destroyed that their extinction was feared. Ironically this tree was named for General John Noble who had devoted much of his life to the cause of forest preservation. A native of St. Louis and 1851 Yale graduate with Republican and abolitionist views, Noble was counsel for many large railroads that received huge Federal land grants. As Secretary of the Interior from 1889—1893, he pushed for legislation to preserve millions of acres of western forests owned by the Federal government. The tree house remained on exhibit for many years as a monument, if not to hypocrisy, at least to the problem of one hand of the government not knowing or caring what the other was doing.[29]

There was sad news in October, 1893, that Clarence King had been committed to a New York asylum after a breakdown following a series of business reverses. Since leaving the government he had travelled frequently between the east and the west on business and, like the Clementes, had difficulty deciding on a place to settle and make a permanent home. After his condition was diagnosed as being due to spinal inflammation rather than mental disturbance, King was released and resumed much of his former activity but not at the same level of intensity.[57]

Edward Beale died in 1893 and his son Truxtun became owner of the Tejon Ranch in California.[30] Truxtun Beale was named after his great grandfather, Commodore Truxtun of the USS Constitution. Truxtun's grandfather, a Navy paymaster, had served with distinction at the battle of Lake Champlain in the War of 1812; and his father Edward Beale, while serving as a Navy Lieutenant, was a hero of the Mexican War.[60] Truxtun did not reflect this military background in his own bearing and demeanor. He bore a general resemblance to his father, even to the flowing moustache, but without the small beard. He had the same facial shape and coloring, but the expression of his eyes was more contemplative, even wistful, as if reflecting on his ability to live up to the gallantry of his ancestors.

When he saw the Clementes in Washington, Truxtun Beale renewed his father's invitation to visit the Tejon Ranch the next time they were on the west coast. Leann and Ramón decided the year of their fiftieth wedding anniversary in 1895 would be a suitable occasion to revisit California, see the ranch and other places and friends in the Golden State, and celebrate their anniversary on the return trip.

At the appointed time, they set out from Washington to Chicago on the B&O and marvelled at its new Chicago terminal called Grand Central Station, a four-story building with a tall corner clock tower topped by the letters "B&O" in electric lights.[31] They admired the handsome exterior of brownstone and brown pressed brick and marvelled at the huge waiting room with ornate columns running its entire length, marble walls, and high arched windows topped by multi-colored glass. Even the doorknobs were made in a floral pattern to contribute to this splendid scene. In addition, the Clementes were told, this was the first building in Chicago to be constructed on top of long clay piles to prevent the possibility of its sinking into the swampy soil on the shore of Lake Michigan.[67]

Fascinating as all this was, they hadn't time to linger as they had to transfer to the Santa Fe depot to complete their journey to California. One of the many changes they noticed since their last trip west nearly thirteen years before, was the adoption of four "standard time" zones to replace the variety of "sun times" that had confused travellers and railroaders alike.[32]

Another change was the travel route beyond Deming, New Mexico, which now went directly west over the former Atlantic and Pacific Railroad route that Santa Fe acquired earlier, through Prescott Junction near Seligman, Arizona, entering California at The Needles. This area of the southwest between the Pecos and Colorado rivers had been left mostly for the Indians as being least suitable for white settlement. Its principal value was for railroads connecting the Mississippi valley with the Pacific coast. The area was sparsely settled with a few mining towns, cattle ranches, and Indian communities. By the mid-1890s it had drawn the interest of railroad passengers attracted by the spectacular scenery and picturesque Indian culture. This also attracted artists who made the area visible to more Americans and desirable to those seeking relief from spreading industrialism and yearning for the old frontier. Artist Frederick Remington commented that "Americans have gashed this country up so horribly with their axes, hammers, scrapers and ploughs, that I always like to see a place which they have overlooked." Many artists regarded it as their mission to record the few surviving Indian tribes still in their native surroundings, such as the Navajo, Hopi, Apache, Zuni, and Pueblo tribes of this area.[33]

Another prominent southwestern subject for artists was the spectacular Grand Canyon of the Colorado River, in the northwestern corner of Arizona Territory. The Clementes viewed it first hand by getting off the train at Williams and joining a guided tour by special coaches travelling about one hundred miles north. Major John Wesley Powell, who succeeded Clarence King as head of the U.S. Geological Survey in 1881, had surveyed the canyon in 1873 and believed it did not result from ordinary erosion. He theorized the river first flowed over flat land which rose in ancient upheavals, so the river cut this unusually deep channel.[34] The exposed strata of the mile-deep canyon walls were said to reveal the geologic history of the western part of the continent. Ramón viewed this at close range on a burro ride down the steep winding trail to the canyon bottom. Leann remained on the rim above, enjoying the magnificent view of the entire area and its ever-changing rainbow of colors, enhanced by transient rain showers passing over different sections of the twisting canyon.

Returning to Williams, they continued by train to The Needles on the California border, where the train stopped at the Harvey House for refreshments. After crossing the Mojave desert they got off the train at Tehachapi where Truxtun Beale's driver was waiting with a four-horse coach to take them to the ranch. Ramón recalled meeting Fremont at almost the same spot over fifty years previously. Before boarding the coach, the driver told them of a disastrous train wreck in 1883 at Tehachapi summit that killed fifteen people, which made the Clementes glad to be off the train at least temporarily. On their way to the ranch headquarters he pointed out to them one of the giant condors that were often seen flying in the area but almost extinct elsewhere.

The land was just as beautiful as Ramón remembered from the time he rode out to meet Fremont's expedition in 1844. It was one of the few things that remained unchanged in southern California. The Truxtun Beales gave them a warm reception on arrival and showed them some of the sights around the ranch, including the first rustic cabin Edward Beale had built after acquiring the La Liebre grant in 1855. When they returned to the ranch headquarters at Paso Creek, Truxtun showed them the pack of Russian wolfhounds he kept to hunt coyotes, which he offered for his guests' amusement. Leann and Ramón politely declined the suggestion. After dinner Truxtun Beale talked about his early experiences at the ranch, such as when he rode with his father into Los Angeles from the ranch in a sulky pulled by a team of camels.[35]

The next morning Ramón arose early to ride with the ranch foreman into the high country where the cattle were grazing in the fresh mountain air—a delightful interlude which he long remembered. Leann slept in and joined the group for a hearty ranch breakfast later in the morning. After farewells at ranch headquarters, the same coach and driver took the Clementes back to Tehachapi, where they boarded the Santa Fe for the trip via Mojave and Newhall to Los Angeles. On the way, they noticed the profusion of eucalyptus trees from Australia, planted as windbreaks along the railroad tracks, and soon began to associate the distinctive eucalyptus aroma with the California scene.

They stayed, as before, at the Pico House and, after getting settled, enjoyed a fine dinner in the elegant dining room, accompanied by string music and attentive waiters.

Ramón's "old home town," the former Indian village of Yang-Na, later the Spanish/Mexican community named El Pueblo de Nuestra Señora La Reina de Los Angeles, was now the fifth largest American city in the west and had just celebrated its first annual "Fiesta de Los Angeles" in remembrance of its earlier days. He barely recognized his former home except for the remaining Spanish street and place names, and the well-preserved Mission San Gabriel Arcangel near where he grew up. The only change in the mission buildings seemed to be the new shingle roof and church ceiling installed in 1886, replacing the old pitched tile roof.[36] Another change from the early days was the absence of the Franciscans who departed in 1852, replaced by secular clergy. The former Clemente ranch and much of the San Gabriel valley was now planted in orange groves, extending east to San Bernardino and Riverside.

Offshore there were boats in Avalon harbor on Catalina Island which had been developed as a summer resort by William and Hancock Banning, who bought the island for $150,000 in 1892.[61] The resort was reached from Wilmington, the seaport founded in 1859 by their father Phineas Banning, an early developer of all forms of transportation in the southwest.[68]

Los Angeles had a new Romanesque-style city hall and county courthouse, reflecting the growing Mediterranean motif. Boosters were promoting southern California as a new center for Anglo-Saxon culture to replace the decadent east with its constant infusion of "undesirable" immigrants from foreign shores, apparently unconcerned that many of these immigrants were from the shores of the Mediterranean itself.[62]

The *Los Angeles Times* had outgrown its first home, and in 1886 a new Times building was erected at First and Fort Streets costing about $50,000. The following year, the Times was the first Los Angeles newspaper to publish seven days a week.[37]

Leann and Ramón visited Jessie and Elizabeth Fremont in their new home on West 28th Street, called "The Retreat," a gift from their friends and admirers, the women of Los Angeles. Jessie was not yet fully recovered from illness following her husband's death. She had known John Fremont since her sixteenth year and they always had been very close. As Jessie talked about their marriage, Ramón realized he had not been aware of all the ups and downs they experienced, and he learned her personal philosophy that helped make their marriage so strong. She believed from the beginning that the most difficult yet most worthwhile part of marriage is trying to understand another human soul. In doing so, she also realized no two people are really alike and, as she put it, "everyone is a minority of one." Thus she learned at the end, as in the case of her own marriage to John Fremont, that no one can ever completely understand another person, but the important thing is trying and the continued search for understanding throughout their lives.[70] When they left, the Clementes felt they knew Jessie Fremont better than before. She and Elizabeth were grateful for the support of their many friends in Los Angeles, including the E.P. Clarks, who did so much to make their lives comfortable.[76]

After visiting the Fremonts, Leann and Ramón had dinner with the Clarks, who lived nearby on West Twenty-third Street. The three Clark daughters, each about one or two years apart, attended the Marlborough School for girls which had been converted from the former hotel. All four children were well-mannered in the New England and middle west tradition of their parents and spoke only when spoken to except for the youngest girl, about ten years old, who seemed more talkative and to be developing a strong will of her own.

Following dinner, Eli Clark described various aspects of how the city had changed. He told of how the oil boom hit town when Edward Doheny and his partner Charles Caulfield came to California and discovered oil near the corner of Second Street and Glendale Boulevard[64] and how Doheny later built a mansion with a private Roman Catholic chapel on Chester Place, not far from the Clarks and the Fremonts. He also told of how the Rancho Topanga Malibu Sequit, one of Ramón's favorite beach locations, had been acquired by Frederick Rindge of Massachusetts for $10 an acre, one hundred times what it cost its former owner in 1857.

The next day, Clark picked up the Clementes at the Pico House, took them for lunch to the California Club, and filled them in on more business and personal news. He and his brother-in-law M.H. Sherman, having completed an electric streetcar line to Pasadena, were working on a similar line to Santa Monica and considering a branch line to a new area called "Hollywood," which they thought might be a good investment for real estate subdivision.[77] Ramón recognized this as an opportunity to participate but felt the payoff might be too far off. He noted the area under consideration was near Cahuenga Pass in which Andrés Pico surrendered to John Fremont in 1847.[63]

Clark told them of another developer, Gaylord Wilshire, who planned a boulevard bearing his name, west to Santa Monica, following El Camino Viejo that Ramón rode down as a young man to visit the seaside ranchos.[65] Clark then showed them around the California Club and Ramón was interested to learn that its membership, though mostly Anglo-American, included a few surviving Californios of Spanish/Mexican descent.

After lunch Clark took them by the new Jonathan Club, another social center for business men downtown, and then through the new Bradbury building at Third and Fort Streets.[38] It was an unusual and impressive structure—five stories high with an interior court extending the entire height of the building, covered by an ornate skylight. Passengers were whisked to the top by cast-iron elevators on external tracks overlooking the courtyard. The surrounding galleries on each floor had elaborate iron railings, crosswalks, and staircases with sculptured columns, bathed in light from descending clerestory windows.[66] The entire effect was a feeling of great spaciousness and light. Leann and Ramón opined that this building would remain for many years as a landmark of architectural style and an inspiration for other architects.

By this time Clark had to return to his office but loaned the Clementes his carriage and driver to continue their sightseeing westward to the sea. He said that the Clementes' favorite community of Santa Monica, located on a portion of the old Rancho San Vicente, was growing in anticipation of his "Balloon Route" streetcar line's scheduled completion in April 1896, which would connect Los Angeles directly with the beach community.[39] On their way to the beach, the Clementes followed close to the new route by carriage, from downtown past "Fort Hill" where John Fremont placed a cannon and "captured" Los Angeles in 1847, northwest towards the

Santa Monica mountains, past scattered residences with indications of more to come, followed by endless orange groves and lemon orchards. Then as they approached Cahuenga Pass leading to the Mission San Fernando, the route veered southwest along the southern foothills of the Santa Monica mountains, through extensive fields of lima beans and other vegetables, to the small village of Sawtelle and nearby "Soldiers' Home" for veterans of the Civil War.

From that point Ramón and Leann could gaze almost directly into the sea, except when the road dipped slightly, then rose again, each time bringing it closer. They could feel the air change when they left the Soldiers' Home as the drier, warmer air of Los Angeles blended into the salty sea breezes. Ramón felt the same excitement at this point of change as he had when riding Cristobal over the same route to the seashore more than a half century earlier.

Arriving in Santa Monica, they noted much more activity than on their last visit. There were several new hotels, many buildings under construction, and there was even a public library in the Santa Monica Bank building.[40] Many handsome residences lined Ocean Avenue atop the palisades and the beach below was flourishing with bathhouses, restaurants, wharves and pavilions, all connected by a boardwalk.

Santa Monica's growth as a beach resort was not hindered and may have been helped by the failure of C.P. Huntington's Southern Pacific Railroad to have it become the principal deep water port for Los Angeles, after having built "the longest wooden pier in the world" two miles north of town.[41] Eventually the San Pedro-Long Beach area was selected for that purpose, as planned by Baker and Beale in 1880, after a group of business men led by the Los Angeles Times teamed up with the Santa Fe Railroad to challenge Huntington's control of the waterfront area. Loss of the harbor may have been Santa Monica's gain in developing as an outstanding beach community instead of an industrialized port city.

Ramón and Leann were urged by their friends to stay through the rest of the year and see the fifth annual New Year's Day Tournament of Roses Parade of flower-bedecked vehicles in the Los Angeles suburb of Pasadena, a few miles north of Mission San Gabriel and near where Don Guillermo had built the Clementes' new home in 1824. This midwinter event, calculated to lure snow-weary easterners to sunny southern California, was enticing, and Ramón would like to have visited the site of his former home, but the Clementes believed they should get home before rather than after the bad weather began in the east.

On the return trip to Washington, Leann and Ramón celebrated their fiftieth wedding anniversary. They chose the Southern Pacific "Sunset Route" via El Paso and San Antonio, Texas to New Orleans, then by steamship to New York on the former Morgan Line which the Southern Pacific had acquired to complete its coast-to-coast connection.[42] The steamship link, advertised as "100 golden hours at sea," paralleled the route taken by Ramón forty-five years earlier after their tour in Mexico, when Leann got off the ship at New Orleans to visit her family in St. Louis and he continued on to New York.

This time they both stopped off in New Orleans and stayed overnight before embarking on their sea voyage. They had thought of staying at the elegant St. Charles Hotel, which had turned them away on their honeymoon in 1846, but it recently burned down and was being rebuilt. The St. Louis Hotel in which they stayed before was still in existence but not operating as a hotel, so they stayed this time at the Cosmopolitan, a smaller establishment on Canal Street, just outside the French Quarter. The Cosmopolitan was operated principally as a New York style-apartment house but also had a hotel section which was most satisfactory.

For old times' sake they sought to revisit the French Quarter but were warned away. They heard it had been taken over by the underworld so that the streets were less safe at night than on their last visit. They learned that the Theatre d'Orleans had been destroyed by fire in 1866 with only the ballroom wing remaining, which was purchased in 1881 by an order of negro nuns—a fitting end for the former locale of the notorious Octaroon Balls. They learned that John Powell, the gentleman riverboat gambler whom they met at the end of their honeymoon, had become a successful businessman and property owner in New Orleans, St. Louis, and Tennessee by the time he was fifty years old but subsequently lost it all and died a pauper in 1870.[43]

The best news was that a new underground sewer system was being installed, making the city less unhealthy. Also public taste in entertainment was changing and there was growing opposition to crime and vice with the beginning of a police crackdown on illicit activities. Local newspapers such as the *Mascot*, first published in 1882, exposed corruption and printed personal items about prostitutes in its "Society Column," as did the *Sunday Sun* in its "Scarlet World" column.[44]

A novel experience for Leann and Ramón was seeing a musical performance in front of their hotel by a local negro group called The

Spasm Boys, who jumped about and shouted "hi-de-hi" and "ho-de-ho" while playing their noisy new type of music. The Clementes learned afterwards that this group, then called The Razzy Dazzy Spasm Band, had serenaded Sarah Bernhardt during her American tour, and the European diva was so impressed she gave them each a coin.[45] Ramón and Leann felt they may have witnessed the beginning of a new American musical movement called "jazz" here in New Orleans.

While they usually enjoyed new experiences, they also realized the past cannot be recaptured, so were ready to resume their journey the next day.

The sea voyage as a setting for their fiftieth anniversary was reminiscent of their twenty-fifth, also at sea. They had no party, at Leann's request, but at dinner they were served a special cake with congratulations from the ship's captain, who was advised of their intentions. After dinner they returned to their stateroom for a quiet time together, just the two of them as they were after their wedding. Leann changed into an emerald silk dressing gown and transferred to it her twenty-fiftieth wedding anniversary gift from Ramón—the gold pin with two birds facing each other on a field of diamonds. Ramón donned a smoking jacket Leann had given him on their fortieth wedding anniversary and a scarf he had worn on their first date. These were articles each had brought along for the occasion, unbeknownst to the other.

They did not exchange elaborate gifts, but each had for the other a remembrance of their half-century of marriage. Leann gave Ramón a small chest containing letters she had kept since they met and the white satin-covered Bible she had carried to the altar. He gave her an illustrated, bound chronology he had prepared depicting all of the significant happenings of their life together up to this point. (Author's note: These gifts were found in Uncle Tony's trunk and provided valuable material for this story.)

After going over the gifts, Ramón called for the room steward, at Leann's request, to bring a tray with one large orange, a knife, a lump of sugar, and a small pitcher of brandy over a warmer. When the tray arrived, Ramón knew Leann was going to do as she had on their wedding night. She cut through the peel's outer layer around the center of the orange, then gently lifted up the peel all around far enough to form a cup on top without breaking the skin in the process. In the center of the cup she placed the lump of sugar and covered it with the warm brandy. She lit the brandy and then handed the orange cup to Ramón, as her grandmother had taught her to give to her true love. Ramón made a toast to Leann and his love for her and their love for each other. They congratulated each other on their marriage which epitomized the "twaining of America" in the truest sense—the "twaining" of two strangers from different cultures, different backgrounds, and different parts of the country. They wished for many more anniversaries, though undoubtedly never another fiftieth.

This led to reconsideration of their own mortality, resulting in Ramón visiting the Oak Hill Cemetery in Georgetown in January 1897 to select a burial site. They liked the location on R Street overlooking Rock Creek just two blocks north of their former home. The cemetery was chartered by an 1849 Congressional Act on land donated by W. W. Corcoran which he had acquired from a great-nephew of George Washington.

Back in Washington Leann and Ramón were still drawn to the west but remained settled in the east, equally drawn to the nation's capital, which was now their home town. They loved all the country in between with its history that made America so great and were glad to have witnessed at least a portion of it. They were proud of their country's role as a free nation welcoming immigrants from all over the world to share in and contribute to its further growth.

They were not so proud, however, of their country's role in the Spanish-American War of 1898, which appeared to be promoted to a large extent by Hearst newspaper editorials against President McKinley's own inclinations. The editorials were part of a circulation war between the rival newspapers of William Randolph Hearst and Joseph Pulitzer, editor of the *New York World*. Hearst took over the *New York Journal* in 1895 after building up the *San Francisco Examiner* as a spokesman for populist causes and attacking entrenched business interests. When he employed Frederick Remington, the talented artist of western scenes, as an illustrator and despatched him to Cuba, Remington was said to have sent Hearst a message indicating there would be no war, whereupon Hearst was reported to have wired back: "You furnish the pictures; I will furnish the war."[11] The anecdote was not intended originally to discredit Hearst, according to correspondent James Creelman, who wrote at the time: "If the war against Spain is justified in the eyes of history, then yellow journalism deserves its place among the most useful instrumentalities of civilization."[46]

The term "yellow" as applied to journalism was not used initially in any derogatory sense. It derived from a character named

"The Yellow Kid" in a cartoon that appeared in Pulitzer's *New York World*. When a controversy arose with Hearst's *New York Journal* over rights to the character, the word "yellow" became a symbol for journalistic excess in the cause of competition.[47]

Many others contributed to the war fervor, including some of Ramón's acquaintance, such as Clarence King, who wrote articles supporting the Cuban insurgents against the Spanish government, and Henry Adams, who drafted the Senate report calling for President Cleveland to mediate with Spain for recognition of Cuban independence.[58]

Lacking the former "safety valve" of an expanding western frontier, the United States now had an excuse for expansion overseas. Since the 1830s America had been absorbed mostly with its own growth, but now was finding renewed interest in other parts of the world and began looking again to Washington for leadership, as in the early days of the Republic.

On the surface, war with Spain seemed to be a popular cause, and the common endeavor helped solidify post Civil War relations between north and south.[14] Ramón believed the origins of the war to be less compelling, however, in justifying the final outcome. The only two Spanish colonies then remaining in the western hemisphere were Cuba and Puerto Rico, and Spain had rejected United States overtures to purchase them. Growing Cuban unrest against oppressive Spanish rule following armed revolt in 1868, led to full-scale uprising in 1895 which was supported by American public opinion in favor of Cuban independence. Thereafter U.S. relations with Spain deteriorated and there was concern for the safety of American citizens in Havana.

The battleship *Maine* was sent to Havana harbor on January 25, 1898, as a diplomatic mission, although some feared it might aggravate existing tensions. On February 16th there was an explosion which killed or injured most of those aboard the *Maine*. Popular belief in the U.S. that this was a Spanish attack was supported by a Naval Court of Inquiry finding on March 21st that the explosion and resultant sinking of the *Maine* was caused by a submerged mine. A Spanish investigation found the sinking to be caused accidentally by an explosion in the ship's forward magazine, but this did not assuage U.S. public outrage. Congressional pressure for a tough stance was fanned by more fiery editorials and slogans such as "Remember the *Maine*."[48]

Finally and reluctantly, President McKinley gave up his search for a political and diplomatic solution to the matter, and on April

25th he asked Congress for a declaration of war. There followed a naval blockade of Cuba while the Pacific fleet attacked and vanquished the Spanish fleet in Manilla. Another ill-equipped fleet was sent hurriedly from Spain to Santiago, Cuba, where it was bottled up in the harbor and destroyed by superior American strength in a two-pronged attack. U.S. Army forces took the critical positions of El Caney and San Juan Hill, which controlled the city of Santiago, while the U.S. Navy completely destroyed the Spanish Caribbean Fleet outside the harbor. An important factor in the American naval victory was the use of new armor-piercing projectiles, manufactured by the fledgling Carpenter Steel Co., using a patented technique of "air hardening" steel.[49] The Spanish admiral's refusal to surrender and his brave efforts to challenge the far superior American fleet earned him the admiration of U.S. naval personnel on the scene.

A new American hero was made when former North Dakota cattle rancher and later New York Governor Theodore Roosevelt organized the 1st U.S. Volunteer Cavalry. He won national acclaim by personally leading his "Rough Riders" in the charge up Kettle Hill at San Juan, and taking the fortified village of El Caney.[50]

The war ended with the Treaty of Paris, at which Spain ceded to the United States for $20 million Guam and the Philippines in the Pacific and Cuba and Puerto Rico in the Caribbean. This terminated Spanish rule in the Americas.

The Spanish-American War seemed to be a later version of the War with Mexico fifty years before, both in the tradition of "manifest destiny." Victory in this later war, and the "Open Door" policy of Secretary of State John Hay towards China in 1899, moved the United States closer to becoming a world power by the end of the 19th century. In spite of its "colonial" presence in the western Pacific with acquisition of the Philippines, and commitment of troops to an international force for restoration of order in China, the United States remained primarily an industrial rather than a military power, as the population indicated its preference for geographic and political isolation over more foreign involvement.

There was distressing news in 1899 from the port of San Francisco of the reappearance of the dreaded bubonic plague, known as the "Black Death" that had originated in India and devastated large parts of Europe and other areas centuries before.[2] The Clementes hoped that the new technological developments and medical improvements in the latter part of the 19th century would stop the currently localized epidemic before it spread further.

The turn of the century, as Ramón and Leann witnessed it, did not mark the end of one period of history and the start of a new one, as could be derived from the fascination with which people awaited the numerical change and imbued it with some special significance. It was the same as the change from any other year to the next—and the same situations continued from 11:59 on December 31, 1899, to 12:01 on January 1, 1900.

The election of 1900 brought in another administration which had to deal with the same problems as the previous ones. The election was the result of the same political system enjoyed in the U.S. since the first president was elected. Some of the factors that brought in the next administration had their roots in previous decades. For example, the U.S. monetary system had been on a de facto gold standard since the 1870s, but the western silver mining interests persisted until Congress passed a law in 1890 mandating purchase of silver for coinage. President Cleveland had this law repealed in 1893 and lost the Democratic nomination to William Jennings Bryan of Nebraska. Bryan won with the slogan "You shall not crucify mankind on a cross of gold!" Incidentally this so-called "boy orator of Platte" was the first presidential candidate to travel by rail across the country to meet voters and address crowds in rural areas as well as in towns and cities throughout the land.

The gold interests supporting Republican nominee McKinley ridiculed Bryan with issuance of two-inch tokens to show how large a silver dollar would be if it contained a dollar's worth of the metal. Referring satirically to an assertion that the U.S. dollar coin contained only 53¢ worth of silver, smaller "dollar" tokens were issued with the inscription: "In God We Trust for the Other 47 Cents."[69] All of these tokens were called facetiously "Bryan money."[51] Furthermore the Democrats were blamed for the 1893 panic and the depression that continued through 1896, so the Republican McKinley was elected. He signed the Gold Standard Act in 1900 and was reelected to a second term the same year.[52]

As Ramón looked back on the early days in California, he compared the different methods used by Spain and England in colonizing the "new world" and the results achieved. Just as western Europe rose above other world power centers in the sixteenth century because it was not centrally controlled, so was the British/United States colonization of the American continent more successful than the Spanish/Mexican effort which presented more obstacles to change. With less central control, the American society and economy

grew and developed more competitively and thus effectively in relation to the geographically larger Spanish/Mexican colonies to the
west and south.

One advantage of the Spanish method over the British/
American was that rather than ignoring or eliminating the native
Indian population as the British colonists in the east and their
American descendants attempted to do, Spain saw how the Indians
could be useful in establishing the "plantation" or mission form of colonizing their territories in the west. This worked very well for a while
under the mission system. However Spain failed to maintain her
foothold because of weak governmental, economic, and social structures. The Spanish had come to America with the primary purpose of
getting gold and riches out of the new land, and only secondary was
the concept of making a self-sufficient and productive community.

The English colonists came with the idea of settling permanently, usually as a family—first the backwoods settlers and later the
independent farmers and ranchers who carved out the beginnings of
the present United States. They brought with them English concepts of law and government, eventually breaking with Britain and
forming their own rules rather than relaying on a far away surrogate
to govern them.

In the south, plantation owners had to rely on enslaved African
peoples to work their lands, having driven away the native Indians
rather than use them as the Spanish had in their mission system. *If
the southern United States had done as the Spanish did, would there have
been a Civil War,* Ramón wondered.

Even though Mexico eventually broke with Spain, it did not
have the cohesion of family and institutional growth such as the
British colonies had from the beginning. Ramón could see, in the
last decade of the century, the ultimate advantages of the British
system of colonization augmented by the new American concepts.
This was demonstrated by the economic growth and industrial
development in the eastern United States which spread inevitably
west and was unequalled by Mexico or any other hispanic colonized
areas in the western hemisphere.

As Ramón had more time to reflect on his experiences and observations, he began to ponder that "other" westward movement, that
of displaced American Indians.[53] Although born in Spanish
California and having been a Mexican citizen, Ramón felt he could
look objectively at the policies of his adopted country with as critical an eye as a native American or a complete foreigner. Perhaps he

was in a better position than either one to look objectively and critically at some policies that seemed at best ambivalent, and at worst cruel, unfair, insensitive, and as imperialistic as those of other nations the U.S. criticized for doing much less.

New York cartoonist Thomas Nast expressed similar concerns in a cartoon published in 1879 concerning efforts to oust Chinese from California. It showed a red man being driven westward by a locomotive and a yellow man trying to catch another locomotive that will take him east. The red man says to the Chinaman: "Pale-face 'fraid you crowd him out as he did me!"

Ramón wondered about those Indians who were forced to leave their homelands in the east and south and relocate further west. He thought of this as the "other" westward migration as opposed to the highly glamorized westward movement of white settlers in the name of "manifest destiny." He recalled that much had been written, painted, photographed, staged, and sung about the phenomenal westward growth of the United States but little about the "other" westward migration of North American Indians to make room for growth of the white man's civilization.

While aided greatly by the railroads and by the Homestead Act of 1862, which promised "free land" to any American claimant, westward expansion of the United States resulted from forced westward migration of the North American Indians and their subsequent concentration into limited areas, which enabled the white man to move into the vacated regions.

Ramón compared this with the California experience, in which Spanish missionaries first trained, taught, and lived with the native Indians. Although maintaining superiority and leadership over the Indians, and often treating them almost as slaves, the Spaniards did not throw them out or destroy them, but rather used them and tried to convert them to Christianity. This is not to deny the frequent mistreatment and abuse of these same Indians, particularly after the missions were secularized.

While California Indians were not forcibly driven off their homelands by Spain and Mexico, after the Americans took over California it was a different story. Many former mission Indians found themselves being packed off to reservations in other parts of the United States to make room for the white man's farms, ranches, roads, towns, and cities.

As Theodore Roosevelt noted in his writings,[34] there were wrongs on both sides, with a tendency for each to consider only their own side and to blame an entire race for individual wrongdoing. Many frontiersmen were brutal and overbearing, while many Indians were treacherous and cruel, but many more on each side were not. Roosevelt found that Indians differed not only as individuals, but by tribe, with Cherokees, Nez Perces, Pueblos, and Cheyennes near the top in relation to white standards, and Apaches, Arapahoes, and "Digger" Snakes near the bottom.[55]

It is little wonder that bitter conflicts occurred between those North American Indians who were still free to function as such and the white settlers, with their U.S. Army defenders. Such conflicts frequently led to full scale warfare, such as: the Black Hawk war of 1837 when Sauk-Fox tribes were pushed west across the Mississippi; the war with the Seminoles resulting in their removal in 1842 from Florida to the territory now known as Oklahoma; and many others down to the last armed conflict between the U.S. Cavalry and the Sioux at Wounded Knee, South Dakota, in 1890.[56]

The "Wounded Knee" conflict was not a war but a massacre. The Ogala Sioux were confined to the Pine Ridge Indian Reservation in the southwest corner of the state. Resigned to their fate after 150 years of fruitless struggle, they took spiritual refuge in a new religious movement called the Ghost Dance. Its central theme that the world was coming to an end was based on the apocalypse as explained to them by Christian missionaries. In the Sioux version, the whites would be destroyed and the Indians would inherit the earth.

By December of 1890, this religious movement was making white reservation officials nervous so they called in the military to round up and arrest the Ghost Dance leaders. On December 19th, a group of 350 Sioux led by Chief Big Foot moved off the reservation in an attempt to evade the soldiers but were captured the following day. They were brought back to the place called Wounded Knee on the Pine Ridge reservation and ordered to disarm. One Sioux brave refused and scuffled with one of the soldiers. Someone fired a shot and the massacre began, ending in only a few minutes with the slaughter of 300 Indians, including women and children. Sixty U.S. soldiers also were killed, mostly by the crossfire of their own comrades. Due to a snowstorm the following day, it was not until New Year's Day 1891 that a pit was dug and the snow-covered bodies of the Indian dead were shoved in.[56]

Ramón recalled from history studies that William the Conqueror's Norman horsemen in 1066 had an advantage over the

Anglo-Saxons through use of the stirrup to steady the rider during attack. Ramón wondered if the American cavalry may have had the same initial advantage over the Indians, who originally rode bareback, without stirrups, which were added later. He also noted the Americans advantage of earlier and greater use of firearms.

There were also westward movements of Indians without wars, such as when the Cherokees were forced to cede their Georgia land in 1835 after gold was discovered thereon and made to cross the Mississippi into Oklahoma territory. There were numerous other examples of uprootings of Indians from east to west, including the original Sioux movement from North Carolina to South Dakota, which led to the American disaster known as "Custer's Last Stand." The Sioux may have sensed another forced move if not their complete extermination and reacted accordingly. There were also the Chickasaw and Choctaw tribes moved from Mississippi and Alabama to Oklahoma, the Shawnee tribe from Illinois and Kentucky to Oklahoma, and many others.

Some said the Indians deserved no help from the U.S. government or expenditure of taxpayers' dollars in their behalf, because they were a defeated nation. But there never was a single unified Indian nation, only a large number of separate tribes, some of which were joined in loose confederations, in common cultural areas, and by linguistic groups, combinations of which were sometimes described as "nations."

In the early nineteenth century, the United States wasn't in much of a position to help anyone but itself. But looking into the future, Ramón could see the United States becoming one of the world's foremost powers, helping other nations, to become U.S. trading partners; and also to see the U.S. trying to right wrongs perpetrated against former black slaves in the cause of human rights and proclaiming the need for such rights in other countries. He wondered if the U.S. would do as much for the native American Indians.

While the abolition of slavery by the United States in the nineteenth century was a tremendous step forward for human rights, Ramón believed treatment of the American Indians would remain a negative factor indefinitely. He noted further that freedom for blacks received a setback in 1896 when the Supreme Court approved racial segregation under the "separate but equal" doctrine after having declared Louisiana's "Jim Crow Car" law unconstitutional.[1,4] In spite of these drawbacks, Ramón felt love and respect for his adopted country that overcame the negative factors.

Altogether he felt his own and his adopted country's course had been generally in the right direction. He fully recognized that he, as well as his country, had made many mistakes and could have done many things a lot better. But if he had his life to do over, Ramón thought he probably would do most of the same things with, he hoped, many improvements. As far as the country was concerned, Ramón believed he could look in vain throughout the world for a better national example with better national and international results.

He and Leann had seen the fruition of "manifest destiny" in the westward growth of America to become a bi-coastal nation with a population of over 70 million, from less than 10 million in 1820, now centered in southeast Indiana, far from the east coast where it began. They believed that the spirit and energy shown by Americans in the nineteenth century would provide momentum to make the United States the greatest nation in the world in the twentieth century to come.

THE END

Illustration No. 42: Shoreham Hotel, Washington, DC,
opened 1889 at 15th and K Street NW.

Illustration No. 43: Richmond Hotel (previously Richmond Flats), Washington, DC, 1890

Illustration No. 44: John Philip Sousa, the March King (center) as leader of U.S. Marine Band, 1890.

Illustration No. 45: Henrietta "Hetty" Howland Green (1834-1916)

Illustration No. 46: "What We Worship" cartoon by Thomas Nast, 1869

THE POWER OF THE PRESS.

Illustration No. 47: "The Power of the Press" cartoon by Thomas Nast, 1869

Illustration No. 48: Sitting Bull with Buffalo Bill

Illustration No. 49: Rose's Station, circa 1989-90; trading post and watering stop for stages. Center of social activities for Tejon Ranch.

Illustration No. 50: Hospital at Fort Tejon, 1888

Illustration No. 51: Tejon Ranch stables, 1888

Illustration No. 52: Tejon Ranch blacksmith shop and men's quarters, 1889-90

Illustration No. 53: Tejon Ranch Vaqueros at majordomo's headquarters, circa 1887

Illustration No. 54: Tejon Ranch cattle boss, circa 1889

Illustration No. 55: Bird's eye view of Los Angeles, 1893

Illustration No. 56: Sixth Street and Broadway, Los Angeles, circa 1890

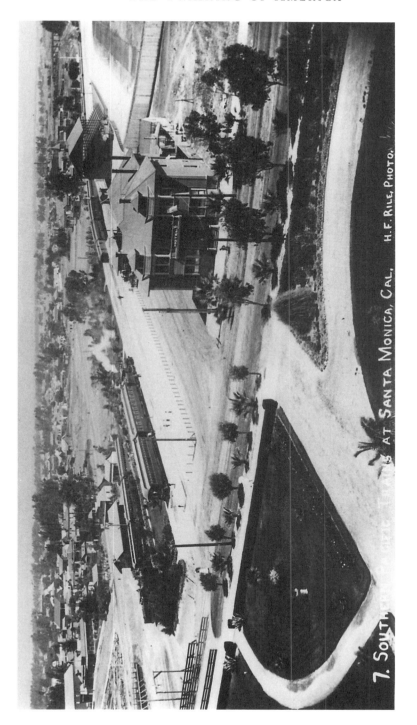

Illustration No. 57: Southern Pacific Railroad depot in Santa Monica, circa 1890

Illustration No. 58: Opening day of trolley line from Los Angeles to Santa Monica, 1896

Illustration No. 59: Georgetown, DC,
3000 block of P Street NW (Formerly West Street)

Illustration No. 60: Georgetown, DC Wisconsin Ave. at M Street (Formerly High and Falls Streets) circa 1900

CHAPTER NOTES

Prologue
1.   Goetzmann, p. 81

Chapter 1—Childhood in Alta California
1.   Barnard, pp. 16 and 65
2.   Ibid., p. 56
3.   Ibid., pp. 57–58
4.   Ibid., p. 59
5.   U.S. Department of Interior, p. 47
6.   Claretian Missionaries, p. 7
7.   Ibid., p. 14
8.   Ibid., p. 10
9.   Barnard, p. 27
10. Claretian Missionaries, pp. 19, 21, and 23
11. Crowe, pp. 34–35
12. Claretian Missionaries, p. 22
13. Ibid., p. 18
14. Barnard, p. 48
15. Claretian Missionaries, pp. 4–5
16. American Guide, Mountain States and West Coast, p. 1203

Chapter 2—Early Experiences in the United States
1.   Crowe, p. 51
2.   California Department of Commerce, p. 22
3.   The source of information is a travel brochure for the Alumni College Abroad *A Voyage of Discovery—Tracing the Route of the Explorers from Cape Horn to Gibraltar, February 27–April 3, 1990*, published for the Association of Yale Alumni, New Haven, CT
4.   Baruch, pp. 13–14

5. American Express, p. 5
6. Adams, p. 174
7. Stover, p. 41
8. Ibid., pp. 36–37
9. Goode, *Capital Losses*, p. 175
10. *American Heritage*, July/August 1988, "The Time Machine," p. 38
11. *Gourmet*, April 1989, "Charleston" by Mimi Elder, p. 140
12. *Southern Heritage*, "Dining In the Low Country," pp. 21–23
13. The source of information is *Chronicle 1823–1983*, a Chemical Bank Special edition of September 1983, published by Chemical Banking Corp., New York, NY
14. Adams, p. 141
15. *Yale Alumni Magazine*, October 1989, "Light and Verity," p. 21
16. Ibid., February 1989, "Old Yale—Medical Beginnings," by Judith Ann Schiff, p. 27
17. Adams, p. 172
18. Ibid., p. 174

Chapter 3—Background for Conquest
1. Woodward, p. 129
2. Eisenhower, p. 197

Chapter 5—Tieing It All Together
1. The source of information is Stack's Catalogue for Public Coin Auction, September 8 and 9, 1988, *Hard Times Tokens*, 270–88, published by Stack's, New York, NY

Chapter 6—How Paths Crossed
1. Fremont, pp. 19–23
2. San Clemente, *History—The View from San Clemente*, by Doris Walker, p. 4
3. Scherer, p. 20
4. Claretian Missionaries, p. 7
5. Crowe, pp. 4–41
6. Fremont, pp. 362–64
7. Brandon, pp. 16–17
8. Starr, *Material Dreams*, p. 82
9. Starr, *Inventing the Dream*, pp. 8–9
10. Ibid., p. 15
11. Ibid., p. 17

12. Lewis, O., p. 90
13. Stone, *Men to Match My Mountains*, p. 31
14. Ibid., p. 34
15. Ibid., p. 39
16. Stone, *Immortal Wife*, pp. 11, 15

Chapter 7—Old Trails and New Beginnings
1. Fremont, p. 365
2. Ibid., pp. 370–71
3. Ibid., pp. 372–73
4. Ibid., pp. 375–76
5. Ibid., p. 381
6. Ibid., p. 406
7. Goetzmann, p. xii
8. Fremont, p. 409
9. *American Heritage*, May/June 1990, "Las Vegas—An Oasis," by Samuel Sifton, p. 38
10. Fremont, p. 388
11. Eisenhower, p. 197
12. Barbour, p. 167
13. U.S. Department of Interior, p. 33
14. Ibid., p. 53
15. Stone, *Men to Match My Mountains*, p. 26
16. Stone, *Immortal Wife*, pp. 99–100, 120
17. Ibid., p. 120

Chapter 8—St. Louis and the California Connection
1. Barbour, p. 20
2. Asbury, pp. 458 and 462
3. Ibid., p. 8
4. Ibid., pp. 92–93
5. Ibid., pp. 137–40
6. *Southern Heritage*, "New Orleans Creole Dinner," pp. 29–31
7. Asbury, p. 145
8. Ibid., p. 130
9. Yeoman, pp. 108, 114, 126, 147, 180, 190, and 197
10. Asbury, p. 172
11. Ibid., pp. 216–17
12. Ibid., 203–04
13. *Smithsonian*, May 1988, "Andrew Jackson Grayson's Avian Art," by Philip Kastner, p. 146

14. Barbour, p. 47
15. U.S. Department of State, "Principal Officers and Chiefs of Mission 1778–1886," Mexico
16. Stover, p. 61
17. Goode, *Capital Losses*, p. 175
18. Miller, p. 3
19. Kelsey, p. 167
20. Ibid., p. 219
21. Adams, p. 214
22. Goetzmann, p. 130
23. Goetzmann, p. 138
24. Kelsey, p. 250
25. Martin, pp. 11–24
26. Starr, *Americans and the California Dream*, p. 26
27. Starr, *Inventing the Dream*, pp. 18–19
28. *Numismatist*, February 1991, p. 210, "The California Mint Debate," by Cole D. Danebower
29. Yeoman, 44th Ed. 1991, p. 234, "Moffat and Co."
30. Lewis, O., pp. 76, 79–80
31. Stone, *Men to Match My Mountains*, p. 71
32. Ibid., p. 112
33. Kirschten, p. 23
34. Ibid., p. 131
35. Ibid., p. 22
36. Ibid., p. 152
37. Stone, *Immortal Wife*, p. 47
38. Ibid., p. 149
39. Ibid., pp. 212–14
40. Ibid., pp. 265, 273, and 276

Chapter 9—Living in Georgetown DC
1. Scherer, p. 34
2. Holmes, pp. 8 and 30
3. Goode, *Capital Losses*, p. 412
4. U.S. Fine Arts Commission, *Georgetown Residential Architecture-Northeast*, p. 52
5. Ibid., p. 129
6. Ibid., p. 191
7. Cutler, p. 25 .
8. U.S. Fine Arts Commission, *Georgetown Residential Architecture-Northeast*, pp. 37 and 113

9. The source of information is brochure *Touring Historic Georgetown*, published by The Georgetowner, Washington DC

10. Goode, *Capital Losses*, p. 451

11. Ibid., p. 408

12. Ibid., p. 310

13. Ibid., p. 453

14. Green, (1800–78), p. 224

15. *American Heritage*, February 1989, "Editor's Bookshelf," review of "Highbrow/Lowbrow" by Lawrence W. Levine, p. 119

16. Martin, p. 61

17. Ibid., p. 70–71

18. Ibid., p. 64–65

19. *American Heritage*, Sept./Oct. 1989, "Post Haste" by Robert L. O'Connell, p. 78

20. *Numismatic News*, 3/21/89, "U.S. Gold Production Heading For Record," by David C. Harper, p. 1

21. *American Heritage*, November 1989, "Chantilly," by Bill Barol, p. 26

22. Barbour, p. 23

23. Scherer, p. 20

24. *American Heritage*, July/August 1988, "The Indispensable Thoreau," by Edward Hoagland, p. 65

25. *Smithsonian*, May 1988, "Andrew Jackson Grayson's Avian Art," by Philip Kastner, p. 148–54

26. Yeoman, p. 180

27. Crowe, p. 59

28. Goetzmann, p. 126

29. Goode, *Capital Losses*, p. 77

30. Ibid., p. 93

31. Cutler, p. 28

32. Stone, *Men to Match My Mountains*, p. 149

33. Stone, *Immortal Wife*, p. 285

34. Ibid., p. 290–91

Chapter 10—Politics and the Civil War
1. Grun, pp. 1843G and 1844F

2. Goode, *Capital Losses*, pp. 293–94

3. Ewing, p. 52

4. *Washington Post*, 9/14/89, p. A1, "Storybook Treasure Found Off South Carolina," by Ken Ringle

5. Barbour, p. 23

6. Ibid., p. 90
7. Crowe, p. 62
8. U.S. General Services Administration, *The Written Word Endures*, pp. 48–50
9. Stover, p. 100
10. U.S. Commission of Fine Arts, *Washington Architecture*, pp. 59–60
11. Paine, p. 73
12. Bally Manufacturing Co., 1987 Annual Report
13. Grun, p. 1861B
14. *Washington Post*, 9/6/89, p. B3, "Personalities"
15. *Numismatic News*, 10/24/89, p. 26, "Civil War Troops Despised Sutler System," by Robert R. Van Ryzin
16. *Smithsonian*, July 1988, "We've Scared Mr. Lincoln Like Hell!" by Thomas A. Lewis, p. 66
17. Carey, p. 371, *The Murder of Mr. Lincoln*, by Walt Whitman
18. Kennedy, James, pp. 8–10
19. *American Heritage*, March 1989, "The South's Inner Civil War," by Eric Foner, p. 47
20. Ibid., March 1990, "The Big Parade," by Thomas Fleming, p. 98
21. Howard, p. 115
22. Ibid., p. 83
23. Ibid., p. 256
24. Ibid., p. 50
25. Ibid., pp. 158–59
26. Gleason, p. 156
27. Ibid., p. 168
28. *American Heritage*, March 1990, p. 18, "Paying For The War," by John Steele Gordon
29. *Washington Post*, 2/25/91, p. D1, "Tracking History on the Underground Railroad," by Avis Thomas-Lester
30. Stone, *Immortal Wife*, p. 355

Chapter 11—Post-War Plateau
1. *Washington Post*, 10/16/88, p. F1, "Where Time Stood Still," by Sarah Booth Conroy
2. Goode, *Capital Losses*, pp. 226
3. Ibid., p. 386
4. Green, (1800–1878), p. 312
5. Ewing, p. 51

6. Goode, *Capital Losses*, p. 257
7. *Smithsonian*, May 1988, "Andrew Jackson Grayson's Avian Art," by Philip Kastner, p. 154
8. Turner, p. 60
9. Ibid., p. 57
10. Ibid., p. 67
11. Green, (1800–78), pp. 341–42
12. Goode, *Capital Losses*, p. 296

Chapter 12—European Adventure
1. Miller, p. 3
2. The source of information is a brochure from the Hotel de Crillon, Paris
3. *Town and Country*, April 1987, "The Grand Tables of Paris," by James Villas, p. 196
4. *France*, Spring 1988, "The Côte d'Azur," by Monique L. Burns, p. 26
5. Ibid., Summer 1986, "The French Riviera," by Gail Forman, p. 79
6. *Washington Post*, 3/19/89, p. E1, "Rome Revisited," by Philip Glazebrook
7. The source of information is a travel brochure of the Venice-Simplon Orient Express, Inc. 1982
8. The source of information is a travel brochure of the National Trust for Historic Preservation, *The Rhineland in Autumn*, 1985
9. Kurtz, p. 232
10. Ibid., p. 216
11. *France*, Winter 1986–87, "Versailles on the Potomac," by Herbert Stein-Schneider, p. 42
12. Davidson, p. 170
13. Kurtz, p. 217
14. Martin, p. 132
15. Kennedy, Paul, p. 186
16. Ibid., p. 192
17. The source of information is a special advertising section of the Monaco Government Tourism Office, appearing in the *New Yorker Magazine*, May 28, 1990.

Chapter 13—Between East and West
1. *Town and Country*, September 1989, "Forever Fifth," by Lindsy van Gelder, p. 170
2. Ibid., p. 174
3. *American Heritage*, December 1988, "The Currier and Ives Print," by Olivier Bernier, p. 20
4. Goode, *Capital Losses*, p. 176
5. *Smithsonian*, May 1988, "Andrew Jackson Grayson's Avian Art," by Joseph Kastner, p. 154
6. Hinckley, p. 126
7. *Improvement Era*, April 1987, "The Tabernacle Organ," by Jay M. Todd, p. 14
8. Utah Travel Council, p. 41
9. American Guide Series, *Nevada*, p. 148
10. Ibid., p. 99
11. Ibid., p. 275
12. Yeoman, pp. 128, 149, 165, 192, and 198
13. American Guide Series, *Nevada*, p. 283
14. Ibid., p. 275
15. Ibid., p. 81
16. *American Heritage*, May/June 1990, "Las Vegas, an Oasis," by Samuel Sifton, p. 38
17. American Guide Series, *California*, p. 279
18. Goetzmann, p. 158
19. Ibid., p. 159
20. Ibid., p. 167
21. Crowe, p. 92
22. American Guide Series, *California*, pp. 58–59
23. Ibid., p. 111
24. Ibid., p. 217
25. U.S. Commission of Fine Arts, *Washington Architecture*, p. 41
26. *American Heritage*, March 1989, "The First 1010," by Nancy Sheperdson, p. 101
27. *Numismatic News*, 12/27/88, p. 16, "Carpetbaggers Once Worked for Wildcats," by Ed Rochette
28. Baruch, p. 32
30. Paine, p. 294
31. Sparks, p. 103
32. Carey, p. 393, *An Immigrant Crosses America*, by Robert Louis Stevenson
33. Crowe, pp. 56 and 72

34. *Washington Post*, 2/13/89, p. A4, "60-foot Sloop Shatters Clipper Ship's NY-SF Record," by Matt Lait
35. *American Heritage*, Sept./Oct. 1989, "Post Haste," by Robert L. O'Connell, pp. 79-81
36. Crowe, pp. 46 and 78
37. Yenne, p. 52
38. Martin, p. 153
39. Berkman, p. 18
40. Jakes, p. 448
41. Goode, *Best Addresses*, pp. 4, 8–10
42. Goode, *Capital Losses*, p. 181
43. Ibid., pp. 262–66
44. *Wall Street Journal*, 4/18/89, p. B2, "American Entrepreneurs—AandP's John Hartford"
45. Goode, *Capital Losses*, p. 344
46. *Numismatic News*, 11/29/88, p. 24, "Silver Dollars Once Unwelcome in St. Louis," by Ed Rochette
47. Freud, p. 13
48. *American Heritage*, July/August 1989, "Bernhardt in America," by John Kobler, p. 52
49. Goode, *Capital Losses*, p. 436
50. *Numismatic News*, 9/6/88, p. 35, "Fabulous Rarities Catalogued in Randall Collection," by Paul M. Green
51. *Numismatist*, December 1988, "Col. Fisk's 'Relief for Chicago' Medal," by Thomas P. Gardner, p. 2094
52. Ibid., p. 2092
53. *American Heritage*, December 1989, "Mephistopheles of Wall Street," by John Steele Gordon, p. 20
54. Adams, p. 163
55. *American Heritage*, Sept./Oct. 1989, "The Public Be Damned," by John Steele Gordon, p. 18
56. *Barron's*, 5/30/88, p. 4, "Good As Gold," by Jay Palmer
57. *Washington Post*, 6/8/89, p. B1, "How Many Democrats did Al Packer eat?" by Lloyd Grove
58. Berkman, pp. 40, 44–46
59. *Wall Street Journal*, 4/25/88, p. 1 article re annual Ramona pageant in Hemet CA
60. Basten, p. 8
61. Wilkins, pp. 81–82
62. Ibid., p. 118
63. Ibid., pp. 253, 269

64. Ibid., pp. 258, 290
65. Ibid., pp. 1, 7, 14, 22, 32, 34, and 39
66. Ibid., pp. 132, 195, and 220
67. Ibid., p. 263
68. Ibid., pp. 158, 185
69. California Department of Commerce, p. 144
70. Starr, *Americans and the California Dream*, p. 182
71. Ibid., p. 244
72. Ibid., p. 366
73. Ibid., p. 192
74. Starr, *Inventing the Dream*, pp. 41–42
75. Ibid., pp. 17, 40
76. Ibid., p. 44
77. Ibid., p. 141
78. Ibid., pp. 23, 24, 26, 30
79. Ibid., p. 38
80. U.S. Department of Interior, p. 87
81. Ibid., p. 89–90
82. *Washington Post Magazine*, 4/28/91, p. 27, "Boss," by Eugene L. Meyer
83. Lewis, O., p. 90
84. Ibid., p. 186
85. Ibid., p. pp. 93 and 95
86. Ibid., pp. 183 and 185
87. Stone, *Men to Match My Mountains*, p. 38
88. Ibid., p. 292

Chapter 14—Home in Washington

1. Goode, *Best Addresses*, p. 11
2. Goode, *Capital Losses*, p. 19
3. Crowe, pp. 79–81
4. Ibid., pp. 56 and 67
5. Goode, *Capital Losses*, p. 268
6. Ewing, p. 55
7. Green (1879–1950), p. 77
8. Ibid., p. 14
9. Ibid., p. 15
10. Cutler, p. 16
11. U.S. Commission of Fine Arts, *Sixteenth Street Architecture*, pp. 324, 337, and 351
12. Ibid., *Washington Architecture* 1791–1861, p. 131

13. Ibid., *Georgetown Residential Architecture-Northeast*, p. 206
14. Ibid., pp. 191–92
15. Sousa, pp. 53 and 66
16. U.S. Commission of Fine Arts, *Sixteenth Street Architecture*, p. 158
17. Ibid., p. 114
18. Ibid., p. 115
19. Cutler, p. 2
20. *Washington Post*, 6/10/90, p. F1, "The Lives of the Lafayette Square Literati," by Sarah Booth Conroy
21. Cutler, p. 7
22. Goetzmann, p. 288–91
23. Ibid., p. 292
24. Goode, *Capital Losses*, p. 259
25. Ibid., p. 357
26. U.S. General Services Administration, *American Image*, p. 4
27. *Washington Post*, 6/26/88, p. 1 of Style Section, "The Club—When Men Were Men," by Sarah Booth Conroy
28. *American Heritage*, December 1988, "When Robert Louis Stevenson Was One of Us," by Margaret Hodges, p. 88
29. Martin, pp. 173–77
30. Ibid., pp. 179–80
31. Fremont, pp. 550–63, 559, 582–85
32. Lewis, A., p. 50
33. Sparks, p. 215
34. Turner, pp. 83 and 89
35. Ibid., p. 88
36. *American Heritage*, Sept./Oct. 1989, "The Public Be Damned," by John Steele Gordon, p. 18
37. *Washington Post*, 5/19/89, p. 106, "George Eastman Said 'Kodak'" by Richard Conniff
39. Greene (1879–1950), p. 91
40. *Smithsonian*, March 1988, p. 70, "Speaking of Snow Jobs," by Ezra Bowen
41. *Farmer's Almanac*, 1988, p. 106, article re Ernest L. Thayer's poem "Casey at the Bat"
42. Goode, *Capital Losses*, p. 346
43. *Wall Street Journal*, 1/25/89, p. B1, Centennial Journal: "A Better Than Average Year—1896"; and Centennial Edition, p. B9, "On The Average—How Dow-Jones Indicator Evolved"
44. Goode, *Capital Losses*, p. 182

45. *American Heritage*, April 1989, p. 20, "The Dread Federal Surplus," by Bernard A. Weisberger

46. *Washington Post*, 6/2/89, Section D, "When The Streets Were Knee-Deep," by Cristina del Sesto

47. U.S. Commission of Fine Arts, *Georgetown Residential Architecture-Northeast*, p. 174

48. *Washingtonian*, July 1990, p. 35, "Painter and Politician," by Stephen May.

49. Wilkins, pp. 348, 352

50. Ibid., p. 268

51. *Gourmet*, April 1989, "Charleston," by Mimi Elder, p. 138

52. Goode, *Capital Losses*, p. 130

53. *Washington Post Magazine*, 4/28/91, p. 27, "Boss," by Eugene L. Meyer

Chapter 15—Differences
1. Scherer, p. 20
2. Kennedy, James, p. 7

Chapter 16—Looking Back and Forward
1. *American Heritage*, December 1989, p. 106, "When Our Ancestors Became Us," by John Steele Gordon

2. Turner, p. 92

3. Goetzmann, p. 295

4. *Washington Post*, 6/26/88, p. C3, "Urban Design," by John P. Eberhard

5. Federal Mogul, p. 5

6. *Automobile Quarterly*, Quatrefoil Catalogue (Jan. 1989), Special Excerpt from "Packard the Pride," by J.M. Fenster

7. *Wall Street Journal*, 1/26/89, p. B1, Centennial Journal: "The Horseless Carriage Struts Its Stuff—1900"

8. *American Heritage*, April 1989, p. 32, "Time Machine—1889"

9. Ibid., November, 1989, p. 37, "Time Machine—1889"

10. *Wall Street Journal*, Centennial Issue, p. B9, "Events That Helped Shape the Century—1890"

11. Martin, p. 183

12. *American Heritage*, July/August 1989, p. 52, "Bernhardt in America, by John Kobler

13. *Town and Country*, September 1989, "Forever Fifth," by Lindsy van Gelder, p. 171

14. Stover, p. 121

15. Baruch, p. 79
16. Lewis, A. pp. 69–73
17. Ibid., p. 74; and Sparks, p. 199
18. See Chapter 14, note 43
19. *Wall Street Journal*, 1/17/89, p. B1, Centennial Journal: "Organized Labor's Turbulent Dawn—1892"
20. *Old News*, p. 1, "Whose Fault Was the Johnstown Flood," by Richard Sheppard
21. *Wall Street Journal*, 1/18/89, p. B1, Centennial Journal: "Stocks Derail and Panic Ensues—1893"
22. Ibid., 1/23/89, p. B1, Centennial Journal: "Pullman Strike Strikes Blow to Labor"
23. Ibid., Centennial Edition, p. B9, "Events That Helped Shape The Century—1894"
24. U.S. Commission of Fine Arts, *A Brief History*, p. 1
25. *Washington Post*, 3/3/89, p. F1, "100th Anniversary of the Zoo," by Karlyn Barber
26. *The Georgetowner*, 3/10–23/89, p. 24, "The National Zoo Celebrates Its 100th," by Gary Tischler
27. *Notes of Interest*, p. 6
28. Goode, *Capital Losses*, pp. 280 and 361
29. Ibid., p. 325
30. Crowe, p. 110
31. Stover, p. 172
32. Ibid., p. 159
33. Gibson, p. 1
34. Goetzmann, p. 183
35. Crowe, pp. 66 and 101
36. The source of information is a brochure *Welcome to Mission San Gabriel*,© Antonio Echezarreta 1971
37. *Los Angeles Times*, "The First 100 Years—A Special Edition of Among Ourselves," 11/20/81, p. 3
38. American Guide Series, *California*, p. 221
39. *Los Angeles Herald*, "Fiesta Number," May 6, 1903
40. Basten, p. 22
41. Ibid., p. 17
42. Yenne, p. 54
43. Asbury, pp. 204–05
44. Ibid., pp. 439–40
45. Ibid., p. 438

46. *Wall Street Journal*, 8/4/89, "Bookshelf," review by Steve Coates of "The Yellow Kids", by Joyce Milton
47. *Washington Post*, 9/3/89, "Book World" review by Harrison Salisbury of "The Yellow Kids", by Joyce Milton
48. *The Numismatist*, January 1989, "Two Coins from the Bottom of Santiago Bay," by Thomas H. Sebring, p. 57
49. Carpenter Technology 1989 Annual Report, p. 8
50. Carey, p. 407, "The Spanish-American War—The Battle of El Caney," by James Creelman
51. *Numismatic News*, 1/31/89, p. 34, "Bryan Money Lampooned Drive for Free Silver," by Robert R. van Ryzin
52. *Wall Street Journal*, 1/30/89, p. B1, Centennial Journal: "Gold Sets a New Standard—1900"
53. *Washington Times*, 8/8/88, "Insight on the News: A Legal and Legislative Indian War," by Miles Cunningham
54. Paine, p. 412
55. Roosevelt, p. 105–07
56. *Washington Post*, 1/29/89, p. E5, "And Where, Pray Tell, Is Wounded Knee?" by John Gattuso
57. Wilkins, pp. 357, 388–89
58. Ibid., pp. 399–401
59. *Washington Post* Magazine, 8/12/90, p. 13, "100 Years of Serenity," by Benjamin Fogey
60. Crowe, p. 57
61. Starr, *Inventing the Dream*, p. 65
62. Ibid., p. 89
63. Ibid., p. 284
64. Starr, *Material Dreams*, p. 125
65. Ibid., p. 82
66. Ibid., p. 183
67. *CandO Historical Magazine*, April '90, pp. 4–7, "Remembering Chicago's Grand Central Station," by Andy Agnew
68. Lewis, O., p. 184
69. The source of information *Stack's American Historical Medals Fixed Price List*, Stack's, New York, NY 1991
70. Stone, *Immortal Wife*, pp. 75, 393, 496
71. Walter, pp. v and 4
72. Ibid., p. 9 and 10
73. Ibid., pp. 12 and 13
74. Army and Navy Club, p. 8

BIBLIOGRAPHY

Adams, James Truslow, *The Epic of America*. New York: Garden City Publishing Co., 1947.

American Automobile Association, *Tour Book of Colorado & Utah*, 1986 Edition. Fall Church, VA: American Automobile Association, 1986.

American Express, *Guide to Country Inns, Northeastern Edition*, 1983–84. American Express Travel Related Services, Inc.

American Guide Series, *California—Guide to the Golden State*. New York: Hastings House, 1939.

_____. *Nevada—Guide to the Silver State*. Portland: Binfords and Mort, 1940.

_____. *The Mountain States and West Coast*. New York: Hastings House, 1949.

American Heritage Magazine, Division of Forbes, Inc., New York, NY

Army and Navy Club, The, *A New Century Beckons—A History of the Army and Navy Club*, Washington, DC 1988

Asbury, Herbert, *The French Quarter,* New York: Old Towne Books, Dorset Press, 1989.

Automobile Quarterly, Kutztown, PA.

Bally Manufacturing Co., Chicago, IL. Annual Report

Bancroft, Hubert Howe, *California Pastoral*. San Francisco: The History Co., 1888.

_____, *History of California*. San Francisco: The History Co., 1890.

Barbour, Barton H., *Reluctant Frontiersman—The Diary of James Ross Larkin on the Santa Fe Trail, 1856–57*. Albuquerque: University of New Mexico Press, 1990.

Barnard, John F., *Ham and Eggs, Spanish Style—A Study of the Spanish Period in California*, Major Thesis for Sociology, Yale University, New Haven, CT, 1940.

Barron's Financial Weekly, Dow Jones & Co., New York, NY.

Baruch, Bernard, *My Own Story*. New York: Henry Holt & Co., 1957.

Basten, Fred E., *Main Street to Malibu—Yesterday and Today*. Santa Monica: Graphics Press, 1980.

Berkman, Pamela, *History of the Atchison, Topeka and Santa Fe*. Greenwich: Bison Books, Greenwich, CT 1988

Blackmar, F.W., *Spanish Institutions in the Southwest*. Baltimore: Johns Hopkins Press, 1897.

Bolton, Herbert E., *The Mission as a Frontier Agency*. New York: The Macmillan Co., 1918.

Brandon, William, *The Men and the Mountain*. New York: William Morrow & Co., 1955.

California Department of Commerce, *Discover the Californias*—1988, Official Travel Guide, Sacramento: California Tourism Co., 1988.

Carey, John, *Eyewitness to History*. Cambridge, MA: Harvard University Press, 1987.

Carpenter Technology Corp., Reading, PA.

Chapman, Charles E., *The Founding of Spanish California*. New York: The MacMillan Co., 1916.

______. *A History of California—The Spanish Period*. New York: The MacMillan Co., 1921.

Chesapeake & Ohio Historical Magazine, Alderson, WV.

Claretian Missionaries, *California's Mission San Gabriel Arcangel*. published by Hubert A. Lowman, Arroyo Grande, CA; made by Dexter Press, West Nyack, NY.

Clinch, Brian J., *California and Its Missions*. San Francisco: The Whitaker and Ray Co., 1904.

Colton, Walter, Rev. USN, *The Land of Gold, or Three Years in California*. Boston: Charles MacDonald & Co., 1866.

Crowe, Earl, *Men of El Tejon—Empire in the Tehachapis*. Los Angeles: The Ward Ritchie Press, 1957.

Cutler, David, *Literary Washington*. Lanham, MD: Madison Books, 1989.

Davidson, Marshall B., *The Horizon Concise History of France*. New York: American Heritage Publishing Co., 1971.

Davis, William Heath, *Seventy-five Years in California*. San Francisco: John Howell, 1929.

de Mafras, Duflot, Translation by Margaret E. Wilbur, *Travels on the Pacific Coast 1840–42*, Santa Ana, CA: Fine Arts Press, 1937.

Desmond, Kevin, *A Timetable oft Inventions and Discoveries*. New York: M. Evans & Co., 1986.

Eayres, Captain of the American ship Mercury, Original Documents of the Mercury Case—letters written to the Viceroy of Mexico from San Diego, February 1814.

Eisenhower, John S.D., *So Far From God—U.S. War with Mexico 1846–48*. New York: Random House, 1989.

Englehart, Zephrim, Father, *The Missions and Missionaries of California*. San Francisco: James H. Barry Co., 1915.

Ewing, Charles, *Yesterday's Washington DC*. Miami, FL: E.A. Seeman Publishing Co., 1976.

Farmer's Almanac, The Old. Dublin, NH: Yankee Publishing Inc., 1988.

Federal Mogul World, Special edition February 1989, *A History of the Federal Mogul Corp*. Detroit: Federal Mogul Corp., 1989.

Flynn, John T., *Men of Wealth* (Chapter IV—Hetty Green). New York: Simon & Schuster, 1941.

Forbes, Alexander, *A History of Upper and Lower California*. San Francisco: J.H. Nash, 1937.

France Magazine, La Maison Francaise, Washington DC.

Fremont, John C., *Memoirs of My Life*. New York: Belford Clarke & Co., 1887.

Freud, Sigmund, *On Dreams* (James Strachey translation). New York: W.W. Norton & Co., 1952.

Georgetowner, The, Washington DC.

Gibson, Arrell M., *A Visual Feast from the Santa Fe Railway Co. Collection of Southwestern Art*. Chicago: Santa Fe Railway Co., 1983.

Gleason, Harold, et al., *Music in America from 1620 to 1920* (Music Literature Outline Series III). Bloomington, IN: Frangipani Press, 1981.

Goetzmann, Wm. H. et al., *The West of the Imagination*. New York: W.W. Norton & Co., 1986.

Goode, James M., *Capital Losses—A Cultural History of Washington's Destroyed Buildings*. Washington DC: Smithsonian Institution Press, 1979.

———, *Best Addresses—a Century of Washington's Best Apartment Houses*. Washington DC : Smithsonian Institution Press, 1988.

Gourmet Magazine, New York, NY.

Greene, Constance M., *Washington, Village and Capital—1800–1878*. Princeton: Princeton University Press, 1962.

————, *Washington, Capital City, 1879–1950*. Princeton: Princeton University Press, 1963.

Grun, Bernard, *Timetables of History*. New York: Simon & Schuster, 1979.

Guedalla, Phillip, *The Second Empire*. London: Hodder & Stoughton Ltd., 1932.

Guide Michelin, France, Pneu Michelin, Paris 1971.

————. Côte d'Azur/Haute Provence, 1957.

Hill, Lawrence C., *La Reina; Los Angeles in Three Centuries*, printed for the Security Trust and Savings Bank, Los Angeles, 1929.

Hinckley, Gordon, *Truth Restored—A Short History of The Church of Jesus Christ of the Latter Day Saints*. Salt Lake City: Corporation of the President of the Church of Jesus Christ of the Latter Day Saints, 1979.

Holmes, O.W., *The City Tavern—A Century of Georgetown History 1796–1898*. Washington DC: Historical Society of Washington DC, 1980; 1995.

Howard, John Tasker, *Stephen Foster—America's Troubador*. New York: Thomas Y. Crowell & Co., 1962.

Hunt, Rockwell Dennis, *Oxcart to Airplane*. Los Angeles: Powell Publishing Co., 1929.

Improvement Era, Historical Dept., Church of Jesus Christ of the Latter Day Saints, Salt Lake City, UT.

Jakes, John, *California Gold*. New York: Random House, 1989.

Kelsey, R.W., *The U.S. Consulate in California*, thesis in partial fulfillment of Degree of Doctor of Philosophy, University of California, Berkeley, CA 1910; Publication of the Academy of Pacific Coast History, Vol. 1, No. 5.

Kennedy, James, *Was Lincoln a Christian?* Ft. Lauderdale: Coral Ridge Ministries, 1989.

Kennedy, Paul, *The Rise and Fall of the Great Powers*. New York: Random House, 1987.

Kirschten, Ernest, *Catfish and Crystal*, 3rd edition, St. Louis, MO: Patrico Press, 1989. Originally published 1960 by Doubleday, Garden City, NY.

Kurtz, Harold, *The Empress Eugenie, 1826–1920*, Boston: Houghton Mifflin Co., 1964.

Laperousse, Jean Francois de Galaup, Comte de, *Voyage Around the World, 1785–88*, Baltimore: Johns Hopkins Press, 1937.

Lewis, Arthur, H., *The Day They Shook The Plum Tree*. New York: Harcourt Brace, 1963.

Lewis, Oscar, *Here Lived the Californians*. New York: Rinehart & Co., 1957.

Los Angeles Centennial Club, Library Committee, *A Historical Sketch of Los Angeles County CA*. Los Angeles: Louis Lewin & Co., 1876.

Los Angeles Herald Examiner, Los Angeles, CA.

Los Angeles Times, Times Mirror Co., Los Angeles, CA.

Martin, I.T., *Recollections of Elizabeth Benton Fremont*. New York: Frederick L. Hitchcock, 1912.

Mellus, Francis, *Personal Diary of several years spent in California during the Mexican period*; property of the Mellus family, Los Angeles, CA.

Miller, Hope Tydings, *Embassy Row—Life and Times of Diplomatic Washington*. New York: Holt, Rinehart & Winston, 1969.

Modleski, Andrew M., *Railroad Maps of North America—The First 100 Years*. Washington DC: Library of Congress, 1984.

Notes of Interest, Quarterly Newsletter of Independence Club of First American Bank, Washington DC, MD, and VA.

Numismatic News, Krause Publications, Iola, WI.

Numismatist, The, American Numismatic Assn., Colorado Springs, CO.

Old News, Susquehanna Times & Magazine Inc., Marietta, PA.

Paine, Albert Bigelow, *Thomas Nast—His Period and His Pictures*. New York: Chelsea House, 1980.

Palou, Francisco, Translation by C. Scott Williams, *New California Missions*. Pasadena: G.W. James, 1913.

Repplier, Agnes, *Junipero Serra, Pioneer Colonist of California*. Garden City, NY: Doubleday Doran & Co., 1933.

Rezanov, Nikolai Petrovich, Count, *The Rezanoff Voyage to Nueva California*, 1806, translated from Russian by Thomas C. Russell. San Francisco: The Private Press of Thomas C. Russell, 1926.

Robinson, Alfred, *Life in California*. New York: Wiley-Putnam, 1846.

Roosevelt, Theodore, *Ranch Life and the Hunting Trail*. New York: St. Martin Press, 1965.

San Clemente, City of, *Community Directory*. San Clemente, CA: Chamber of Commerce, 1989.

Sanchez, Nellie de Grift, *Spanish and Indian Place Names in California*. Los Angeles: Powell Publishing Co., 1927.

_____, *Spanish Arcadia*. Los Angeles: Powell Publishing Co., 1927.

Santa Monica Outlook, Santa Monica, CA.

Scherer, James A.B., *Thirty-first Star*. New York: G.F. Putnam & Son, 1942.

Simpson, George, Sir. *Narrative of a Voyage to California Ports, 1841–42*. San Francisco: The Private Press of Thomas C. Russell, 1930.

Simpson, L.B., *The Encomienda in New Spain*. Berkeley: University of California Press, 1929.

Slater, Ronald L., *St. Joseph Light and Power Co.—A Century of Progress, 1883–1983*, St. Joseph, MO: St. Joseph Light and Power Co., 1983.

Smithsonian Association Magazine, Smithsonian Institution, Washington DC.

Sousa, John Philip, *Marching Along—Recollections of Men, Women and Music*. Boston: Hale, Cushman & Flint, 1928.

Southern Heritage "Company's Coming" Cookbook. Birmingham, AL: Oxmoor House, 1983.

Sparks, Boyden, et al., *The Witch of Wall Street—Hetty Green*. Garden City, NY: Doubleday Doran & Co., 1931.

Standard & Poors *Security Owners Stock Guide*. New York: Standard & Poors Corp., Feb, 1991.

Starr, Kevin, *Americans and the California Dream*, 1850–1915, New York: Oxford University Press, 1973.

———, *Inventing the Dream*, California Through the Progressive Era. New York: Oxford University Press, 1985.

———, *Material Dreams—Southern California Through the 1920s*. New York: Oxford University Press, 1990.

Steele, James, *Old California Days*. Chicago: Merrill-Higgins Co., 1892.

Stone, Irving, *Men to Match My Mountains*. Garden City, NY: Doubleday & Co., Inc., 1956.

———, *Immortal Wife*. New York: Doubleday & Co., Inc., 1944, reprinted by Signet Books, 1969.

Stover, John F., *History of the B&O Railroad*. W. Lafayette, IN: Purdue University Press, 1987.

Thompson, David, *Democracy in France Since 1870*. London: Oxford University Press, 1964.

Town & Country Magazine, New York, NY.

Turner, Charles W., et al., *Chessie's Road*. Alderson, WV: C&O Historical Society, 1986.

U.S. Commission of Fine Arts, *The Commission of Fine Arts—A Brief History*. Washington DC: The Comm. of Fine Arts, 1984.

———, *Georgetown Architecture—The Waterfront*. Washington DC: 1968.

_____, *Georgetown Residential Architecture—Northeast*. Washington DC: The Comm. of Fine Arts, (undated).

_____, *Sixteenth Street Architecture*, Vol. I, Washington DC: U.S. Govt. Printing Office, 1978.

_____, *Washington Architecture 1791–1861*, Washington DC: U.S. Govt. Printing Office, 1971.

U.S. Department of Interior, *Exploring the American West, 1803–1879*. Washington DC: National Park Handbook #116, 1982.

U.S. Department of State, *Principal Officers of the Department of State and U.S. Chiefs of Mission, 1778–1986*, Washington DC: Office of Historian, Bureau of Public Affairs, Washington DC.

U.S. General Services Administration, *The American Image— Photographs from the National Archives 1860–1960*, New York: Pantheon Books, 1979.

_____, *The Written Word Endures—Milestone Documents of American History*, Washington DC: National Archives and Records Service, 1976.

Utah Travel Council, *Utah Travel Guide—1988*, Salt Lake City, UT: Utah Travel Council, 1988.

Vancouver, George, Captain, *A Voyage of Discovery to the North Pacific Ocean and Around the World*, printed for G.G. and J. Robinson, London, 1798.

Wall Street Journal, Dow Jones & Co., New York, NY.

Washington Post, Washington DC.

Washington Times, Washington DC.

Washingtonian, The, Washington DC.

Watson, D.S., *The Spanish Occupation of California*. San Francisco: Grabhorn Press, 1934.

Walter, Elizabeth Brainerd, *The Washington Club—The First One Hundred Years 1891–1991*. Washington DC: The Washington Club Preservation Fund, 15 DuPont Circle, Washington DC, March 1996.

Wilkins, Thurman, *Clarence King—A Biography*. Albuquerque, NM: University of New Mexico Press, 1988.

Wilner, Frank N., *Railroad Land Grants*. Washington, DC: Association of American Railroads, 1984.

Woodward, John, et al., *A Treatise on Heraldry*. Rutland, VT: Charles E. Tuttle & Co., 1969.

Yale Alumni Magazine, New Haven, CT.

Yenne, Bill, *History of the Southern Pacific*. Greenwich, CT: Bison Books, 1985.

Yeoman, R.S., *Guide Book of United States Coins*. Racine, WI: Western Publishing Co., (published annually).

INDEX

LIST OF ILLUSTRATIONS
AND CREDITS

11. Carson's Men, by Charles M. Russell, 1913, oil on canvas. From the collection of Gilcrease Museum, Tulsa, OK (#0137.2295).
12. Domes of Yosemite, by Albert Bierstadt, chrome lithograph circa 1868. Courtesy Amon Carter Museum, Ft. Worth, TX. (Museum No. 1968.42)
13. Jessie Benton Fremont. Courtesy Denver Public Library, Western History/Geneology Dept., Denver, CO (Neg. #F12067).

PARTS IV–V: (pages 154-166)
14. The Broadway, St. Louis, from the *Illustrated London News*, 1858. Courtesy of Missouri Historical Society, St. Louis, MO (Neg. #SS–571; Lic. No. 5165, 11/22/96).
15. Naval Sketches of the War in California, Battle of the Plains of Mesa (near Los Angeles), original water color by William H. Meyers, January 9, 1847. Courtesy of the Franklin D. Roosevelt Library, Hyde Park, NY.
16. Col. John Charles Fremont, "The Pathfinder of the Rocky Mountains," drawing. Courtesy of Denver Public Library, Western History/Geneology Dept., Denver, CO (Neg. #F26927).
17. San Francisco, Lithograph, S.F. Marryat, 1851. Courtesy Amon Carter Museum, Ft. Worth, TX. (Museum No. 1972.97)
18. Los Angeles, Los Angeles County, Cal. 1857, Lithograph Charles C. Kuchel and Emil Dresel. Courtesy Amon Carter Museum, Fort Worth, TX. (Museum No. 1972.61)
19. George-town on Potomack, an eighteenth century map published in 1934 by the National Society of Colonial Dames of America of the District of Columbia. Courtesy of The Historical Society of Washington, DC. (No. 7287.)
20. President's House (aerial view about 1845) showing the grounds, public buildings and private residence. National Archives and Records Administration, Washington, DC (#66–G–21K–17).
21. Willard (City) Hotel and View to White House, sketch. National Archives and Records Administration, Washington, DC (#66–G–21K–6).
22. Georgetown, 1860, litho by E. Sachse, Baltimore, MD, circa 1860, Machin Collection, courtesy of The Historical Society of Washington, DC. (M91 print from slide)

23.   The USGS Field Party of 1864 (Clarence King at far right). Courtesy of Denver Public Library, Western History Dept., (Neg. #F27319).

24.   Edward F. Beale, 1862, first Superintendent of Indian Affairs for California and Nevada, and founder of Tejon Ranch. Courtesy of Tejon Ranch Co., Lebec, CA.

25.   Georgetown and the City of Washington, 1864 map by Johnson and Ward, courtesy of The Historical Society of Washington, DC. (No. 2140.)

26.   Map of the Defences of Washington, 1864–5. Courtesy of The Historical Society of Washington, DC. (No. 3622.)

PART VI: (pages 222-236)

27.   Nice's Promenade des Anglais (at the turn of the century). Copyright: ND-Viollet, Roger Viollet, Paris, France.

28.   Interior of Palace Car—Ohio Railway, about 1875, photographer unknown. National Archives and Records Administration, Washington, DC (American Image #45).

29.   Zion's Cooperative Mercantile Institution, Salt Lake City, 1869, William H. Jackson photograph. National Archives and Records Administration, Washington, DC (Photo call No. 057–HS–810).

30.   The Great Palace Reclining-Chair Route, Chicago and Alton Railroad. Lithograph by Ballin & Liebler, New York. From the collection of the Library of Congress, Washington, DC (LC–USZ62–1371).

31.   Across the Continent on the Pacific Railroad—Dining Saloon of the Hotel Express Train, wood engraving in *Frank Leslie's Illustrated Newspaper*, January 15, 1870. From the collection of the Library of Congress, Washington, DC (LC–USZ62–14133).

32.   The Portland Flats (Washington's first apartment house). The Gramstorff Collection, Photographic Archives, National Gallery of Art, Washington, DC (#5635A).

33.   Harvey's Restaurant, Washington, DC, photo by National Photo Co. From the collection of the Library of Congress, Washington, DC (LC–F82–2539).

34.   Garfield Inaugural Arch (1881) with parade passing under arch on Pennsylvania Avenue at 15th St. NW; the largest of 15 such arches erected along Pennsylvania Ave. Photo by G. Prince, Washington, DC, from the collection of the Library of Congress, Washington, DC (LC–USZ62–22842).

(engraving). The Bettman Archive, New York, NY (#SF8388).

48. Sitting Bull with Buffalo Bill, Denver Public Library, Western History Dept., Denver, CO. (B348)

49. Rose's Station, circa 1889-90. Trading post and watering stop for stages. Center of social activities for Tejon Ranch. Courtesy of Tejon Ranch Co., Lebec, CA.

50. Hospital at Fort Tejon, 1888. Fort founded in 1854 and used as headquarters for the U.S. 1st Dragoons, abandoned in 1865 and used thereafter by Tejon Ranch hands and farm workers. Courtesy of Tejon Ranch Co., Lebec, CA.

51. Tejon Ranch Stables, 1888, courtesy of Tejon Ranch Co., Lebec, CA.

52. Tejon Ranch blacksmith shop and men's quarters, circa 1889–90. Courtesy of Tejon Ranch Co., Lebec, CA.

53. Tejon Ranch vaqueros at Majordomo's headquarters. Don Juan Jesus Lopes on white horse. Circa 1887. Courtesy of Tejon Ranch Co., Lebec, CA.

54. Tejon Ranch cattle boss, circa 1889. Courtesy of Tejon Ranch Co., Lebec, CA.

55. Bird's Eye View of Los Angeles, 1893. Panoramic Maps of Cities in the U.S. and Canada, page 20, entry no. 27.1, from the collection of the Library of Congress, Washington, DC.

56. Sixth Street and Broadway, Los Angeles, California, photograph circa 1890. The Bettman Archives, New York, NY (F9237).

57. Southern Pacific Railroad Depot in Santa Monica, circa 1890; H.F. Rile photo, courtesy of University of Southern California Library, Regional History Collection (No. 32495).

58. Opening day of trolley line from Los Angeles to Santa Monica, 1896. Courtesy of University of Southern California Library, Regional History Collection (No. 1943).

59. Georgetown, DC, 3000 block of P Street, NW, north side, (formerly West Street between Congress and Washington Streets); courtesy of The Historical Society of Washington, DC. (No. 5446).

60. Georgetown, DC, Wisconsin Avenue at M Street, circa 1900. 1100 block of Wisconsin and 3200 block of M Street; (formerly High Street and Falls Street). Courtesy of The Historical Society of Washington, DC. (No. 6774.)